ORGANISING FEMINISMS

Organising Feminisms

The Micropolitics of the Academy

Louise Morley

Senior Lecturer
Centre for Higher Education Studies
University of London Institute of Education

First published 1999 by
MACMILLAN PRESS LTD
Houndmills, Basingstoke, Hampshire RG21 6XS
and London
Companies and representatives
throughout the world

ISBN 0–333–73934–5 hardcover
ISBN 0–333–73935–3 paperback

A catalogue record for this book is available
from the British Library.

This book is printed on paper suitable for recycling and
made from fully managed and sustained forest sources.

10   9   8   7   6   5   4   3   2   1
08   07   06   05   04   03   02   01   00   99

Printed and bound in Great Britain by
Antony Rowe Ltd, Chippenham, Wiltshire

 Published in the United States of America by
ST. MARTIN'S PRESS, INC.,
Scholarly and Reference Division
175 Fifth Avenue, New York, N.Y. 10010

ISBN 0–312–21676–9 clothbound
ISBN 0–312–21678–5 paperback

Contents

Acknowledgements

I would like to thank Stephen Ball, Debbie Epstein, John Head, Meg Maguire and Mary Maynard for reading chapters and for offering such perceptive comments. Thanks are also appropriate to Chiz Dube and Julia Harris for transcribing the tapes. My colleagues at the Institute of Education, University of Sussex, deserve acknowledgement too for their support and encouragement to me to complete this work. Most importantly, I would like to appreciate the forty women, in different parts of Europe, who shared such rich and fascinating insights.

Abbreviations

AUT	Association of University Teachers
CUCO	Commission on University Career Opportunity
CVCP	Committee of Vice-Chancellors and Principals
DES	Department of Education and Science
ERASMUS	European Community Action Scheme for the Mobility of University Students
HEFCE	Higher Education Funding Council for England
HEQC	Higher Education Quality Council
HMI	Her Majesty's Inspectorate
UCCA	Universities Central Clearing and Admissions
UCG	University Grants Committee
PCCS	Polytechnic Central Clearing System
RAE	Research Assessment Exercise
TEMPUS	Trans European Mobility Scheme for University Students (in Eastern European countries)
THES	*Times Higher Education Supplement*
WSN	Women's Studies Network (UK) Association

Introduction: The Micropolitics of Academic Feminism

The intellectual beginnings of this book can be found in an autobiographical account of my engagement with feminism and education as a student, a lecturer, school teacher, educational policy-maker and community activist. I taught women's studies for 11 years and from the moment I entered the academy, I have been attempting to theorise why universities are experienced as such alien terrains by many women. I wish I could say that this was all a massive projection on my part, and that the problems reside in my personal history, with individuated internalised oppression as a consequence of a conjunction of class and gender disadvantage (Morley, 1997). But the problems do not seem to disappear that easily, as I am forever hearing narratives from women students and staff about subtle and overt practices which leave them feeling undermined, confused and disempowered (Morley and Walsh, 1995, 1996). This is an account of the academy as perceived from the margins – the discursive location of 'other', examining how behaviours, structures and values create a sense of dominance in the academy.

I became increasingly interested in micropolitics as a political adjunct of process-oriented humanistic psychology. I wanted to decode the symbiotic parallelism of pleasure and pain which appeared to haunt both women's studies and women's engagement with the academy. As a feminist academic, I have frequently questioned the location of my constituency, as at times it has felt as if I have been open to attack from all sides. The problematisation of power in counter-hegemonic subjects such as women's studies can sensitise students to evaluate their relationships with each other and with authority figures such as tutors. As a feminist tutor, I have often represented a safe space for students to rehearse their discontents. This results in my undertaking substantial emotional labour, operating within quasi-therapeutic discourses in organisations dedicated to the life of the mind.

1

I have also known colleagues who have applied their creativity to making my life as difficult as possible, in order to ensure that I never soared above them in the academic hierarchy. One former colleague, a total inactive in every other respect, always managed to manipulate structures, such as timetabling or representation on decision-making committees, to my disadvantage. He withheld important information, but made strenuous efforts to tell me anything that would unsettle or destabilise me. He infused every transaction with me with sarcastic, undermining remarks. Nothing he did was ever tangible enough to warrant a formal complaint – he always stopped just short of that point. To have raised these problems with my dean or head of depart-ment would have resulted in my being labelled oversensitive or small-minded. I soon learned from feminist colleagues elsewhere that relations such as these were widespread, and that there was nowhere to take the outrage and confusion that many of us were experiencing. Micropolitics began to acquire an urgent significance.

It would be erroneous to degenerate into essentialised binaries, suggesting the victimhood of women and the easy denunciation of all men. I have also had extensive experience of women's organisations and have witnessed debilitating and destructive internecine struggles based on exclusions, confinements and domination. A micropolitical perspective recognises control and conflict as essential and contra-dictory bases of organisational life. Grounded in quotidian practices, the study provides feminist readings of the academy, capturing some of the ambiguities, paradoxes and uncertainties of women caught between their commitment to an international political movement and their location in dominant organisations of knowledge produc-tion.

My study is based on interviews with 40 informants in Britain, Greece and Sweden. It is not, however, a three-nation case study. Rather, it aims to explore, via some cross-cultural triangulation, what academic feminism means in different locations. I have attempted to decode and disentangle gendered message systems, such as pedagogy and organisational culture, and the matrix of power relations in the academy. In order to challenge the theoretical parochialism of so much of educational research, I have had to assemble a montage of academic disciplinary approaches. Consequently, I have utilised concepts from the sociology of education, feminist theory, policy studies, organisation studies, postmodernism and critical social research.

Initially, my research question focused on the introduction and

maintenance of women's studies in the academy. After several interviews, it soon grew into a far larger project, as data increasingly
revealed that what I was being presented with was multiple, cross-
cultural feminist readings of the academy, often posed in micropolitical terms, accounts and anecdotes. While not an ethnography in
the traditional sense, the use of ethnographic methods meant that I
fed the data back into the process of collection. What has emerged is
a study of the micropolitics of the academy.

Lennon and Whitford (1994: 1) have argued that 'Feminism's most
compelling epistemological insight lies in the connections it has made
between knowledge and power.' They believed that 'legitimation of
knowledge-claims is intimately tied to networks of domination and
exclusion' (p. 1). The conceptual framework of micropolitics in my
study reveals the increasingly subtle and sophisticated ways in which
dominance is achieved in academic organisations. The connection
between knowledge and power is unpacked and interrogated in fine
detail. As such, it provides an analytical corrective to traditional
notions of disembodied objectivity and meritocracy. Paying attention
to the micropolitical enables emotional as well as intellectual readings of gender in the academy to surface. This can challenge the
Cartesian dualism of rationality in opposition to emotion.

The radical feminist mantra, the personal is political, recognised
that intra- and interpersonal relationships form an arena in which
macro-processes of patriarchal power are enacted and challenged.
While initially appearing somewhat reductive, it can be a useful
summary of the extent to which macro discourses of power invade
psychic and social landscapes. Feminism and postmodernism show
how power relations at the micro-level of society both enable and
reflect global effects of domination. Feminist academics, as visible
change agents, require increasingly complex micropolitical literacy,
strategies for self-care and evolved theoretical frameworks for their
daily engagement with patriarchal power relations. This is an
intensely political project. Ball (1994a: 27) reminded us that according to Foucault:

> the real political task is to criticise the working of institutions which
> appear to be both neutral and independent, and to criticise them in
> such a manner that the political violence which has always exer-
> cised itself obscurely through them will be unmasked so that we can
> fight them.

The idea that the academy might be a violent place appears at first to be a bizarre juxtaposition, but feminist 'unmaskings' soon disclose the myriad ways in which women are undermined and excluded from access to resources, influence, career opportunities and academic authority. Exposing the minutiae of the quotidian turns our attention to the multiple points at which power is exercised. As Luke (1994: 215) pointed out:

> the production of academic knowledge … is structured on one of the oldest organizational models – the university – to survive the medieval era into the 21st century.

Anachronistic practices and hierarchical structures may account, in part, for women's subordination in the academy, but other complex forces are at work too. Said (1994: xv) pointed out that the 'challenge of intellectual life is to be found in dissent against the *status quo*'. This idea was also articulated in The Higher Education Quality Council (HEQC) Report (1994: 315):

> universities are organizations like no other; that they are institutions where the principal product is *dissent*, or opposition to received wisdom.

A key consideration in my study is whether dissent has different consequences for different groups. Habermas (1981) described feminism as a new ideological offensive. My study turns feminists' theoretical offensive on to the academy itself, by documenting how the micropolitics of gender oppression permeates intellectual frameworks, organisational cultures and women's psychic narratives.

CONCEPTUALISING MICROPOLITICS

The workplace has become a major site of gender politics. Micropolitics focuses on the ways in which power is relayed in everyday practices. The concept entered organisation studies in the 1980s, suggesting that there is a way of conceptualising a 'darker side' of organisational life (Ball, 1987: 270). Micropolitics has been read as a subtext of organisational life in which conflicts, tensions, resentments, competing interests and power imbalances influence everyday transactions in institutions. Hoyle (1982: 87) described micropolitics as 'an organisational underworld which we all recognise and in which we all participate'. Micropolitics is about influence, networks, coalitions, political and personal strategies to effect or resist change. It involves rumour, gossip, sarcasm, humour, denial, 'throwaway remarks', alliance-building. Blase (1991: 1) defines micropolitics as being

> about power and how people use it to influence others and to protect themselves. It is about conflict and how people compete with each other to get what they want. It is about cooperation and how people build support among themselves to achieve their ends.

Feminists in the academy need both to read organisational micropolitics and evolve their own micropolitical strategies for intervention and change. The problems of the academy are both structural and played out in micropolitical struggles. Micropolitics exposes subterranean conflicts and the minutiae of social relations. In my study, women with power-sensitive analyses outline how power is relayed through seemingly trivial incidents and transactions. In so doing, they demonstrate how patriarchal power is exercised, rather than simply possessed.

The exercising of power in organisations can be overt and identifiable, but also subtle, complex and confusing. Blase and Anderson (1995: 13) suggest that in a postmodern world, power is used and structured into social relations so that it does not appear to be 'used' at all. The cultural and feminist approach to the micropolitics of organisational life contributes to an understanding of the distorting effects of power and the ways that power is exercised invisibly (Marshall and Anderson, 1994: 175). A micropolitical analysis renders the competition and domination visible; exposing processes of stalling, sabotage, manipulation, power bargaining, bullying, harassment and spite.

Feminism, through theory and practice, can also make hidden meanings of the academy visible, and expose them as gendered processes of power. While there is often some hegemonic struggle between feminism and postmodernism, micropolitics and feminist theory can be complementary paradigms for the analysis of organisational life. Like many aspects of racial and gender oppression, bullying and sexual harassment at work, micropolitics can also be subtle, elusive, volatile, difficult to capture, leaving individuals unsure of the validity of their readings of a situation. What appears trivial in a single instance acquires new significance when located within a wider analysis of power relations. The attribution of meaning and decoding of transactions, locations and language is an important

Organising Feminisms

component of micropolitics. Both feminism and micropolitics privilege processes, rather than structures. Both can label unnamed feelings, experiences, practices and transactions, because the language in which oppressed groups express these phenomena is often politically and socially subjugated and rendered irrelevant or illegitimate by dominant discourses.

It could also be claimed that, as feminist scholarship has entered into conventional reward systems and power networks in dominant organisations, it has its own micropolitics. Furthermore, in spite of the impact of the policies of the New Right and the transition from welfare to market values in education, academic feminism continues to flourish in Britain today. The presence of oppositional discourses within dominant organisations of knowledge production produces interesting tensions and questions. The margins/mainstream debate has always harboured suspicions of the micropolitical aspects of the academy's acceptance of feminist knowledge and inquiry within its ivory towers, fearing incorporation and dilution in the mainstream and ghettoisation on the margins. Campbell (1992: 20) warned that while feminism has been allowed to flourish as it represents good economic sense, it is important to have strategies for its future development:

> the prevailing straitened economic climate seems hostile to all but narrowly economic considerations, it seems especially important to maintain momentum and prevent feminism becoming stalled at this point.

Agger (1993) argues that the market for women's studies and academic feminism *depends* on patriarchy. As a 'reverse discourse', feminism is both oppositionally located in the academy and also defined by patriarchy. It could be argued that feminism is flourishing in the academy *because of* patriarchy.

Feminism represents a major piece of change. The arrival of the feminist product highlights the gendered micropolitics of the institution. As change agents, feminist academics have to destabilise current culture and practices to some extent, in order to establish a new order. Lacey (1977) claims that change, or the possibility of change, brings to the surface those subterranean conflicts and differences which are otherwise glossed over in daily routines. The academy, like any other organisation, is full of contradictions – structures are both fixed and volatile, enabling and constraining. Feminist academics can be knowledge agents, micropolitically making interventions, not only in course provision and organisational practices, but also about the discourses and regimes of truth that inform them.

GENEALOGY OF ACADEMIC FEMINISM

Feminism takes many forms in the academy, representing different theoretical strategies and formations. Women's studies courses have flourished throughout Europe, North America, Australia, New Zealand and Canada and have more recently been developed in China, India, Zimbabwe, Mexico, Thailand, Korea, the Philippines, Brazil, Nigeria and South Africa. Women's studies courses in Britain originated in adult education in the 1970s and entered the academy in the early 1980s. The first women's studies MA commenced in 1981 at the University of Kent. Now courses exist in the majority of British universities, some at undergraduate level, but the majority at post-graduate level. However, feminism also exerts a strong presence in academic disciplines, and the question of mainstreams/margins location of academic feminism has been a rich debate (Aaron and Walby, 1991; Bowles and Klein, 1987; De Groot and Maynard, 1993). Feminists have indicated a need for academic disciplines to broaden their parameters of inquiry and identified traditional disciplines as epistemological enforcers. As Campbell (1992: 16) indicated:

> In the last twenty-five years especially feminist academics have brought to light more and more of the distortions perpetuated in traditional 'objective' studies that misrepresent the world and women particularly.

It has become an orthodoxy of feminist analysis to draw attention to the micropolitical functions of academic disciplines, believing that separation only mirrors and reinforces the fragmentation of most spheres of social life (Campbell, 1992). Furthermore, the development of feminist knowledge is obstructed by conceptual boundaries. These can decontextualise knowledge and sustain horizontal segregation. The disciplines themselves are gendered, with ensuing hierarchies of 'hard' and 'soft' subjects. The promotion of interdisciplinary or transdisciplinary approaches to learning suggests that feminism refuses to think and act in accordance with the 'rules' of knowledge and academic life. However, it has also been argued that women's studies *is* a discipline. According to Elam (1994: 100):

Women's studies is thought by many to be a discipline created by feminism as a response to a society and a university structure that did not meet its needs. Almost by definition, then, women's studies is an attempt to rethink the disciplinary organization of the academy.

The issue of boundaries and definitions has been problematic. For example, not all women's studies courses have feminist theoretical underpinnings, and feminism, as a constellation of signs, is differently interpreted (see Seller, 1994). This can be attributed to cultural, political and historical differences. Rose (1994) outlines shifting feminist priorities for higher education over the decades in Britain:

> Feminist struggle at the turn of the century took, after the vote, the issue of access to education and science as one of its central objectives ... Second-wave feminism took place in the context of more or less continuous expansion in higher education ... The expansion did, however, provide the conditions in which feminist intellectuals, as an increasingly large and visible group, have been able to move from a weak position largely outside the publicly financed production and transmission system of knowledge to one where ... they are a visible and influential presence. (Rose, 1994: 57)

The struggle to become a 'visible and influential presence' has not been problem-free. After initial battles of access for women students, and the abolition of the marriage bar for women academics (Dyhouse, 1995), feminist influence was able to turn to the message systems of curriculum, epistemologies and pedagogy. As Rose (1994) indicates, the origins of these interventions took place against a political backdrop of expansion in higher education. The expansion was not just in material terms, but also in intellectual terms, as new universities in Britain in the 1960s such as Sussex, Lancaster, Kent, Warwick and York developed new maps of learning, with opportunities for interdisciplinary work and the development of relatively new disciplines such as sociology and cultural studies.

The curriculum illustrates the way in which hegemonic definitions of education, culture and knowledge are contested (Cherryholmes, 1988). Feminists were among those who decoded these secret complicities between power and knowledge, and identified how power functioned to determine what students had the opportunity to learn and what was forbidden to them. The notion of exclusion was paramount, as Rich (quoted in Sinfield, 1994: 16) described: 'When someone with the authority of a teacher describes the world and you are not in it, there is a moment of psychic disequilibrium, as if you looked into a mirror and saw nothing.' Feminist scholarship represented a new paradigm in social and critical inquiry, as it deconstructed and reconstructed concepts, methodology and grand theories. Recovery of lost knowledges, recognition of the partiality of existing knowledges and reflexivity about the validation and production of social knowledge formed the foundation of feminism in the academy.

While academic feminism is perceived by some as a 'reverse discourse' (Ramazanoglu, 1993), for others it is merely a reformist measure. Currie and Kazi (1987: 77) expounded the anomalies associated with the organisational location for feminist academics:

> as feminists trying to create new ideas and alternatives, we are opposed to the university as it currently exists. In this way, as well as struggling to end the sexual oppression of both women and men, we are at the same time struggling with a demoralizing source of opposition – a process which appears and claims to be impartial, but which in practice operates to render feminism incompatible with academia.

Hennessy (1993) also warns that feminists need to forestall efforts to absorb and domesticate feminism, and that feminism must maintain its potential as an oppositional discourse in the university. My study traces the contours of some of the personal and professional challenges involved in negotiating a radical intellectual home for feminism in the academy.

Feminists are not a monolithic group. While it has become almost an orthodoxy of feminist scholarship to rehearse the tripartite ideologies of feminism, outlining theoretical differences between radical, socialist and liberal feminism, I have chosen not to do so. These have been important analytical tools in theorising and promoting feminism, but have also implied forms of distinction and closure, while not necessarily paying attention to 'race', disability or age. Stanley (1997) argues that the certainties of the divisions between different types of feminisms are no longer there, and questions whether they were ever there in the first place for 'few of us understood our ideas and praxes for long within such confined and static terms' (p. 9). It could also be argued that the only identity permitted to feminists in organisations is that of liberal feminists, working within existing structures to reform, rather than revolutionise. Postmodern feminism challenges all these assumptions, suggesting that identity is not fixed or stable, but contingent and constantly in flux.

Feminism has been substantially criticised for its culturally-specific and ethnocentric distortions (Maynard, 1996). I specifically aimed to include diverse European countries to interrogate commonalities and differences in micropolitical experiences and meanings. Walby (1990: 227) indicates that an international perspective is essential as neither class, 'race' nor gender can be understood within one country alone. Practically, this can mean that at times the data in my study from women for whom English is a second or third foreign language contain the odd error in grammar or syntax. But the feelings and intellectual and political analyses seem to transcend these patriarchal linguistic rules!

1 The Challenges of Feminist Research

THE POLITICS OF INQUIRY AND SITUATING MYSELF

In this chapter I aim to provide a description of my methods and methodologies, while also providing critical analysis of the research process itself, drawing on feminist theory and literature which problematises the issues of power and method (Fonow and Cook, 1991; Gitlin, 1994; Maynard and Purvis, 1994; Stanley and Wise, 1993). I outline some of the developments in feminist epistemology and relate them to critical social inquiry methodologies, such as grounded theory, reflexivity and standpoint theory. I also consider convergences and disjunctions between feminism and postmodernism. By so doing, I aim to locate this piece of research on the micropolitics of feminism in a wider critical context and demonstrate some of the problematics associated with power relations and the politics of inquiry.

What constitutes valid and reliable feminist knowledge is a key question. As assertions of 'knowledge' frequently both reproduce and guarantee domination and power, there is a problem as to how feminism can legitimately claim to be a site of knowledge about the oppression of women, without reproducing the power relations it questions. As a feminist academic, I share Fine's (1994: 13) anxiety about 'how best to unleash ourselves from our central contradiction – being researchers and being active feminists'.

Exposure to theoretical complexities can be an essential constituent in reflexivity and help explain some of the resistance I feel to social research. My feminist consciousness warns me not to exploit informants for the enrichment of my creative endeavours, and to seek ways of knowing which avoid domination and subordination. I question whether research automatically objectifies the researched and privileges the researcher, who has the power to name, describe and frame questions and experiences. My interest in postmodernism, with its potential nihilism, makes me wonder if there is an inherent futility in the entire process! I also frequently question the rise of the 'consumerist ethos towards knowledge' (Skeggs, 1991: 257). In Britain, this has been exacerbated by New Right educational policy which demands reductive indicators of academic productivity. In the midst of these intellectual and political complexities, I attempt to hold on to what might be described by postmodernists as an enlightenment, rationalist project, i.e. a belief in the connection between intervention and outcome, and see some social research as minor pieces of political action, located in particular historical moments. Policy archaeologists such as Scheurich (1994) have argued that research questions and social problems are social constructions, and that certain issues come under the gaze of social researchers at particular political and historical moments. As McRobbie (1982: 48) observed:

> No research is carried out in a vacuum. The very questions we ask are always informed by the historical moments we inhabit.

The historical moment I inhabit is characterised by the growth of feminism in the academy and the increase in the number of women undergraduate students, alongside an alarming under-representation of women in senior posts. This raises questions about how new counter-hegemonic knowledges are being introduced into the academy, and what change agency strategies are employed by those in structurally disempowered locations.

The issue of 'location' can be challenging for feminist academics. For many, academic feminism is a contradiction in terms, an oxymoron, selling out feminists' commitment to everyday praxis (Elam, 1994; Morley and Walsh, 1995, 1996). Ladwig and Gore (1994: 234) asked:

> How is writing a volume to be read by other academics going to contribute to the overall political concerns of the author?

On the other hand, 'academic feminism is also frequently viewed by the establishment as being insufficiently academic' (Morley and Walsh, 1995: 1).

My research into the micropolitics of feminism in the academy generated feminist data in the process as well as the content. First, I soon saw that I had 'othered' myself in mainstream research communities. My feminism was not seen as knowledge, but rather as an obstacle to overcome, or a pollutant in the otherwise hygienic process of knowledge production. Elsewhere in the feminist research community, I was conscious that my dilemmas had been theorised for at least two decades, so how could I provide an original angle? (Roberts, 1981; Stanley and Wise, 1983, 1984).

Second, there was the issue of access, which meant that many of my informants were either known to me, or knew me through my work in women's studies. This raised ethical questions about social and professional boundaries. Third, the issue of power relations and internalised hierarchical thinking were also features of the research process. When I interviewed the elite, such as professors, I was disadvantaged because of my relatively low status. I had to ensure that my internalised oppression did not allow me to be overawed and dominated (Ball, 1994b; Morley, 1997; Neal, 1995; Walford, 1994). When I interviewed students, I was often conscious that some of them related to me as a lecturer, an authority figure, and I had to make sure that I did not dominate them. When interviewing peers, I tried to allow them their privacy and separateness, and not make assumptions about shared tacit knowledge.

A fourth challenge was to undertake empirical work, while simultaneously engaging with literature on critical social inquiry and discussions on feminist methodologies – i.e. ideological, epistemological and ontological concerns. This raised anxieties about the power relations involved in data collection and analysis, and the controversial areas of interpretation and representation. A fifth and complex area related to how I could engage with postmodernist analysis of the micro-physics of power and undertake research from a feminist standpoint.

FEMINISM, POSTMODERNISM AND EDUCATIONAL RESEARCH

In relation to educational research, feminism is not just of theoretical significance. Griffiths (1995a) argued that educational practices and outcomes are damaged by sexism, and that sexism distorts the way in which such practices and outcomes are understood and researched.

> This is precisely the concern of feminist epistemology: how to improve knowledge and remove sexist distortions. (Griffiths, 1995a: 219)

The issue of how knowledge can be 'improved' has produced a rich debate. There is no identifiable formula which can guarantee quality assurance as knowledge production *per se* is a heavily contested area. The insertion of postmodernism into theorising about feminist research has raised questions about standpoint, social change and the privileging of experience. It is debatable whether feminism and post-modernism are compatible or in opposition, or both, as would befit the postmodern assertion of contradictory, discontinuous and unstable relationships. My view is that they are linked in a homeopathic relationship, with small doses of postmodernism mobilising feminist antibodies. While it initially feels poisonous, it can be successful in sharpening and strengthening our theory-building. As Griffiths (1995a: 220) observed:

> Both feminism and post-modernism challenge traditional conceptions of epistemology ... Both ... made their challenges, in part, by refusing to assume away politics. Both of them draw attention to the deep and irreducible connections between knowledge and power.

A common feature of feminism and postmodernism has been the importance of reconceptualising categories such as 'truth', 'objectivity' and 'knowledge', and to demonstrate how power relations and politics are deeply embedded in social research and knowledge production. As Popkewitz and Brennan (1997: 295) indicate:

> There is not a single, universal standard truth but rather a contingent and politically strategic concern with how truths are produced.

Feminists, Hughes (1995) reminds us, have argued that there is no objectivity disassociated from the social and economic politics of the inventors or users of specific scientific methods. Postmodernism disrupts the notion that there is a singular 'truth' existing that awaits to be discovered (Tierney, 1994). A feature of postmodernist thought is the unsettling of certainties and the formerly firm foundations on which knowledge claims were based (Gipps, 1993). Feminism too has challenged patriarchal paradigms and raised questions about whose knowledge is being validated and produced via social research (Harding, 1991). Both feminism and postmodernism are critical of universalistic grand theories and meta-narratives, focusing instead on fragmentation and flux. Both question many conventional notions about the nature of science and appear to celebrate difference and pluralism; both share concerns that research is part of the technology of regulation. Maynard (1993) questions whether it is ever possible to develop research techniques that do not involve the researcher in strategies of surveillance and control.

However, the relationship between feminism and postmodernism is complex and fraught. This has been described as a 'hegemonic war'

(Skeggs, 1991: 256), with postmodernism seen as an obstruction to the feminist agenda for social change, as its nihilism could lead to political inaction and hopelessness. Postmodernism is sometimes perceived as leading to an irresponsible relativism, which undermines feminist standpoint theory. The fear is that 'woman' has become such an unstable category in the postmodern discourse of the death of the subject, that feminists have no location from which to speak. Furthermore, there is a futility contained in the postmodern condition which challenges the notion of interpretation in social research.

> Educational research, or any ethnography, that attempts to understand the words and deeds of others is redundant for postmodernists. The world, according to postmodernists, is opaque; it is all lived on the surface. There is nothing that hides behind its surface appearances. It is not a case of people saying what they mean – rather they don't mean anything – for there is no meaning to be had ... (Skeggs, 1991: 259)

Much of the debate on the relationship between feminism and postmodernism is posed in modernist binaries. Furthermore, these are gendered and competitive, with postmodernism sometimes viewed as a new variety of white male, academic dominance. The competing paradigms analysis has led to suspicion and rejection of postmodernist theories of social research by many feminist academics:

> in allying themselves with postmodernist positions, feminists, willy nilly, are getting ... entangled in a set of assumptions which may leave their position untenable. (Benhabib, 1992: 210)

An irony is often indicated in the way in which postmodernism articulates a commitment to difference without reference to two major structures of inequality: 'race' and gender (hooks, 1991). Whereas postmodernist perceptions of the dispersed nature of power and the irrationality of organisations inform my inquiry, the project is from a feminist standpoint.

THE TENSION OF OPPOSITION: FEMINIST STANDPOINT THEORY

A central theme in standpoint theory is the relationship between women's personal knowledges and the generation of scientific or propositional knowledges (Henwood and Pidgeon, 1995). Studying the social world from feminist perspectives can reveal forms of understanding traditionally excluded from inquiries undertaken by the 'ruling gender' (Maynard, 1994). Standpoint theory involves the attribution of epistemic privilege to socially marginalised groups, enabling those who have otherwise been objectified to enter the research process as knowledge-makers (Harding, 1991). Braidotti developed de Beauvoir's earlier claim (1972) that the world is masculine but coded as universal. The mark of sexual difference falls on women, as there is a tendency to conflate

> the masculine viewpoint with the general 'human' standpoint and the confinement of the feminine to the structural position of 'other' ... marking them off as the second sex ... whereas men are marked by the imperative of carrying the universal. (Braidotti, 1992: 26)

McRobbie (1982: 46) predicted tensions when she argued how the 'urgency of the polemics of politics ... are at odds with the traditional requirements of the scholarly mode'. Referring to feminist researchers, Fine (1992: 230) observes:

> Because we acknowledge that politics saturates all research but are usually the only ones who 'come clean', we run the risk of being portrayed as distinctly 'biased' and thus discounted.

Dubois (1983: 108) coined the term 'passionate scholarship' to describe the politically engaged premise of feminist research, a premise that breaches the academic rule of disembodiment. Social sciences cannot be value-neutral according to Rosser (1988), because society is not neutral on issues such as gender, 'race' or sexual preference. Fine (1992: 214) highlights how researchers 'pronounce "truths" while whiting out their own authority, so as to be unlocatable and irresponsible'.

A criticism of standpoint theory poses questions about whose standpoint it is. Finch (1984) asserted that there is an added dimension when women interview women because both parties share a gendered, subordinate structural position. This early thinking has been challenged for excluding consideration of 'race', disability, sexuality, social class and age, and for incorporating these social structures in one universalising category: 'women' (Bhavnani, 1993; Hill Collins, 1990; hooks, 1991; Morris, 1995; Maguire, 1996; Phoenix, 1994; Siraj-Blatchford, 1995; Stanley and Wise, 1993). The establishment of feminist standpoints is perceived as critical. However, Maynard (1994: 20) suggests that once the existence of several standpoints is admitted, 'there will necessarily be contested truth claims arising from the contextually grounded knowledge of the different standpoints'. To describe this simply as pluralism understates the differing power relations between women.

There is also widespread rejection of the notion of 'double', or 'triple', disadvantage and the 'additive' approach when researching, for example, women with disabilities. Morris (1995) believed that research itself is part of the 'problem' for disabled women as it perpetuates the image of victimhood. Furthermore, it is invariably undertaken by non-disabled people, who hold certain cultural assumptions about disability. When standpoints do not consider diversity and power relations, they can imply limitations and constraints, and provide further evidence of how all knowledge is partial, situated and potentially exclusionary.

RESEARCHING THE MICROPOLITICAL – IS THERE A FEMINIST METHODOLOGY?

A question for me in this research has been what form feminism should take in textual terms (Stanley, 1991: 216). Smith (1992) maintains that social scientific inquiry ordinarily begins from a standpoint in a text-mediated discourse or organisation. It could also be argued that experience of sexist oppression is a valuable source of data for theorising gender, exemplifying a postmodernist concept that power can be productively linked to knowledge (Giroux, 1991; Morley, 1995b). While Stacey (1988: 21) argues that 'there is no uniform canon of feminist research principles ...', Stanley (1991) summarises the basic tenets of what constitutes feminist research. She emphasises how feminist theory is derived from experience; the feminist researcher locates herself on the same critical plane as the researched and that there is a rejection of the dichotomous myth of subjectivity/objectivity. Stanley suggests that what these premises signify is actually better described as a feminist epistemology rather than a methodology. Stanley (1991: 208) asserts that the debate on feminist research has misunderstood that what is being proposed is a different *method* or technique, rather than a specifically feminist theory of *knowledge*. Maynard (1993: 327) concludes that rather than the method *per se*, it is the questions asked, the way the researcher locates herself within the questions and the political purpose of the work, that distinguish feminist from other forms of research. In other

words, feminist research is being freed from some of its earlier ortho-
doxies and is engaging with methodological pluralism, rather than
the quantitative/qualitative binary oppositions challenged by
researchers such as Kelly et al. (1992).

Feminist objections to quantitative methods have been potently
argued:

> Quantitative approaches have foundationalist origins – they rest on
> an epistemological position which sees a single unseamed reality
> existing 'out there' which the special expertise of science can inves-
> tigate and explain as it 'really' is, independent of observer effects.
> (Stanley and Wise, 1993: 6)

In social research, numbers have traditionally been perceived as the
ultimate expression of objectivity. Feminist critics argue that the
pretence of objectivity has led to disembodiment and objectification.
Hughes (1995: 403) believes that statistical analysis becomes a powerful tool in constructing the Other, and that 'domination and
exploitation would be impossible to sustain if difference was not
created and maintained'. Kelly et al. (1992: 150) maintain that what
makes feminist research is not so much the method used, but rather
its application and purpose. For example, the quantification from
surveys can give an indication of the scale of a problem, such as
domestic violence.

The positivistic imperative for 'objectivity' and the banishment of
emotion from the research process has been heavily criticised and
exposed for its dishonesty by a range of counter-hegemonic research
theorists (Eichler, 1988; Fine, 1994; Lather, 1991; Rowan and
Reason, 1981; Stanley and Wise, 1993). Harding (1991) and Haraway
(1988) argue that 'objectivity' has always been about a particular and
specific embodiment. Therefore, there can never be an unmediated
account. Haraway (1988) believes that feminist objectivity means
quite simply situated knowledges. She suggests that feminists could
view objectivity as a 'particular and specific embodiment', rather than
as a 'false vision promising transcendence of all limits and responsibility' (pp. 581–2).

Some feminist researchers have questioned whether there are any
inherently liberatory methods and the extent to which liberation itself
is an enlightenment concept (Maynard and Purvis, 1994). Some have
attempted to clarify issues by inserting typologies and taxonomies
into the debate. Haraway (1988) believes that there are three central
questions to pose in relation to whether research is feminist or not.

First, there is the issue of accountability, not just to the research participants, but to feminism in the wider sense. Researchers need to ask if the researched are reinscribed into prevailing notions of power-lessness. Second, in relation to sensitivity to the power relations embedded in the process, researchers should ask themselves if the micropolitics of the research relationship is discussed. And third, in recognition that 'woman' is not a unifying category, researchers need to consider how their studies engage with questions of difference.

Skeggs (1994a) has summarised three areas to consider in relation to what constitutes feminist research: Ontology, that is, what is knowable? Epistemology, that is, what is knowledge and what is the relationship of the knower to the known? And, methodology, that is, how do we find things out? Skeggs maintains that the ways in which these different questions are answered, or ignored, in the research process will demonstrate the different theoretical positions held by researchers. Differentiating feminist from non-feminist research, Skeggs (1994b: 77) claims that in response to the ontological question, 'feminist research begins from the premise that the nature of reality in western society is unequal and hierarchical'. However, this is not distinctively feminist as the claim could also be made in relation to post-colonialism or Marxism. Fine and Gordon (1991) believe that feminist research should involve the study of *what is not* by disrupting prevailing notions of what is inevitable, what is seen to be 'natural' and what is considered impossible. A key idea here is that of disruption, or deconstruction, with feminism a marker of an oppositional, challenging stance. In attempting to define how feminist research differs from the mainstream, Jacklin (cited in Farnham, 1987: 102) asked: 'do feminists ask different questions?'

REFLEXIVITY

Reflexivity demands emotional and theoretical literacy on the part of the researcher, who can engage sensitively with the research study while/because s/he is aware of her/his own responses, values, beliefs (Morley, 1995b). This can take the form of recognising that research is a social activity 'which intrudes on people's lives' (Troyna, 1994a: 6). It can also mean hesitancy, uncertainty and caution as a result of being acquainted with the theoretical complexities of the subject. Cain (1990) implies that there is a difference between personal and theoretical reflexivity, the former being individualised thoughts, feelings and responses of the researcher, the latter a theoretical under-standing of the site from which one works. Stanley (1991) talks about alienated knowledge and discusses how traditional scientistic knowl-edge hides, through a series of textual means, its labour process. Reflexivity, she argues, acknowledges that our descriptions are mutu-ally constitutive. Indexicality of knowledge demonstrates that it is contextually dependent. Reflexivity is also often located in opposition to ventriloquy, exemplifying engagement and ownership, rather than performance. But recently, personal reflexivity has been represented as self-indulgent, confessional, cathartic and a selective reconstruc-tion of the research process (Troyna, 1994a). Both Meg Maguire and Stephen Ball noticed that, in an earlier draft of this work, I had avoided the use of the first-person singular. I realised that I was attempting to resist self-indulgence, while struggling with a discom-fort about claiming authority. I continue to experience difficulty negotiating the boundaries between abstract and embodied processes of knowledge production while simultaneously maintaining a balance between authorial dominance and invisibility.

TAKING THE PLUNGE (REFLEXIVELY)

In my study I opted for semi-structured, in-depth interviewing as my primary research method. I rejected the idea of surveys and ques-tionnaires as data already exist on the range and location of women's studies courses and feminist academics in Britain (WSN, 1995). As this was a study of the *micropolitics* of feminism, I sought examples of the quotidian and the extent to which feminism influenced social and professional relations and opportunities in the academy. I opted for narrative as I wanted to hear the stories of women teaching, studying and researching as feminists (Lieblich and Josselson, 1994; Shotter and Gergen, 1989). I was keen to discover how they inserted, devel-oped and sustained their feminisms via their academic practices, and I wanted to interrogate their agency, influence and strategies for interest representation. However, this is not a classical ethnography. It is a theoretically-driven inquiry, which draws on ethnographic tactics for illuminatory purposes.

In the interviews, I focused on three broad areas: (1) the organisa-tional context, i.e. culture, ethos, equity policies and practices; (2) provision and experiences of feminism into the academy, i.e. women's studies courses; feminist pedagogy, feminist modules on mainstream courses and (3); experiences of being feminist academics/students, i.e. promotion and tenure, career development and opportunities, interpersonal relations. At the end of all the interviews, I asked what changes they would like to see.

I attempted to build triangulation into the research design, by selecting informants located in diverse locations and organisations. Conscious that much feminist research focuses on the Anglophone community, I included other European countries in the study, with a North/South dimension. I interviewed 40 women in the UK, Sweden and Greece from 25 institutions. Ten were in Greece, seven in Sweden, 22 in the UK, of which six were from overseas (three from the USA, one each from Nigeria, Argentina, Finland) and one in Spain. Twenty-five were in academic posts of whom two were professors, one an associate professor (reader), four assistant professors (overseas universities) six senior lecturers (new universities in the UK), nine lecturers (of whom two are part-time and one untenured), eight researchers/doctoral students and seven postgraduate students.

All the women interviewed identified themselves as feminists, and 24 had been involved in women's studies programmes either as students or lecturers. Twenty-two had introduced feminism into their disciplines. I gained access to informants by contacting women's studies departments and individuals listed in the Women's Studies (UK) Association Members' Handbook (1995). I asked women I knew who had been involved in introducing feminism into the academy. I also contacted women I had met at conferences and seminars overseas. A process of snowballing ensued, during which I visited institutions and was introduced to colleagues or provided with addresses of significant actors. This was especially the practice in Greece and Sweden, where women made strenuous efforts to find interesting informants from their networks for me to interview.

Mindful of the problematics associated with the research process, I invariably enter my studies with a degree of reluctance and resistance. I found asking for interviews or access to institutions or individuals uncomfortable and exploitative. I also find that there is a degree of emotional labour involved in the process, which often leaves me depleted after paying such close attention to narratives. Equally, there is the risk of stirring previously occluded painful memories for informants. I know that I am a researcher, not a counsellor or therapist, and cannot offer follow-through support. Measor (1985: 63) described how the interview involves entering another person's social world and their perspective, but remaining alert to its configurations at the same time ... There is a contradiction in aiming for ultimate rapport and yet treating the person's account both critically and sociologically.

Holland and Ramazanoglu (1995: 279) stated how research based on interviews also brings in the subjects of research, which makes interviews social events and research more clearly a social process. Everywhere I visited I was treated with outstanding hospitality and interest. In spite of busy schedules, women slotted me into lunch hours, coffee-breaks and in some cases, invited me to their homes. This felt very nurturing, but also increased my sense of being a receiver rather than a provider (more evidence of my binary thinking?). After introducing the context of my research, interviews frequently started with informants expressing self-doubt by asking, 'I don't know if I'm the best person for you to talk to'; or, 'I hope I will be of some use to you.' I always scheduled in time for discussion/winding-down time after interviews. This posed questions about the social relations aspect of interviewing. One enormous frustration was that often, after the interview, with the tape recorder absent, women would continue to peel back layers of their memories to reveal significant critical incidents they had previously forgotten. To have asked to recommence recording in a quasi-social situation would have felt quite predatory and anti-social. As a result many important insights are not in the transcripts. However, I included them in research memos, formulated as soon as possible after the interview.

There can be an artificiality about a transaction based on questions. It can appear clinical and abrasive. I frequently adopted the agenda of interviewees, paying careful attention to issues that were 'on top' for them. I tried to be sensitive to voice, non-verbal communication and the issue of boundaries. As some of the informants knew me through different networks, I stressed confidentiality, both in the sense of making the data anonymous, but also in the more complex domain of not referring to interview material in another setting.

Following the interviews, I was often stimulated, but quite disoriented, after entering other people's worlds. At times, my excitement felt akin to that engendered by investigative journalism, as I was so stunned at what I had 'uncovered'. I was also very wary of ghoulishness, opportunism and tokenism, checking my delight at discovering that informants had particularly vivid incidents of sexual harassment, racism, disablism to relate.

This study revealed the enormous strength of feminist networking in the academy. On very few occasions was I refused an interview. As a white woman, I felt certain that I would appear, to black women, as yet another researcher trying to adjust her research sample to meet the requirements of anti-discriminatory practices. Yet this was not the case, and several black women participated with considerable support and enthusiasm. A group of MA students were happy to talk, but refused a taped interview on the basis that they disagreed with research and did not want to be statistics in someone's book. This refusal to play the research game struck me as exceedingly refreshing but made me question why so many of us do.

FEMINISM AND GROUNDED THEORY

Further theoretical tensions exist between feminism and grounded theory. Central to the concept of grounded theory is the belief that the researcher starts with a *tabula rasa*, and elicits theory from the data (Glaser and Strauss, 1967; Strauss and Corbin, 1990). The aim is for theory to follow data rather than precede it. This inductive approach was developed in opposition to the positivistic notion of hypothesis testing and deductivism, in which a predetermined theory was used with the rigidity of a grid on the research data, and lived experiences were reduced to matrices of standardised variables. Lather (1986) described grounded theory as an attempt to minimise researcher-imposed definitions and avoid the problem of conceptual overdeterminism and theoretical imposition. Reinharz (1983) advocated not undertaking an extensive literature search before an investigation, in order to avoid self-fulfilling prophecies. Strauss and Corbin (1990) claimed that the research question in grounded theory study is a statement that identifies the phenomenon to be studied, with insight and understanding increasing with data interaction. Grounded theoreticians are advised to maintain an attitude of scepticism as all theoretical explanations should be regarded as provisional. Everything should be checked, played against the actual data and never accepted as fact. Grounded theory, according to Strauss and Corbin (p. 55), should 'help the analyst to break through biases and assumptions brought to, and that can develop during, the research process'. The researchers' perspectives are altered by the logic of the data.

I considered the use of grounded theory as at one time it was seen as highly compatible with feminist ideology. First, it was concerned to locate theory in participants' worlds, and second, it was thought to aid the process of breaking out of the confines of androcentric theory (Henwood and Pidgeon, 1995). Some feminist researchers who initially rejected deductivism now reject grounded theory, on the basis that no feminist study can be politically neutral, completely inductive or solely based on grounded theory as *all* work is theoretically grounded (Maynard, 1994: 23). Kelly et al. (1992: 156) believe that:

> As feminists, we cannot argue that theory emerges from research, since we start from a theoretical perspective that takes gender as a fundamental organizer of social life.

Holland and Ramazanoglu (1995) indicated that we cannot read meaning *in* texts, allowing them to pose their own meanings, without also reading *into* them. While accepting the need to take women's experiences and accounts seriously, Cain (1986: 265) reminded us of the need 'to take our own theory seriously' and 'use the theory to make sense of ... the experience'.

One complexity of data-led theorising is articulated in the term 'false consciousness'. Lather (1986: 269) described how

> Sole reliance on the participants' perceptions of their situation is misguided because, as neo-Marxists point out, false consciousness and ideological mystification may be present.

Applying Gramsci's theories of hegemony (1971), Lather (1986) emphasised how most people to some extent identify with and/or accept ideologies which do not serve their best interests. Smith (1992) suggested that since knowledge is essentially socially organised, it can never be an act or an attribute of individual consciousness. For example, in this study, when informants reported that their gender had never impeded their career progress in the academy, or that feminist students were only able to talk in slogans, should this be taken at face value, or was it an example of false consciousness? Or was the accusation of false consciousness a way of rationalising the occurrence of contradictory or uncomfortable data? Did this display an inability of some participants to read power relations or evidence of the micropolitical enactment of macropolitical power relations? Whatever the case, who was I to say, and why was my reading more valid than theirs?

INTERPRETATION AND ARTEFACT

The question of whether an artificial and patriarchal order is being imposed on the raw data is a recurring theme in feminist research. Feminists in the 1990s have argued that there is an inherent fragmentation and fabrication in the research process, as people's lives are dissected, according to the researcher's frame of reference. Maynard (1994: 11) indicated how:

> Only one part of experience is abstracted as the focus for attention and this is done in both a static and atemporal fashion ... Often the result of such an approach is a simple matrix of standardised variables which is unable to convey an in-depth understanding of, or feeling for, the people under study.

Fine (1994: 22) also drew attention to how social research invariably involves 'carving out pieces of narrative evidence that we select, edit, and deploy to border our arguments'. Condor (1986) suggested that the emphasis on isolating 'variables' excludes aspects of meaning inherent in the context and totality of women's lives. The process of interpretation also implies that there is a knower and a known (Henwood and Pidgeon, 1995). A further concern is that feminist researchers dissect women's narratives and subject them to analysis heavily influenced by male theorists of social science. Smith (1989: 35–6) cautioned about the dangers of feminists turning talk into texts and texts into sociology. Holland and Ramazanoglu (1995: 274) commented that even if the researcher identifies politically *with* women, this does not necessarily give us the methodological tools with which to avoid the conceptual distancing of women from their experiences. They highlight how feminists have had to accept that there is 'no technique of analysis or methodological logic that can neutralise the social nature of interpretation' (p. 281). Interpretation is perceived by contributors to Maynard and Purvis (1994: 7) as a social process, and as such, is a 'political, contested and unstable activity'.

The interview method exposes the dynamic link between social and technical processes. Social relationships enrich, distort and constrain data collection, and the techniques used affect social relationships. Part of reflexivity is to notice and understand the relationship between the two. As with all social science studies, knowledge claims must be problematic. I recognise that an interview is a specific account given to a particular interviewer at a particular moment

(Holland and Ramazanoglu, 1995: 288). But data analysis in this study has revealed strong patterns and features across national and institutional boundaries.

2 Equity and Change in Higher Education

MARKET CULTURE AND NEW MANAGERIALISM IN THE PUBLIC SERVICES

A central concern of this study is feminism as change in the academy, and the consequences and challenges for feminist change agents. In this chapter, I examine processes that link macro-changes to micro-consequences by focusing on the dynamic relationship between political and organisational change in higher education in Britain. By so doing I hope to describe the complex configurations of power and organisation in higher education into which feminisms are introduced, with attention to economic, cultural and intellectual changes. This involves interrogation of policies and discourses of New Right reform, new managerialism, mass expansion, equity and postmodernist theories of power, with questions raised about the interconnection of demographic changes and equality of opportunity. Equity is considered in relation to the democratic rhetoric of enhanced access, and connections are made between equality and quality by questioning what is being accessed by changing student populations.

In Britain, the market has become a policy alternative to public monopolies. By 1983 universities were beginning to be perceived by the government as offering poor value for money, being too distant from the wealth-creating sectors of industry and commerce, and being too dependent on government funding (Walford, 1992). As a result, the academy has undergone cultural changes in the last decade. New discourses have been introduced, with new authority, activated by the concept and practice of new managerialism. New managerialism relates to both macro-economic policy and post-Fordist work regimes. A fundamental premise of new managerialism is the belief that objectives of social policy can be promoted at a lower cost when the appropriate management techniques are applied to the public services. New managerialism bases its status on early Taylorist claims that management is a scientific discipline. Hence, a technicist industry has developed, based on a rationalist epistemology of change. Pollitt (1993: 15) describes how the aim has been to evolve a 'scien-

neo-Fordism?

tific' approach so 'public officials would be better protected against the irrationality of "political interference"'. The New Right made a commitment to 'roll back the frontiers of the state' (Maidment and Thompson, 1993: 25) and change the way Britain was managed. In 1980, the Secretary of State for the Environment, Michael Heseltine, said:

> Efficient management is the key to the [national] revival ... And the management ethos must run right through our national life – private and public companies, civil service, nationalised industries, local government, the National Health Service. (Heseltine, 1980, quoted in Pollitt, 1993: 3)

The result has been the development of competing moral systems, with welfare principles in opposition to market principles or 'guardian versus commercial' syndromes (Jacobs, 1992). Applying commercial values to 'guardian' contexts results in considerable tensions, currently exemplified in New Labour's intention to charge students tuition fees in higher education (Richards and Tysome, 1996). Central to new managerialism is the promotion of a corporate mission, with goals, monitoring procedures and performance measurement. Responsibility is devolved and increased responsiveness to clients/customers is alleged. Clarke, Cochrane and McLaughlin (1994) argue that these developments are part of a wider ideological process which is transforming relations of power, culture, control and accountability, and that this is linked to social policy changes which reflect an ongoing reconceptualisation and restructuring of the state.

The emphasis in new managerialism is on the three Es: economy, efficiency and effectiveness. Noticeably, a fourth E – for equity – is absent. (The fifth E is for 'environment'.) Ranson and Stewart (1994) observed that values, particularly those relating to social justice, are perceived as irrelevant to management theories based on marketisation. As Ball (1994a: 71) indicates, the reform process in the UK is not simply structural or technical, but also cultural and ideological. As concepts of consumerism and individual rights and choice gain currency, questions arise as to how equity values can be sustained in the increasing emphasis on economic/efficiency models. Pollitt (1993: 7) commented:

> First, ideology is said to consist of values, ideas and beliefs about the state of the world. That managerialism consists of a set of ideas and beliefs has already been established, but what of *values*?

Ball (1994a: 125) asserts: 'Equity is off the agenda, inequality is a cornerstone of the market.' The emphasis on quality, evaluation, accountability and value suggests consumer empowerment, without acknowledging social inequalities (Morley, 1995a). Under the guise of political neutrality, the market economy poses as a technology, but represents a range of values which confirm and reinforce the established social order of wealth and privilege. Ranson and Stewart (1994: 48) decoded the cultural transition:

> freedom rather than equality, individualism rather than community, efficiency rather than justice, and competition rather than co-operation ...

Competition is a primary feature in the market economy and, as Sidgwick et al. (1994: 469) comment, is believed to 'expose and eliminate waste, inefficiency, inertia and antiquated methods of working'. In a market culture, state monopolies and producer capture are perceived as enemies of democracy. According to Hayek (1944), the market is a neutral mechanism; it has no morals. There are winners and losers and focusing on the 'losers' is inefficient. The new culture in the public services obscures the fact that what counts as efficiency and effectiveness is itself both a political judgement and a social construct. Ball (1990) maintains that whilst new managerialism appears to be linked to enhancing efficiency, it is a mechanism for the New Right to gain more precise control over education. This has been accomplished, in part, by deregulation and the introduction of competition or 'quasi-markets' (Le Grand and Bartlett, 1993).

Negative images of the public services were amplified by the anti-Left media. By characterising them as wasteful, inefficient and dominated by reactive policies of municipal socialism, the New Right were able to justify dirigiste policies in the public sector. Deregulation and the introduction of a free market would ensure a more rigorous deployment of resources. Inflation had supposedly been caused by the unbridled expansion of public services beyond the financial means of the state. The belief being that

> Public organizations have, purportedly been self-interested and unresponsive to the public and have failed to fulfil the expectations of the postwar years of leading to the creation of a fairer, more equal society. (Ranson and Stewart, 1994: 3)

Higher education policy is a 'discourse of power' (Shore and Roberts, 1995: 8). Prior to education reform, universities appeared to be run like 'publicly funded corporations' (Harrison, 1994: 52). Before universities could enter the marketplace, it was believed that they had to change their organisational structures and operations to become 'more managerial' (Walford, 1992: 188). The Jarratt Report (1985) suggested that vice-chancellors should be seen as the chief executives, and governing bodies were to perform as Boards of Directors. The Croham Report (1987) recommended performance indicators for universities' finance, management, teaching and research, and major changes in the way universities received funding from the Universities Grants Committee. The concept of measurement was introduced via interventions such as teaching quality audits and research assessment exercises, with government funding directly linked to acquisition of research contracts and production of the written word and publication of the results in competitive league tables (Morley, 1995b; Shore and Roberts, 1995).

These changes in the academy appear to have been accommodated with minimal resistance and opposition (Davies and Holloway, 1995). Emphasis on productivity and the resulting intensification of workloads has contributed to the development of a compliance culture, with increased docility of academics. Shore and Roberts (1995: 13) argue that 'the system, above all, plays on the insecurity of the disciplined subject'. Power has also become more diffuse with the simultaneous regulation and deregulation of public services. Changes have been accomplished by a mechanism Kickert (1991) described as steering at a distance. According to Jeffs and Smith (1994: 24), central government has been able to distance itself from direct responsibility for unpopular decisions such as school and hospital closures, or the introduction of fees for higher education, through the creation of markets and managers. Shore and Roberts (1995: 12) indicate how state intervention is disguised through 'recruitment of intermediary agencies'. In higher education, for example, there has been an insertion of the quality discourse and public accountability. This has been implemented largely through a system of peer review such as the HEFCE teaching quality audits and research assessment exercises. A postmodern reading would suggest that this process reflects Bentham's panopticon, a system through which, having internalised the values of the ruling group, professionals regulate themselves. There has also been the internalisation of the notion that absolute standards of truth and excellence are achievable (Harrison, 1994). Hence some academics are theoretically wedded to postmodern theories of power, but are operating with modernist discourses of objectivity and measurement.

It would be unwise to degenerate into an Orwellian dualism and suggest that all that was associated with the old regime was good, and the new culture is uniformly bad. The situation is more complex than that. The discourse of choice and consumer power can be attractive to members of the community who have traditionally experienced powerlessness and frustration in relation to powerful organisations. As Cox (1992: 23–4) stated:

> There is a powerful resonance in assertions that contrast the benefits of being a consumer in a free market with the dependence and subordination implied by being a client, patient, tenant or pupil in a professionally dominated and often patronizing, sexist and racially biased public service.

The idea of destabilising the complacency of public service organisations, by making them more accountable, less financially secure and subject to consumer choice has its attractions. However, consumer choice is not a neutral mechanism. Bourdieu and Passeron (1990: 51–2) – have observed how the education market presupposes 'possession of the cultural code required for decoding the objects displayed'. Sidgwick et al. (1994) point out that research into the 'marketing' of both education and health has discerned marked disparities in the information and awareness which different socio-economic groups possess when entering into market transactions. Arguments for reform have been based on the suggestion that

> public service provision in local government (as in the rest of the welfare state) has historically operated in the interests of the group which run it. (Cochrane, 1993: 221)

This is particularly true in the case of Britain's 'old' universities, whose much cherished autonomous self-government, in the name of academic freedom, has protected these institutions since the Renaissance. Tritter (1995: 420) explains how the 'cosy world of higher education' has been disrupted by recent changes:

> the creation of the Higher Education Funding Council (HEFC) and the Higher Education Quality Council (HEQC), and the quasi-market created by the Research Assessment Exercise (RAE), have dramatically altered traditional notions of academic accountability. (Tritter, 1995: 420)

The new economy of power in the public services has produced paradoxes in higher education. For example, progressive discourses and practices of adult learning, access and opportunity have grown at the same time as resurgent right-wing applied economics. Expansion is represented as beneficial to members of subordinate groups by enabling them to gain access to cultural capital in the form of academic and professional training. However, it is argued that whilst quantitative representation of 'non-traditional' students has increased, qualitative changes in service delivery have failed to occur (Edwards, 1993; Evans, 1995). The result is that the client group in Britain may have shifted, for example, to incorporate 50 per cent female undergraduate students (Coffield and Vignobles, 1997), but organisational cultures and priorities of the academy are still geared to the needs and interests of the dominant group. The opportunity discourse can rapidly transmute into exploitation of the 'consumers' in the market economy. While mass higher education is an inherently democratic concept, in the current context, it is the democracy of the marketplace (Harrison, 1994). For example, if black and white students from working-class backgrounds enter unreconstructed courses in underfunded mass educational provision in the academy, whose interests are being served?

BROADENING THE MARKET: MORE MEANS LESS?

The former Conservative government in Britain made a commitment in the 1992 election to provide higher education for one third of 18–21 year olds by the year 2000. This was accepted by all parties, and higher education, unlike the school sector, was not an election issue. The dominant view was that increased access to higher education would strengthen the economy. Britain had been shamed by comparison with other industrially developed countries. From its elite medieval beginnings to the period immediately preceding the second world war, only 3 per cent of the population, mainly young, ruling-class men, attended British universities. The University of London opened its doors to women students in 1878, while Cambridge did not follow suit until 1947. By 1962/3, the number of the total population in higher education had grown to 7.2 per cent (Ainley, 1994: 11). In 1963, the influential Robbins Report ignored gendered, racialised and social-classed power relations, and reinforced the myth of disembodied age-related meritocracy, stating that courses of higher education should be available to 'all young persons who are qualified by ability and attainment' (Robbins, 1963: 49). 1987 saw the adoption of the North American model of mass higher education, and by 1990 the age participation ratio reached 20 per cent for the first time. In spite of these recent changes, Britain still lags behind the Netherlands, Sweden, the USA and Japan, who all have over 80 per cent of their 18 year olds in higher education. Half of the new student intake in the UK is now outside the 18–21 age range, but the term 'non-traditional learner' is still used for students over 21. This nomenclature, adopted to describe mature students, insidiously reinforces normative constructions of students (Morley, 1993). Halsey (1993) and Pring (1992) still focus on access to higher education in relation to school leavers. The academy not only defines what knowledge is, but also defines and regulates what a *student* is.

Demographic trends according to Edwards (1993: 5) mean that there is, and will be for some time, a shortage of conventionally qualified 18-year-old students to enter full-time higher education in many Western countries. In Britain and the United States, for example, widening access for mature students, women, the working class and those from 'minority ethnic' groups has been an aim (DES, 1987; HMI, 1991). It is debatable whether this came about as a commitment to equity or as a market strategy to widen the consumer base. 1994 was the first year in which women constituted 50 per cent of the total number of students in higher education. In Britain, the figures show that between 1979 and 1988 there was a 37 per cent increase in full-time mature students, with the proportion of women rising steadily from 41 per cent in 1979 to 48 per cent in 1988 (DES, 1991). This statistical evidence is perceived by some as both a result of 'feminist advocacy' and as evidence of a decrease in 'gender inequalities' (Halsey, 1993: 130).

Theorists of higher education have highlighted the part it plays as a vehicle of class domination and social control (Morley, 1997; Shore and Roberts, 1995). While only 7 per cent of young people are educated in independent schools in Britain, they represented 25 per cent of the intake to higher education in 1987, and 19 per cent in 1991. However, the proportion of these students at Oxford rose from 37 per cent in 1988 to 48 per cent in 1991 (Heward and Taylor, 1993: 77–8). From 1990 the UCCA and PCAS asked candidates to specify their ethnic origin. Admissions in 1990 and 1991 recorded that 'ethnic minority' students made up 8 per cent of all students in higher education in the UK, with the former polytechnics receiving a higher proportion of applications from 'minority ethnic' groups than established universities. There have been differing interpretations of statistics. Modood (1993) suggests that the term 'ethnic minorities' disguises gender and class variables:

> For while Africans have a representation at more than three times their size, Indians and 'other Asians' ... at about two and a half times their size, the Chinese at somewhat more than twice and Pakistanis at somewhat less than twice, the Black Caribbeans have an over-representation of about 50 per cent which is mainly based on performance of the women ... (Modood, 1993: 169)

However, the working group set up by the Committee of Vice Chancellors and Principals to analyse Universities Central Clearing and Admission (Taylor, 1992) recorded that African-Caribbean and Bangladeshi students were significantly under-represented, particularly in the older universities (Henry, 1994). Participation of disabled students is also a cause for concern (Gibson, 1996; Iantaffi, 1996). An estimated 0.3 per cent of higher education students are recorded as disabled, although they comprise 3 per cent of the 21–29 age group. The elitist pattern continues, as the composition of students in high status institutions remains largely unchanged, with women and 'ethnic minority' students clustered in what Halsey (1993: 131) describes as 'cheaper and less prestigious forms of institution ...' Halsey concluded that the British binary line has lost its official status and a post-binary system has begun (Halsey, 1993: 139). Mass expansion appears to be reinforcing the hierarchical structure of higher education. It could be argued therefore that the terms 'old' and 'new' universities are new codes for the insider/outsider discourse.

Transition to mass education in Britain is set against a political backdrop of underfunding. In 1981, the subsidy for overseas students was removed. The 1981 Public Expenditure White Paper announced a reduction of 20 per cent in higher education expenditure. Cuts were not evenly distributed across institutions, with newer, more technically oriented universities, such as Aston and Bradford, receiving higher penalties than Oxford and Cambridge. By 1984, it was evident that financial cuts were a continuing feature of academic life, and in the past decade there has been an increase of 64 per cent in overall student numbers and a rise of only 11 per cent in staff. Tritter (1995: 420) points out that in 'English universities, the ratio of pupils (*sic*) to full-time academic staff has climbed from 9.7: 1 in 1980–81 to 14.2: 1 in 1992–3.'

In the early 1990s, it was estimated that, by mid-decade, direct public funding for teaching would have fallen to around 25 per cent of the total costs, with universities required to find new sources of income and become less reliant on government sources (Davies and Holloway, 1995). A vice-chancellor of a new university commented:

> It is those who restrict access by accepting only students with the highest traditional qualifications which receive status, privilege, honours and resources. (Wagner, 1989: 36)

The expansion in student numbers was perceived by Epstein (1995) as driven by economic necessity rather than by a commitment to equality of opportunity. The market economy, Evans argued (1995: 74), means that some universities have adopted the old supermarket slogan of 'pack them in and pile them high'. A cynical interpretation of the mass expansion in higher education in Britain is that economic recession and high unemployment require that people are relocated from the employment market. In terms of mature students, lack of career opportunities and social disadvantage in a depressed economy can motivate some to seek cultural capital via educational qualifications.

There is a complex interaction between mass expansion and selective forces which continues to shape the composition of the student body. Benn (1995: 3) believes that widening access must include improving retention as well as entry. Epstein (1995: 61) highlights how her former institution was successful in attracting black and working-class students, but staff were unable to support them and ensure their successful progress through degree courses. This was not, she stated, because of lack of goodwill or commitment to equal opportunities, but 'because of the very pressure of numbers resulting from market success of attracting and accepting these students'. In other words, mass expansion had led to potential shortchanging of the new consumer, as the organisation is not geared to differing educational needs. As Lorde (1984: 115) noted:

> institutional rejection of difference is an absolute necessity in a profit economy which needs outsiders as surplus people.

Epstein (1995) also mentioned the concern expressed by the external examiner in relation to the large proportion of black, working-class women among those who failed the degree or had to re-sit part of it. This exemplified how educational values cannot remain unblemished by the demands of the market and the economically

driven enterprise culture. It further serves to illustrate how the
market functions as a class strategy and the penalties incurred by
recruiting 'value-added' students.

The 1992 Further and Higher Education Act removed the binary
divide between polytechnics and universities. Ainley (1994) thought
that this resulted in the widening of social and academic divisions in
higher education. Evans (1995: 74) believed that the transition from
elitist institutions to large-scale teaching machines means that 'the
mere acquisition of a first degree no longer carries the immediate
cachet and promise of occupational privilege it did thirty years ago'.
Speaking from a different ideological position, Amis said in 1961 that
'if more lower-class people [*sic*] are let into higher education, standards will decline. More means worse' (quoted in Sinfield, 1993: 4).
Bourdieu (1979) predicted this development when he argued how
culturally arbitrary qualifications can change their worth as badges of
distinction acquired by different social groups. He believed that new
signs of exclusion can be evolved by traditional elites to preserve privileged access to the powerful positions they previously inherited but
which are now ostensibly open to meritocratic competition. It would
appear that increased access seems to be leading to educational inflation and negative equity, with the value of qualifications tumbling as
more representatives from marginalised groups acquire them. Rather
than associating widening access with enhanced quality and diversity,
it is perceived as dilution, or pollution; a situation which challenges
the very notion of equity in higher education.

EQUITY IN THE ACADEMY

Thomson (1995: 283) argued that during the 1970s and early 1980s
the social movements of feminism, anti-racism and gay liberation
began to make an impact on education in the form of equal opportunities philosophies.[1] The ascent to power of the Left in several
metropolitan local authorities meant that there was an articulation,
both in policy and practice, of the place education played in the
production, reproduction and transformation of the major dimensions of social inequality. Compared with other public sector

---

[1] Eisenstein (1984) believed that feminist influence on education could be
traced back to the fifteenth century, whilst others argue that Sappho in the
fifth century was an early feminist educator (Purvis, 1994).

institutions, local authorities, schools and colleges of further education for example, equity discourses have scarcely permeated the
academy. This point will be developed further in the next chapter.

In 1986 an investigation in Britain for the Commission for Racial
Equality discovered that 20 of the 42 universities replied citing their
charters as sufficient evidence of their commitment to equal opportunities, and that former polytechnics were more likely to have
policies than established universities (Heward and Taylor, 1993).
Only two out of five universities offer equal opportunities training for
staff responsible for recruitment, and in half these cases training is
not compulsory (Personnel Management, 1994). Enquiries of the
Commission on University Career Opportunity (CUCO) in the late
1980s suggested that over 90 per cent of universities had formally
adopted equal opportunities policies, a little over half had examined
their criteria for appointments, promotions and regrading, but only
37 per cent had devised implementation plans (CUCO, 1994; Davies
and Holloway, 1995).

In their study of the representation of 'ethnic minority' groups in 53
university prospectuses in the academy, Jewson et al. (1991)
concluded that 80 per cent of universities did not offer any sort of
explicit or implicit equal opportunities statement in their prospectus.
Organisational segmentalism was also seen as a barrier to change.
Leicester and Lovell's study (1994) found that even when equal
opportunities were mentioned in universities' mission statements,
fewer than in one in ten departments had any written policy on 'ethnic
minorities', and just 2 per cent had a formal policy on women. The
long tradition, or pretence, of academic freedom and beliefs in the
disembodiment and purity of knowledge meant that these concerns
are often perceived as largely irrelevant to higher education (Evans,
1995). Jewson et al. (1991: 184) believes that universities have rarely
regarded themselves as institutions that could, or would, engage in
unfair discrimination, as they have been traditionally 'wedded to an
ethic of individual academic achievement which purports to recognise
no boundaries or barriers other than that of merit and ability'.
Leicester (1993: 1) observes that 'the "higher" one goes through the
education sectors, the more resistance to progressive antiracist and
pluralist change'. Her explanation was that 'the more privileged,
elitist and hierarchical the arena, the more resistance to democratiz-
ing developments one might expect to find' (Leicester, 1993: 2). In
terms of broader social policy, more than 20 years of equality legislation has done little to shift the substantial difference in men and

women's employment positions in the academy (Morley, 1994 and 1995c). The cliché of the gender gap indicates that there is both verti-
cal and horizontal segregation in the academy, with women staff under-represented in positions of seniority, and women students under-represented in the disciplines of science and technology.

When policies and statements do exist, it is questionable how much impact they have had on employment practices, organisational cultures, epistemology, curriculum development, dominant academic discourses and pedagogy. One explanation is that equality discourses are too rooted in liberalist ideology to alter structures. It is also argued that located as they are within a framework of discriminatory practices and prejudices, equal opportunities policies, whether liberal or radical in their conception, remain ameliorative. They are often anchored in a superficial perspective of racism and sexism which neglects to address the structural and institutional determinants of social inequality (Rassool, 1995). Jewson and Mason (1986: 314–15) interrogated central divergences between liberal and radical interpretations. The liberal conception is embedded in notions of fairness and justice, conceiving talent and ability as individual attributes. This analysis derives from early thinking such as that of Stuart Mill (1869: 445), who argued that human beings should be free to develop their faculties and not be 'chained down by an inexorable bond to the place they are born to'.

Equality of opportunity has had a particular connection with gender politics, originating from seventeenth- and eighteenth-century campaigns for improvements in the legal and social standing of women in Europe (Forbes, 1991: 17). When applied to policy, there is a preoccupation with procedures and rules, ostensibly to guarantee fair play. The radical approach, Jewson and Mason (1986) argue, seeks to intervene directly in workplace practices and structures and is more concerned with outcomes than with rules. The preoccupation with end state arguments is invariably implemented by monitoring and positive action programmes. An example of these ideological differences is Arends and Volman's (1995: 121) comparative study of equality policies in the Netherlands and the UK. They indicate how the Inner London Education Authority (ILEA) combined egalitarian and radical terminology and focused on structures that produce difference, by considering educational establishments as both instruments of change and producers of inequality. Dutch policy, they concluded, individualises the issue and aims to change 'mentality' and meet 'needs' in education. It is widely believed that it was the ILEA's

radicalism that contributed to its abolition by the New Right (Jeffs and Smith, 1994).

Equity discourses have been vulnerable to attacks from the New Right, and have had limited support from the Left. Feminist critics claim that equity discourses are inappropriate for the complexities of difference, diversity and pluralism. For example, Kulke (1993: 132) argues that equality discourses of modern times in general have not fundamentally altered the gender hierarchy, because concepts of equality and gender differences have been formulated and constrained by the form of patriarchal rationality within which they are embedded. That is, belief systems and values enable the identification of areas for change, which transform into political inception and develop into mediation, outcomes and effects on social justice. Furthermore, the trajectory analysis for equity insufficiently acknowledges that inequalities in the private sphere influence ability to participate in the public sphere. Spivak (1987: 103) identified how the political, social, professional, economic, intellectual arenas are ascribed to the public sphere, whereas the emotional, sexual and domestic are the private domain. The collective is dissolved into the individual. A common criticism of the 'equality' discourse is that it has a relativity problem. Franzway et al. (1989: 96) ask: 'equal with what, or whom?' They believe that 'equality' fails to challenge the model by which the male individual is taken as the universal case. The normative connotations of policies for equality can separate the individual from the wider social context and perpetuate hegemonic value systems. hooks (1987: 62) suggests that equity language is simplistic and glib and, referring to sexual equality, asks: 'Since men are not equals in white supremacist, capitalist, patriarchal class structure, which men do women want to be equal to?'

Considerable scepticism exists regarding the use of equity policies to influence social and organisational change. Whereas Maidment and Thompson (1993: 2) define policy as 'any conscious attempt to mobilize resources and personnel to achieve an objective', equity policies are often perceived as tokenistic, ineffectual and dishonest. For example, McAuley (1987: 162) asserts that equity policies are damaging to women, because the statement comes to be accepted as a representation of the truth. Jewson and Mason (1986: 317) discovered that policies were often an excuse for inactivity, and were often

seen as evidence of deceit or bad faith on the part of management … the existence of the policy made official, and in particular legal, complaints more difficult to sustain. Such consequences were taken by some as evidence of a cunning strategy aimed at continuing with *de facto* discrimination while undermining officially accepted grounds for complacency.

Jewson and Mason also established (1986: 328–9) the manipulative use of equity by suggesting that 'The existence of a policy may, in certain circumstances, assist an employer in defending a tribunal case'. This is reinforced by Troyna (1994b: 73), who analysed micro-political functions of the equality discourse in education in terms of Edelman's concept of 'symbolic political language' and 'condensation symbols' (Edelman, 1977). Troyna explains how 'condensation symbols' are designed to create symbolic stereotypes and metaphors which reassure supporters that their interests have been considered. However, they are so framed that the proposed solutions may also be contradictory or ambiguously related to the way supporters first viewed the issue.

As I mentioned before, policies for equality have had few product champions. The ideology of new managerialism, with its emphasis on efficiency and elimination of waste, has facilitated the targeting of Equal Opportunities programmes for reform. Arnot (1995: 169) indicates how feminist demands for educational equality have been perceived as 'ideological extravagances'. The notion of redistribution of resources to further the interests of subordinate groups is perceived as undesirable and expensive social engineering by the contributors to Quest's edited collection of papers (1992) attacking equal opportunities. Utilising the economic rationale, Quest states that in 1991 the Equal Opportunities Commission spent over £4.5 million promoting and enforcing sex equality. Conway (1992: 57) also claims that:

> Hiring a woman, when an equally well-qualified man was available, would be an unsound economic move for any employer looking to make a long-term appointment … it would appear that current equal opportunities legislation is causing society to produce less wealth than it would do in the absence of such legislation.

Contributors to this volume employed arguments similar to those used to defend pornography; that is to say, essentialist views about women's differences in preferences and abilities, and the location of equity in the range of coercive, bureaucratic discourses which censor and violate individual freedom. The book would not be worthy of comment if it were not written by senior members of the academy, and thus represents a discursive site, where prejudice is legitimated by academic authority.

CULTURE CHANGE IN THE ACADEMY

New Right discourses, linked to public policy and income streams, have influenced significant cultural changes in the academy whereas equity discourses have not. Culture in the broadest sense is political (Sinfield, 1994). In society and in organisations, while culture is diverse, there is inevitably a dominant culture. The academy is also one of the innumerable places where production of culture occurs. A central obstacle to cultural change in academia is the belief that knowledge is decontextualised, and constructed and communicated with impartial power and authority. This belief in itself confers power on those identifying what constitutes pure, absolute knowledge. Gramsci's concept of hegemony implies that dominant groups can conceal their power by projecting their particular way of perceiving and defining social reality so successfully that its view is accepted as 'common sense' (Jaggar, 1983). Spender (1982: 16) developed this concept:

> Men have provided us with a false picture of the world ... not just because their view is so limited, but because they have insisted that their limited view is the total view.

Counter-hegemonic discourses, such as equity, cannot enter organisations without a degree of struggle. This can be particularly stressful for change agents, a point I return to in Chapter 3. Williams notes that:

> While there is a dominant culture ... its dominance depends on continuous processes of adjustment, reinterpretation, incorporation, dilution ... The dominant may tolerate, repress, or incorporate these other formations, but that will be a continuous, urgent, and often strenuous project. (quoted in Sinfield, 1994: 25)

Hearn et al. (1989: 1) believe that 'Until recently, academia ... has obscured life rather than reflected it.' Evans (1994: 171) suggests: 'Unfortunately, the academy exists in a world in which homogeneity is an increasingly prized feature of social life.' This can mean that when minorities enter dominant cultures, there can be a resulting cultural dissonance in which members of under-represented groups are required to detach themselves from subcultural allegiances and ventriloquise dominant discourses. However, remaining loyal to one's 'subculture' can have the effect of positioning members of subordinate groups in oppositional location. Bourdieu (1988) maintains that the right to speak, in other words, legitimacy, is granted to those possessing 'cultural capital' (recognised resources and values). Similarly, Ainley (1994: 156) maintains that elite higher education legitimates the 'pre-existing cultural capital of some'. At the other end of the spectrum are those motivated to participate in higher education to acquire cultural capital and counter social disadvantage. This raises interesting questions as to how organisational cultures can be influenced and changed. The dominant group has accrued the legitimacy to influence equity changes, but can lack the political motivation to do so, while members of subordinate groups can have the political motivation, but not the cultural legitimacy.

Ranson and Stewart (1994: 43) describe how the powerful decide which issues enter the arena and also control when issues do not arise. For example, the politics of non-decision making has been theorised in relation to the micropolitics of organisational change, demonstrating how issues and demands can be suffocated, maimed or destroyed before they gain access to the relevant decision-making arena (Lukes, 1974: 18–19). If equity initiatives are successful, they represent major examples of organisational change. As Ball (1987: 32) argues:

> Innovations are rarely neutral. They tend to advance or enhance the position of certain groups and disadvantage and damage the position of others ... Vested interests may also be under threat: innovations not infrequently involve the redistribution of resources, the restructuring of job allocations and redirection of lines of information flow.

In the academy, change processes are complicated by the autonomy that accrues as a result of expert power. It can mean that those beyond the boundary of knowledge cannot question a professional judgement. This is particularly pertinent in the case of academic promotions, where judgements of academic worth remain nebulous and are in the hands of the dominant group (Morley, 1994). Equally, new knowledges are validated by members of the profession credentialised in existing disciplinary and intellectual frameworks.

POSTMODERNISM IN THE ACADEMY

There have been changes in the policy framework and in the composition of the student population. Additionally, postmodernism has
been a major theoretical influence in the academy, providing new
ways of understanding power and change processes. When discussing
equity and change in higher education, it would be easy to frame the
analysis in modernist polarities, depicting the past as a golden era of
collegiate scholarship and the present as a vulgar, consumer-led
enterprise. Postmodernism exposes dualistic thinking and argues that
organisations and social life are full of messy contradictions and shifting certainties. The pluralism and irrationality embedded in
postmodernism mean that it is fruitless to subject change processes in
the academy to rational analysis. Equally, there is a perception of the
futility of recently introduced changes, and the extent to which new
managerialism is embedded in a modernist rational epistemology.

> Given then, the persistent pluralism of postmodern forms and the
> heterogeneity of its institutions, the pursuit of 'pure' academic
> standards or absolute notions of academic quality become as futile
> as the pursuit of 'pure' socialism. (Harrison, 1994: 64)

Postmodernism recognises fragmentation, dispersal, discontinuity
and plurality as common features of the social world. New forms of
academic provision in the academy, such as modularisation and credit
transfer, could be seen as reflecting the disintegration and fragmentation denoted in postmodernism.

Postmodernism continually connects knowledge with power. In this
analysis, meaning is not fixed in language or in consistent power relations of domination and subordination, but shifts according to a range
of linguistic, institutional and cultural contextual factors.
Furthermore, there is a hostility to notions of human nature, and an
argument that subjectivity is multiple and contradictory and constituted by discourses. This view encapsulates a suspicion of any
discourse which promises enlightenment and freedom (Kenway,
1995: 131). In this reading, the naive rationalism of equity discourses
could be exposed and displaced by postmodernism.

Propounding a view that power is not a possession nor something
that can be distributed between people, the postmodernist rejection
of the 'zero-sum' model confuses some of the aims of the equity
discourse's goals of fairness and resource redistribution. Ransom
(1993: 129) observes that 'Power is not like a cake; it does not follow

that if I have more, you have less.' This can be a challenging concept for members of marginalised groups whose personal, material and political disempowerment through patriarchy, racism and capitalism influence their potential to participate in higher education.

A dilemma posed by postmodernism is how to influence organisational change in the academy if there is no fixed standpoint from which to negotiate. Purvis (1994) questions whether postmodernism, with its apolitical notion of dispersed power, can be an effective tool for challenging patriarchy in education. Equity issues have been confounded by the postmodern reconceptualising of identities and subjectivities. Walby (1994) indicates that in contrast to the totalising framework of traditional Marxism, which attempted to subsume all other forms of social inequality under that of class, the focus on fragmentation expounded in postmodern social theory denies the coherence of classic analytical concepts such as 'woman', 'class' and 'race'. In their dispersal of identity and power, Walby argues that postmodernists neglect the social context of power relations. She believes that, in spite of the reconceptualisation of power inherent in postmodernist theory, 'patriarchy and racism remain potent social forces, and capitalism has not withered away ...' (Walby, 1994: 226). Whereas postmodernism has had a significant theoretical impact on the academy, the modernist notion of a unified, disembodied subject unaffected by gender, 'race' and social class power relations dominates academic culture.

There are fears that postmodernism could dismantle feminist and equity changes. As Lown (1995: 119) warns:

> Those of us who have struggled, or are seeking to struggle, to find a voice for our experience in the 'margins', need to be mindful of those who might wish to use postmodernism as an argument against political critique and collective action.

The 'finding a voice' theory is itself problematic and could be said to emanate from liberatory beliefs which ignore the way in which many oppressed groups are themselves oppressors in other arenas. However, feminists continue to articulate concern that postmodernism has eroded the hard-won and minimal intellectual and political space allocated to marginalised groups in the academy. The new, scarcely established and differentiated 'female' identity is being decontextualised. Rose (1994: 51) ascertained that:

> when feminism has massively delegitimised the hegemonic voice of

the white bourgeois male and valorised the voices of oppressed women in all their diversity, then postmodernism declares the 'death of the subject'.

In contrast, Aronowitz and Giroux (1991: 61) discern some commonalities between postmodernism and oppositional politics:

> Postmodernism's refusal of grand narratives, its rejection of universal reason as a foundation for human affairs, its decentering of the humanist subject, its radical problematization of representation, and its celebration of plurality and the politics of racial, gender, and ethnic difference have sparked a major debate.

They also warn that while postmodernism articulates a commitment to recognition of difference, it has a tendency to 'democratise the notion of difference in a way that echoes a vapid liberal pluralism' (Aronowitz and Giroux, 1991: 72). Rose (1994: 53) rejects the imperative of a dichotomous choice between either materialism or postmodernism and prefers a 'nuanced attention to discourse while locating it within the materialist constraints within which it is produced'. Discourses form the academy and are, in part, formed by it, but there are social and material factors influencing who participates and how in the process of knowledge production and consumption.

SUMMARY

In this chapter, I have argued that there have been empirical changes, ideological shifts and competing discourses in higher education contributing to change processes. There are paradoxes and dilemmas posed by the discourses of new managerialism, quality, access and equity. For example, there is a sinister side to mass expansion and academic accountability, but also a seductiveness which makes it a difficult area around which to contest and mobilise. Ironically, New Right reforms have ostensibly created a greater demographic shift in the academy than several decades of equity initiatives, flawed and inadequate though these might have been. There have been some moves away from intense selectivity to a culture of entitlement of access to higher education. This has been achieved largely through redefining the nature of the academy. The New Right removed the overt binary line, forcing new forms of covert stratification in higher education, with members of marginalised groups participating largely in non-elite institutions, often underfunded and unsupported.

While postmodernism is heavily theorised by intellectuals, the dominant structures and values of the academy remain rooted in modernist, rationalist beliefs of objective standards of excellence and the universal subject. Participation in some parts of the higher education system has been broadened. While the 'racial' and gendered composition of consumers has been partly transformed in non-elite institutions, its impact on epistemologies and organisational cultures remains questionable. In the economically led expansion of the market, under-represented groups are perceived as a lucrative new market for recruitment, but their racialised, gendered and classed subjectivities have not yet been addressed. In spite of managerialist efforts to ensure quality, excellence and objective standards, the very nature of cultural capital has changed, with inflation of certification in the labour market. Just as members of marginalised groups succeed in decoding and accessing the system, the market value of their qualifications is called into question. This raises profound questions about equity in higher education.

3 Feminism and Equity: Political Partners or Discordant Discourses?

SPREADING THE WORD: DISSEMINATION AND DISRUPTION

This chapter consists of feminist readings of equity discourses and the extent to which equity has enabled development of academic feminism. It also questions how policies for equality have impacted on women's employment and access to the academy. The implementation gap – that is the discrepancy between policy text, intention and practices – is evaluated in terms of micropolitical interference, policy symbolism and competing hierarchies of oppression. As such, it explores a complex matrix of variables. The discussion has a cross-cultural perspective as Swedish informants locate their experiences in the context of state feminism and liberal welfare bureaucracies. Greek informants discuss legislative changes for equity as liberalising measures in the post-Junta democratisation period.

In her historical research, Dyhouse (1995: 3) showed that even before the end of the nineteenth century, some universities outside Oxbridge were advertising themselves as making 'no distinction of sex'. She added:

> The sceptical feminist may be forgiven for wondering if the claim is analogous to that made so frequently today: 'the university of X is an equal opportunities employer. (Dyhouse, 1995: 4)

This scepticism often extends to a profound pessimism about change in dominant organisations. My study demonstrated that the mobilisation of academic feminists in equity work was uneven. This was often the result of fatalism about the likely success of their interventions rather than an inability to recognise and resent grievances. Those who had introduced feminist scholarship and women's studies had not necessarily been supported by the existence of equal opportunities policies. Indeed, the juxtaposition of equity with feminism in my interview questions appeared strange to many respondents, and scepticism about the effectiveness of policy to further women's interests was very apparent. A university lecturer gave examples of how the policy for equality failed to shift gender and class privilege embedded in recruitment practices, and continued to favour graduates from elite institutions:

> I feel that my institution mouths all the right things about equal opportunities and access and all the rest of it and then blithely carries on, on the whole employing Oxbridge young men whether they have got their PhD or not. There's all the goalposts for us that *we* have got to finish our PhD, we have got to publish ... But when it comes to it, if someone from Oxbridge comes along, then the man from Oxbridge gets the job whether he has finished his PhD or not. So that says it all as far as I am concerned ...

This lecturer's observations about elitism and the prolonged dominion of Oxbridge have been demonstrated statistically in Halsey's study (1992). His evidence shared that in 1989 more than one third of university teachers and more than a tenth of polytechnic teachers in Britain had been students or teachers at Oxbridge. In this sense, there is a tacit and often explicit assumption of the perceived superiority of Oxbridge. In spite of equity policies, there appears to be a relentless reproduction of gender and class privilege. The embedded properties of this process call into question the effectiveness of relatively small-scale policy interventions.

Feminist scepticism about policies for equality can relate to the reformist theoretical underpinnings of the enterprise and also to the extent to which policy development and implementation both reproduce and are dependent on existing power relations. Marshall and Anderson (1994: 176) state that 'traditional policy activity, policy analysis and policy studies will not sufficiently capture the issues of the disempowered'. This highlights the mediated and complex character of the policy cycle. The 1980s saw the beginning of the insertion of equity policies in the public services in Britain, with varying degrees of feminist involvement. Newman (1994: 200) describes this climate as one of 'progressivism (gradual, incremental change towards a distant but desirable goal)'. While equal opportunities policies were introduced in Britain as a consequence of anti-discrimination and equal pay legislation in the 1970s, their effect on access, employment and curriculum development in academic institutions has been marginal (Heward and Taylor, 1993). The Equal

Opportunities Commission, set up to monitor the legislation, is perceived by many feminists as 'underfunded and politically nearly toothless' (Rose, 1994: 61). In 1990, the Hansard Society Commission recommended that all higher education institutions should appoint an Equal Opportunities Officer who would produce regular audits on the progress of women within the institution, but failed to emphasise the importance of where these posts would be located in the management structures (Hansard, 1990). Jackson (1990: 321) saw that this enabled senior staff to abdicate responsibility. She asked:

> Why is it so difficult to get equal opportunities issues discussed? Why, in the UK, do these issues get shunted down the line to working parties of staff and students without executive authority?

Policy development and implementation are often located in existing structures of social and hierarchical relationships.

A senior lecturer in my study emphasised the dissemination problem, with equity initiatives located and contained within management rather than in the wider institution, something that illustrates how policy agents and the political decoding of policy text are of vital importance to implementation. Her observations articulated questions about which actors are dominant in the relationship between shaping and implementing policies for equality. She suggested that policy interpretation is dependent on the possession of cultural capital to enable understandings of rights and benefits and how engagement with equality policies is constrained and distorted by power inequalities:

> there are a lot of policies around and they mean nothing, nobody knows about them. That's the major problem. Nobody actually knows that they have these entitlements. And I don't think they have much encouragement to find out that they have them. We have a very very insular Personnel Department with no vision or reaching out at all. They very much see themselves as part of management, you know, and designed to just keep the lid on it.

The consciousness, status and intention of policy agents can have a profound effect on closing the gap between text and practices, raising questions about recontextualisation in the policy cycle. Policy-makers are rarely a homogeneous group, and values and understandings of key actors can differ. As Marshall and Anderson (1994: 171) indicated:

people with power in political, institutional, and professional cultures that created sexist and differentiated access are being relied on to create new power and access processes and to willingly and thoughtfully give up their power and privilege.

A senior lecturer pointed out how the micropolitical processes of her institution effectively produced and inflected their policy for equality. Locating change in existing structures of domination gave the work authority, but also subtly reproduced inequalities in equality procedures:

> the Vice-Chancellor's view on equal opps is that it's a jolly good thing but we report directly to him and any suggestion that that might not exactly be in the spirit of equal opportunities is, you know, he wouldn't see it like that at all ... So as long as he has the power in his hands or he and his little clique. And in terms of working relations and management styles it's *so traditionalist and* so line management and obtuse in terms of understanding things like the effect of having an all-male interview panel when you're a woman who's, you know, hoping to get promoted or whatever. I mean, you know, they're so blind [*sic*] to all of that.

A senior lecturer in a college of higher education also noted how recruitment and selection procedures often bore no resemblance to good practice in equity policies, and how she was attacked and discriminated against on the basis of age, gender and motherhood:

> I started in the Institute about five years ago as a part-timer doing contract work, and I was teaching across two institutions: X University and this institution. X University was horrendous, all equal opportunities rules were broken, the person interviewed me told me I'd wasted too much time having kids, that's why I was too old for the job and then after they appointed a young man of 24 who was less qualified than me to teach the courses they wanted him to teach. They turned round and offered me a part time job and I basically told them where to go and left.

In the absence of an analysis of gender and power, the victim of inequalities was blamed, as an individual, for her loss of cultural capital, exemplifying how the perception of equity issues politically defines the observers as well as the observed. Furthermore, it provides an example of how organisational policies for equality frequently fail to theorise the boundaries between public and private spheres (Marshall and Anderson, 1994).

Ideally, equity should include consideration of access and employment issues *and* services delivered by organisations, such as curriculum, pedagogy and epistemology. There are connections between the composition of the workforce, organisational cultures and the type of services delivered. For example, all interviewees in my study commented on links between patriarchal organisational cultures and lack of career opportunities for women. Both of these impact on knowledge production. Just how equity policies can break this hegemonic cycle is not always clear to those responsible for development work. The result is often a series of fragmented and seemingly tokenistic gestures. There is also the issue of the feminisation of equity, with women bearing the major responsibility for introducing and sustaining change. This is another example of political commitment as overload, with women over-extending themselves in order to influence change. This practice also relates to a belief in the epistemic privilege of the oppressed, that is, the idea that people who have experienced oppression will have insights into how to combat it. However, it is questionable whether equity has been subjected to the same theoretical rigour as feminism in the academy. A principal lecturer in a new university outlined how feminism is more evolved than equity in her institution:

> The equal opportunities policy does not help women's studies, quite the reverse in fact, as women's studies is more advanced in the institution, and generally more theoretically sophisticated ... we are always being asked to sit on equality committees. So far, the policy only relates to employment, certainly not to service delivery.

Elsewhere, women's change agency, perceived as self-interest, is exposed to the types of attitude they seek to challenge. As one senior lecturer in a new university observed:

> The Equal Opps Group has been described, and I think is perceived by a lot of people, as being a group of women nagging. Because there are ... I think there's ten of us and I think seven of them are women. The other side to that is that, you know, as always happens, it's the women in the group that have done *huge* amounts of work and it's the men that say, 'Oh sorry, you know, I've got a research term so I can't do anything', or, 'Oh sorry, I'm giving a paper next week.' I mean you know it's exactly the case of the people who get exploited are the ones that care about equal opps.

This observation raises questions about the productive aspects of

power relations. That is, whether change processes are more effectively driven by the energy of those who translate ontology into
epistemology.

A perception gap often exists between ideological intentions and
organisational images of equity initiatives. A senior lecturer noted
how economic stringencies influenced the status of equity in her new
university, and how there was little collective ownership of potential
outcomes:

> I think that equal opportunities is not perceived as a good thing.
> Generally, it's seen as a waste of money and in these times of hard-
> ship jobs are more important than Equal Opps and people should
> stop banging on about it. I don't think the people who could benefit
> from it see it as being about them either. In terms of access to
> promotion I mean.

Women's studies was seen as an interim measure, a holding opera-
tion, by one senior lecturer, while equity work was being developed in
more detail, with feminist academics as policy advocates:

> We are ... fighting for ... equal opportunities policies and to get
> them into practice is such a huge issue ... Until that is fully
> addressed I don't see that we can develop a great deal except
> through areas like women's studies.

A senior lecturer in a college of higher education reflected on the
separate trajectories for equity and feminism in her organisation:

> I think it is institutionally helpful to have an equal opps policy and
> I think maybe it's helpful for the institution to have women's
> studies as well, but I don't actually think they are working together
> in the long term really.

Another senior lecturer perceived curriculum development and
teaching of women's studies as a more satisfying form of influence
than equity policy development work:

> Women's studies and equal opportunities are actually almost
> different routes into some of the same things – frustrated equal
> opportunities person takes up women's studies.

A senior lecturer in women's studies in a new university advanced her
belief in agency and speculated that the development of feminist
scholarship came about as a result of individual feminist interventions
rather than policies and structures for equality:

The institution has a very strong equal opportunities policy ... But it hasn't helped us. I feel that we as individual strong women have fought for, you know, all the things that we wanted to do.

Two informants from new universities in my study had been required by their institutions to relate the organisational policy for equality to their course development, with management directives to include equity in curriculum, as well as recruitment issues. This type of directive was perceived as surveillance and regulation by many academic staff. A senior lecturer in a college who was also a member of the equal opportunities working party commented:

we'd highlighted the curriculum as an absolutely key area in terms of changing the culture of the institution. That, I think, they really found very difficult to cope with. You know, the idea of anybody ... going in and monitoring, even at the level of saying, 'OK, we'll call in everybody's bibliographies, for a start.'

A lecturer in a new university described how her institution's policy for equality had to be addressed in the validation of a new women's studies course:

when we wrote the validation document we had to put an equal opportunities statement in there and to say how the degree related to that equal opportunities statement for the university, then where did we fulfil it and how did we fulfil it, the equal opportunities statement. I then set up an equal opportunities interview training course ... So I suppose that's had a direct impact on it.

This exemplified an organisational attempt to apply equity strategically to women's studies curriculum development, thus structurally linking feminism with equity. It was also an example of an institution moving beyond a preoccupation solely with employment issues and starting to consider equity in relation to epistemology. However, in my study, it was rare to encounter this corporatist approach to policy implementation.

THE IMPLEMENTATION GAP

As many informants in my study noted, there are frequently discontinuities between policy intention, texts and practices. Deem (1992a: 125) asserts that 'policy ... is a process not a statement and words have to be turned into deeds and changes monitored and evaluated.' This has been a predominant view of equity activists and implies a rational strategy for bringing about change. This approach, however, relies on universalising the decoding of the links between problem analysis and options for action, the cause and effect. A poststructural analysis would indicate how meaning is not fixed in language or in consistent power relations. Rather, it shifts according to a range of linguistic, institutional and cultural contextual factors (Kenway, 1995). Ball (1994a: 10) constructed policy as:

> both text and action, words and deeds ... policies are crude and simple. Practice is sophisticated, contingent, complex and unstable.

Analysis of equity implementation includes assessing the ways that micropowers intersect, articulate and rearticulate. The processes on which action must be based involve negotiation, compromise and a degree of loss. There is often a perceived loss of autonomy, for example, and attempts to standardise practices are sometimes seen as coercion. From my experience and from much of the data in this study, it was evident that equality policies also operate at a symbolic level. They remain as linguistic formations only, and do not disturb power, status and material opportunities. Policy symbolism has been theorised by Edelman (1977), who claims that policies may often be more effective in giving the impression that action is being taken. Policies are developed in order to avoid resistance or rebellion, or to meet statutory requirements. The implementation of equality measures carries an implicit binary that the alternative or current picture is one of inequality – something that many senior staff will find threatening, as it calls into question their legitimacy, implying their status has been achieved via privilege rather than merit. Hence equity work is often an elaborate ritual or charade, with carefully mannered, but ultimately meaningless performances.

I have noticed how discussion about equity issues in this research, and in the 20 years I have spent as an equity activist, is frequently accompanied by non-verbal gestures of exhaustion and powerless-ness. The energy ebbs out of the conversation and there is a sense of being overwhelmed by the vast scale of both the embeddedness of inequalities and of the change agency task. This was very appar-ent in my interviews, with feelings of powerlessness, and even rage, dramatised by sighs, slumped bodies, tight lips. Foucault believed that a prime site for discursive regulation is the body itself. He suggested (1980: 151) that the 'micro-physics' of power operates 'through progressively finer channels, gaining access to individuals themselves, to their bodies ...' Power, he wrote, 'seeps into the very grain of individuals, reaches right into their bodies, permeates their gestures, their posture ...' (quoted in Martin et al., 1988: 6). Shilling (1993: 125) argues that:

> social relations, inequalities and oppressions are manifest not simply in the form of differential access to economic, educational or cultural resources but are *embodied.*

This was substantiated in a survey of equal opportunities personnel conducted by Kandola et al. (1991). They discovered that 90 per cent of their subjects showed a higher than average incidence of symptoms of physical illness. As Ball (1994b: 111) indicates:

> Policy is ... an assertion of voice, or a cannibalization of multiple voices. Policy influence is a struggle to be heard in an arena where only certain voices have legitimacy at any point in time.

The struggle to be heard can wear down change agents, and the appraisal of an issue as stressful can sometimes indicate memory of previous failures. As Spence (1992: 13) says, 'activists get ill'. Activists in dominant organisations often function from a structurally and personally disempowered location. As Shaw and Perrons (1995: 4) note, 'social identity clearly makes a difference to the strategies that can be pursued, as well as to the outcomes.' For example, being male or female, black or white can be as significant, at the conscious and unconscious level, as one's hierarchical position, both in terms of self-image and in the perceptions of others.

Equity work in this research, in the form of committee work, policy development, consciousness raising and dissemination, was felt to be draining and uncreative by many of those involved in it. This related to how it was being introduced into organisations with competitive, individualistic cultures, where notions of collective challenges to disadvantage were counter-cultural. This raised important strategy questions about the incorporation of feminists into the equity policy cycle. Feminists in my study indicated that their participation in deci-sion-making arenas for textual production did not necessarily equate with influence on practices, as a senior lecturer observed:

> The most frustrating bit has been being on the Equal Opportunities Action Group – formulating policies, putting a huge amount of work into reading other people's policies and pointing out the

equal opportunities gaps and implications. And knowing that you'll go to a meeting, you'll all sit round, everyone will nod sagely and say, yes this is very good, and it will make *no* difference to the reality of how people get treated. I just cannot bear it, you know, I'm so sick of that kind of time wasting. I think policy-making in this institution just doesn't connect up with what happens ... Because the people who are responsible are either naive or overworked or don't share ... aren't committed to the spirit of the policy. And because there's a dominant liberal individualist ethos which is that, you know, the institution is not a nanny and should not do this and should not do that and, you know.

Wildavsky (1979: 387) reminds us that 'policy is a process as well as a product'. The complexity of decision-making is not always apparent in the end-product. A senior lecturer highlighted the labour intensity of the policy development process and how this was concealed by distillation of discursive material into policy text:

it took a number of years to actually get the thing. I mean, it was unbelievable how long it took to actually get it on to paper. When it was on paper, it was substantially reduced. You know, I mean, when you think of what we did and all the kind of fine detail that we had in, and we end up with this little single leaflet ... this little glossy thing.

While time is necessary to evolve policy, it can also be used to sabotage and demoralise participants in the process. Ball (1994a: 20) warns that 'some emancipatory policies are subject to creative non-implementation'. A senior lecturer in a college of higher education observed how prolonged equity initiatives can be, especially when micropolitical factors impede its development and implementation:

we did get a policy out in the eighties ... Certainly the Equal Opportunities Policy has been through a few crises ... The feeling has been that ... despite having the policy for quite a long time – it was re-drawn, it was lost, it was invisible ... So, a new committee was set up with the new institution that gave us an opportunity to look at it and there has been a feeling at the top, never mind at the bottom, that it has not been effective so it's under review, not the policy but how best to put that into action, and I feel very positive about that, I feel that this has just got to be good, we just never grabbed it in the first place, with targets and all sorts of things that you need. How can we review something we didn't know where it was supposed to be going? So it was rather woolly. It was a crisis really, but I'm glad it's treated seriously as a crisis and so that is good, maybe that is in the interest of women's studies.

These observations raise questions about the locus of change and influence in equality policies. There are levels of decision-making, action and lower-level actors sometimes referred to as 'street-level bureaucrats' (Lipsky, 1980). There have been increasing discussions focusing on policy implementation and disjunctions at a local level (Bowe, Ball and Gold, 1992; Ham and Hill, 1993). General statements of intention within organisations are implemented by individuals and groups, who often have discretion in interpreting policy statements. This problematises who is responsible for a policy's 'meaning' and how the text is decoded and translated into action or inaction. Micropolitics at the local level can involve complex forms of resistance, compliance, sabotage and accommodation. The relationship between the policy text and agent(s) of implementation is inscribed by power relations.

STUDENTS AND EQUALITY

Data from students, particularly in Britain, were very weak on equity issues. Many did not understand my questions, did not know if their institutions had policies and could not think how equity policies had impacted on them, as students. This was certainly not an indictment of the students themselves, but partly illustrated the absence of equity discourses and effective implementation and dissemination in the academy. Those who were aware of policies were very dismissive of their effectiveness, believing that their rights and well-being as gendered consumers had been untouched by the existence of policies for equality. An MA student commented:

> I don't know if they were just a piece of paper they had ... No, I don't think I can think of any way in which they impacted on me ... I can't think of any.

An American MA student was unclear about where her institution, and indeed Britain, stood on equity issues. When asked if her institution had a policy for equality, she replied:

> I don't know ... I think so, but I really couldn't say ... Yes, I'm just going to assume they have one. But I also assumed that there would

be, you know, a Civil Rights Bill for disabled people in this country, which there isn't!

A postgraduate student was uncertain both about the existence and the impact of equity policies:

the EOP? ... I'd really need to think about that, it's not something I ... in many ways I think it's not much good to me, but I'd have to go away and think about it.

A young black MA student, while not a representative for the entire 'black community', attempted to capture some of the despair relating to equity and 'race':

I don't think you will find any black person who takes equal opportunities seriously. This university says it has a policy and yet all the teachers are white and there are only two of us – black students – on the women's studies course.

An MA student provided an example of how she used the Student Union's policy, with varying degrees of success, to challenge the hidden curriculum of sexist imagery:

Just recently we went down to the college bar and there were some coasters for the tables which we found horrible ... which were advertising this woman – they were selling the pleasure of the drink but they hadn't got a picture of the drink, they'd got a picture of a woman with hardly any clothes on ... So I took it to the Union Council and they said, 'Yeah, we agree ...' The president went down to speak to the bar manager and he laughed at him and said he'd take them off, and then the next time they were still in there.

A postgraduate student who had also been a member of Senate in her university, felt it was hypocritical to claim it was an equal opportunities organisation. She also highlighted how power relations were embedded in the processes of policy development in the male-dominated University Senate:

Well, I haven't felt the benefits of it [the Equal Opportunities Policy] at all. I've questioned whether they are entitled to put it on job adverts and I've suggested they ought to use things like 'working towards' because it quite clearly doesn't exist ... And they've now made – I mean the Equal Opportunities Officer was full time and is now a part-time post. So I mean they think they have done it all basically with the job adverts. But you know, I have challenged this in Senate and said this is just simply not happening ... but certainly time and time again there have been issues that affect women you know ... and I had to come along and stand up and say something ... You know Senate itself was something like 80–90 per cent men. The women consequently, who also tended to be much junior, never said anything particularly controversial. And I would come away at the end of Senate with all kinds of women that I didn't know rushing up to me saying, 'I'm really glad you said that, but we don't feel able to.'

This account is an important example of how women who have already been silenced by discriminatory cultures are unlikely to feel comfortable enough to challenge patriarchal authority.

A lecturer in a new university observed that while the organisational policy for equality had had a limited impact on the development of women's studies courses, she believed it gave a positive message to students, and linked equal opportunities culture with potential career opportunities for women's studies students:

I know that some students who come to us with concerns about doing a degree in women's studies and wondering if that is the right thing and is it mainstream enough? Is it a proper degree? and things like that. I think the fact that there is a strong equal opportunities culture here and in other institutions, if they look around and see that it is a very important aspect of institutional development. In many places now it feels somehow more legitimised, that it feels like these are important issues and there may be a space for us in the job market and there may be more acceptance of it later on.

However, politicised, conscious students often had no expectations of equity effectiveness, and engaged with declared and hidden curricula and organisational culture with an anticipation of their oppositional status, as feminists.

SWEDEN: 'REAL PROFESSORS AND PROFESSORS THAT HAVE BREASTS!'

Comparative work can be a useful mechanism for highlighting different stories influenced by different logics and discourses of nation states. Equality has a strong history in Sweden, where there is extensive state welfare intervention (Forbes, 1989). The codification of Swedish equality policies began in 1972 when the Social Democratic government appointed the Equal Opportunities Advisory Committee, attached to the office of the Prime Minister. In 1983 and for the next five years equality questions were assigned to a separate unit within the Ministry of Labour. Initiatives are implanted in structures of the national and local state, with a corporatist approach to policy-making and implementation. There are equal opportunities plans for public services, committees at municipal level and an Act on Equality Between Women and Men at Work (Equal Opportunities Act, 1980) (Eduards, 1991). Many Scandinavian feminists have been critical of the liberal, pluralistic basis of equality policies, perceiving them as state patriarchy and a means of silencing radical feminism (Dahlerup, 1987; Eduards, 1991; Haavio-Mannila et al., 1985; Siim, 1987). Eduards (1991: 686) draws attention to a situation known as 'women's reforms on men's conditions'. There are many tensions between feminism and equality, as a Swedish lecturer in my study indicated:

> Feminism in Sweden I think is ... well that depends on which group is talking ... But, of course, I think that it is viewed as something disturbing the process of equality many times ... Well, there is a very broad view that women, feminist women, are radical. And that they disturb, so to say, the tranquil reformist way of development that is going on in one way, as people believe. And that it shouldn't be disturbed by women who want a quicker development! I think it's quite a common view ... it's a very common way of viewing from the point of view of men ... Because they all say they are ... they like the idea of equality. But they don't like the women screaming about it!

A Swedish research student also drew attention to schisms that had arisen between feminism and equality:

> I think it is related to the social democracy policy during the 1970s, which I think is a very big split between feminism and equality research. I think the equality research was beginning during the 1960s here with women and men actually, but mostly women, and they were looking at equality issues which is not the same as feminist issues. And during the 1970s when we got a very strong welfare state you could say that you were feminist, but the feminist perspective did not have any influence within, for example, the University.

But the University said because of the government, you have to have women's studies, you have to deal with the women's studies issues, but it is not actually women's studies politics that they are running. They are running some kind of equality policy, which is not a good equality policy even, that is bad. It's very, very conservative.

The association of equality with liberal reform and feminism with radicalism was also commented on by a Swedish postgraduate student:

we even have a Board, an Equality Board, they don't do anything. I don't know what they do. I've never seen any of their work, but I think they have small pamphlets ... It's not the feminist politics, definitely not, it's the neoliberal, nice equality politics, which is very problematic.

While Scandinavia is often the envy of feminists struggling for equalities elsewhere, Rose (1994: 104) pointed out how:

Scandinavian academic institutions cling to their patriarchal power and have been rather successful at resisting structural reform. In Sweden, where university teachers are part of the civil service ... there are still only 4 per cent women full professors.

Swedish feminists had differing views of the extent to which equality policies had facilitated the development of feminism in the academy. Whereas one associate professor commented that her university's policy for equality had had no impact on the development of women's studies, a Swedish postgraduate student disagreed: 'especially during the 1970s – because women's studies centres started all over Sweden ...'

An associate professor in Sweden described how government-led equality initiatives were also about to be applied to recruitment and selection in the academy:

But with reference to this latest proposition, like a white paper, it's just looking at the question of when you apply for a position, the committee that looks at your application, are women there, are there women that know anything about gender, women's studies? That is something that is on the books at the moment ... it's like a white paper – 'Equality between men and women in the area of education'. It's propositioned and it is discussed all this Spring and then it will be passed. These are the kind of things that are being discussed to try and make it better for women.

A Swedish associate professor described how she had used equality legislation as a lever to counter discrimination she perceived had taken place against her. Her example demonstrated how equity had made recruitment procedures more transparent:

> Yes I used it [the Equal Opportunities Policy] once, actually. I applied for a position in a small university ... We were two applicants, one colleague of mine from here and the assessor, he wrote and put me in the first place and the man in the second. But my colleague, he had taught up there before and they wanted him, so they said 'we will hire him', and then I wrote and I got it ... I wrote first a letter to the University, saying that if you don't hire me I will go to the State, so they hired me.

I recognised that this bold gesture was uncommon in Britain, where the arbitrary nature of academic judgements means they are difficult to challenge in any systematic, procedural way. I asked if many academics in Sweden used the equal opportunities policies in this way. She replied:

> No, not very many because women, they are ashamed of using it and I don't understand why, because finally we have got a rule that helps us, why do we not use it? I am telling people about that rule all the time because if you have come so far that you are in a competition you won't get a job because you are not worse or less qualified than a man. You might even be more qualified, it's just very hard to say. It's arbitrary competition and evaluation.

The issue of shame and self-recrimination in response to rejection was analysed by Lieberman (1981), who offered this advice to academic women:

> They will try to persuade you you are being denied tenure (or promotion, or reappointment) because of your deficiencies. The argument most certain to take you in is the one that speaks to your self-doubt, so they will tell you your publications are mediocre, your teaching weak. Don't believe it. (Lieberman, 1981: 3)

So, a circular argument emerges. Women's confidence has been undermined by sexist oppression, but high degrees of confidence are required to challenge discriminatory decision-making. Thus, those most damaged by oppression are culturally, socially and emotionally in the weakest location to confront it. Bettelheim (1979) observed that victims will only fight their oppressors when they believe they have nothing left to lose. Using litigation to challenge discrimination can have severe micropolitical consequences for women who wish to remain in their organisations. Ironically, using equity policies has gender implications. The Equal Opportunities Commission in the UK now receives more complaints of discrimination from men than from women. In Sweden, too, a major criticism of their Equal Opportunities Act is that it has invested resources in supporting men wishing to enter sectors traditionally 'dominated' by women. The former deputy equal opportunities ombudsperson wrote that 'the Act has become an offensive instrument for strengthening men's position in the labour market' (quoted in Eduards, 1991: 692). Measures to promote equality in Sweden and Britain can be thought to be superficial and individualistic, to maintain gender neutrality, and have an emphasis on rights, rather than outcomes.

It is questionable how gender policies include consideration of other forms of inequality, such as 'race' and social class. Political parties in Sweden have an informal quota system, with a 40/60 rule for nominations. This means that neither men nor women should have more than 60 per cent nor less than 40 per cent of the seats (Eduards, 1991). A Swedish postgraduate student commented on how quota systems imposed by Swedish equality policies tokenised women, and worked in favour of privileged, non-feminist, white middle-class women:

> It is not a feminist politics within those 50 per cent of women in government for example, it's women, but it's not feminist politics ... I think that is the problem. I think that equality politics during the 1970s and 1980s was very good within some kind of ways, but it's very problematic when you compare it to what has actually happened in many aspects. For example, if you look at all those women who are excluded, harassed, whatever they are, black women, ethnic women, working class. They are not disappointed about this, because you have got 50 per cent, which is really good isn't it? But you do make a very big group of women invisible in this kind of politics.

This exemplifies Cockburn's observation (1989: 217) that the central concern of equal opportunities policies is 'gaining power, not changing it'. Quota systems can also discriminate against women working in academic areas where there was already a significant representation of women, as they provide the opportunity for employers to 'pull up the drawbridge' once prescribed numbers have been achieved, as a lecturer in Sweden discovered:

> I mean it's interesting that I am going to apply for a lectureship job now at the Sociology Department and I was up to get the papers from the faculty and the woman there – who I thought was not very helpful ... then I was saying, 'but it says on this paper that they will try to get more women'. Then she said, 'well it won't help you because in the sociology department it's about 50/50 anyway, so this won't help you.'

A lecturer described how, in spite of robust equality policies in the Swedish academy, feminist scholars are still perceived as representing minority, specialised interests:

> In personal terms there are lots of ways you get discriminated. I remember one time when a colleague and I were applying for research money and it was for a project about the Labour Market, working life, and you get to read the referees' point of view, and it was interesting how the referees managed to exclude you. It would be like, 'well X and Y are obviously excellent women's studies researchers but it's harder to know their competencies in the area of working life ...' So, they find ways to exclude you.

The focus on policy is sometimes perceived as a diversion from feminist, theory-driven work (Rose, 1994). A postgraduate student in Sweden observed how the increase in number of policy active women as a result of equity policies had not necessarily incorporated feminist theory into public policy-making:

> So, we have a much more troubling identity than feminists in other countries. We have a lot of strong women, but not feminists. There are a lot of tensions there.

Some of these tensions were rehearsed by Siim (1987), who alleged that while the Scandinavian welfare model has enabled some entry of women into the labour market, women have none the less remained essentially objects in policy development. As Gherardi (1994: 607) argues, 'any equal opportunities program is bound to fail if it is implemented in an organizational culture which thinks of women as the second sex.' This was illustrated in a Swedish postgraduate student's description of how recent proposals to change the gender composition of senior academic staff had resulted in an equality/quality debate. This measure, intended to promote women, served to humiliate them and expose them to further hostility and classification as the second sex, illustrating how one of the most pervasive ways in which power relations operate is through myth and rumour:

> They [the universities] are really male-dominated, so the way to solve this, and they want from the Department of Education, they want more women to be professors, but they don't have the strength or the power to go in and criticise the Universities' procedures of how to recruit the professors ... Instead they go to the Law of Equal Rights. We have to appoint more women professors even if they are less qualified ... it has been a big debate in the newspapers ... and some male professors say that it's very frightening that women who are less qualified should get this professor title. Some women say, like I am saying, 'that's not really the question, it's not that they are less qualified, it's that they are less known in the system ...' It will come to a point when we talk about real professors and professors that have breasts!

As this student illustrates, inserting reformist policy measures into unchanged structures means that new and more inventive modes of distinction will be evolved! Women, like other under-represented groups in the academy, continue to be defined as outsiders. This has also been highlighted in the case of women students. While the number of women undergraduates is increasing in many countries, the percentage of women who receive higher degrees remains low (Stiver Lie et al., 1994). If women are screened out of academia at an earlier stage than men, this could have implications for the composition of the academic labour force. According to one Swedish postgraduate student, her university's equal opportunities policy did nothing to challenge universities' gatekeeping role in determining access to postgraduate work:

> It [the Equal Opportunities Policy] is that way at an external side but not inside the University really, because more men become doctors for example than women.

Sweden's reputation for effective equality policies, lower wage differentials and a high participation rate of women in all spheres of economic and political activity is of long standing. However, it appears that gender discrimination within higher education is as entrenched in Sweden as elsewhere in Europe.

GREECE

My questions about equity in Greek universities were universally met
with references to the 1975 Constitution. This 'guarantees by special
explicit provisions the equality of men and women' (Moussourou and
Spiliotopoulis, 1984: 136). Organisational policies for equality do not
exist in Greek universities, but the academy is regulated by the
government, to the point of specifying promotion criteria. After the
collapse of the military junta, a Socialist government was elected in
1981. This introduced extensive welfare policies, during which the
principle of equality was promoted and, in 1983, the General
Secretariat for Equality of the Two Sexes was established (Balaska,
1994). Equity legislation was perceived as an important liberalising
reform after the junta. This period was also accompanied by significant socio-economic development and urbanisation – both of which
have led to demands on the education system. Many of my informants
believed that progress for women has been rapid in Greece, particularly as a consequence of its membership of the European Union. For
example, in 1971 21.3 per cent of the female population were illiterate (Moussourou and Spiliotopoulis, 1984). However, in the
post-junta period, the percentage of women students in higher education began to increase, from 32 per cent in 1972–3 to 39.2 per cent in
1978–9.

A Greek professor outlined the effectiveness of women's organisations' influence on constitutional development:

The new Constitution in 1974 ... had a radical provision claiming
that ... all the Greeks are equal – in front of the law. But the new
Constitution said that Greek men and women – it retained the
classic provision of Greeks are equal before the law but it had ...
the second paragraph which stated that men and women are equal
... And also there is another article, another provision, which
obliged the Legislator to abolish all the inequalities ... between
men and women ... You see we have a new Constitution ... And
new laws which have settled this equality problem in our society.
And yet also the Constitution has some provisions which facilitate
the place of women. Provisions for assistance to mothers, married
or not married. Provisions for equal pay for equal work ... Of
course, Greece also has ratified the main Treaty of 1979 of the
United Nations which abolishes all the inequalities and which
obliges the State to take these affirmative actions to make women's

positions better ... And mainly it was the Socialist Party during the previous decade which has ... brought many changes in favour of women. And it was not only the Government. But after the fall of the junta in 1974 we have a revival of the Women's Movement ... Because during the junta period all political activities were outlawed.

Several Greek informants commented on the correlation between the fall of the dictatorship and the rise of the women's movement. However, they also emphasised family responsibilities as a major obstacle in academic women's career development, especially as an important aspect of cultural capital related to time spent studying and working overseas (Cacoullos, 1991). They made crucial connections between women's academic production and reproduction. In this sense, gender in the academy, as elsewhere, is produced by the sexual division of labour.

The academy has been described as a 'greedy institution' (Acker et al., 1984; Edwards, 1993). Career development requires a significant time investment. An assistant professor believed that there was no overt discrimination in her university, rather it was the failure to accommodate women's role in the private sphere that created disadvantage:

> Trying to cope, and how you lag behind in terms of being able to travel abroad, to take the opportunities, especially if you have children, especially during a certain period of your life ... most of the time nowadays, I suspect at least with our university, it isn't a case of open discrimination. Or openly saying, no you won't be promoted or, you won't be chosen to go to this project or that project or this and that because you're a woman ... It does not follow that women get less opportunities. I wouldn't say so. I think it is, to a very great extent, the ... how would I put it? ... the objective, so to speak, difficulties ... which however are not taken into consideration.

An associate professor gave examples from her life history to exemplify how social practices override legislation:

> Of course, I didn't start my education right after graduating from the high school because I belong to the women of the older generation who had all these difficulties to follow what they wanted to. So I started as an assistant which was the lowest position in the university. And since I was married and I could not leave my family

– I had no children but … I had many obligations and I was working too. I could not avail myself of the regulations that the university had to send each staff abroad – with a scholarship – And so, since I couldn't leave Athens, I had to stay in the university while all male colleagues … There is discrimination which is not … due to this time … in any discriminations according to law, no. The law treats men and women equally … But reality still makes all these inequalities survive.

Her poignant description of being left behind while her male colleagues travelled abroad captured the Cinderella status many women academics inhabit in terms of relative opportunities for promotion and career development.

It is evident from feminist scholarship in Greece that there is also an implementation gap between social policy for equality and educational and employment practices. Kassimati (1993) writes that while feminist bodies have created pressures for equality legislation, education and the labour market maintain their own laws and practices. This implementation gap was theorised by a Greek researcher, who observed that the equality movement had been a western import, and as such it had failed to acknowledge cultural specificities and social conflicts:

I think there are many social changes in Greece over the last 20 years and which are quick changes and all of us don't know how to adapt to these and we have practices from our past socialisation, which is not so much adapted to life today in Greece. There is a social conflict there and I mean my generation has also the idealism of socialism and social movements and so on what is not true for today for young people. And my generation brings up children not knowing exactly what the values to be transmitted should be … Because also maybe some things were very exaggerated, and I think in Greece, well, this movement was not produced. We were influenced by what happened in Europe and in America, we did not have time to absorb it, to make it ours and to adapt to it to what our reality is, in our terms of speaking.

Comments about the 'otherness' of Europe and America exemplify Herzfeld's observations (quoted in Cowan, 1996: 62) that '… contemporary Greek selves are fashioned precisely through the exploration of the tensions of *being*, yet at the same time as *not being*, "western" or "European".' Hence a dichotomy has evolved with the 'West' epitomising progress and modernisation, and southern European countries representing the traditional, with the latter perceived as a major impediment for reform. However, gender issues cannot be so neatly or rationally categorised. While Greek feminist academics often cited traditional family responsibilities as an explanation for women's horizontal and vertical segregation in the academy, the percentage of full female professors in Greece in 1990 was 6.3 per cent (Balaska, 1994). This is similar to Britain (7.3 per cent). Greece only mentions equality in its Constitution, whereas Britain has both legislation and organisational policies for equality. However, Sweden, along with Denmark, has some of the most extensive public child-care provision in Europe and over two decades of heavily promoted equality legislation, but still has only 4 per cent full female professors.

HIERARCHIES OF OPPRESSION

In much of the above discussion, equity issues are conceptualised in terms of gender politics, with few references to how gender relates to other structures of inequality. While equity discourses are constituted to combat discrimination, they are often held guilty of perpetuating it by selective inclusion and exclusion of particular structures of inequality. 'Race' and gender are frequently positioned as competing paradigms, while social class, disability, age and sexualities are often considered optional extras, with product champions expressing the singularity of their exclusion:

> Economic class is a form and arena of oppression that has been the focus of certain kinds of [class] politics and has been massively theorized, and indeed has been the basis of one particular grand narrative. Despite this, and the activities of trade unions, class and classism do not seem to feature strongly in most of the debates around equal opportunities. (Hearn and Parkin, 1993: 153)

> It is no accident that the lesbian and gay agenda constitutes the most marginal and vulnerable area of organizational politics, and are usually excluded from equality policies. All women, then, are organizationally constituted as 'heterosexual' women. (Newman and Williams, 1995: 11)

I agree with both the above quotations, in as much as social class and sexualities are frequently overlooked in policy debates. However, the challenge remains how to maintain equity, with consideration of the interconnections between different structures of inequality, on political, organisational and social agendas without degenerating into rival claims. Even in the 1990s, with access to complex theoretical frameworks with which to analyse power relations, it is not uncommon for groups to assert the seriousness of their oppression by differentiating it from the 'easy ride' enjoyed by other oppressed groups. Fuss (1989: 16) suggested that 'the politics of experience sometimes takes the form of a tendency amongst both individuals and groups to "one down" each other on the oppression scale'.

Luke (1994: 220) describes this pattern as:

> much like inverse cultural capital: identity markers (e.g. colour, lesbian, disabled) can easily become the ontological ground on which to base a 'superior' insider knowledge of more 'authentically' experienced, 'real' embodied oppressions ...

Lynch and O'Neill (1994: 307) theorise social class in relation to higher education and emphasise how

> working class people occupy a structurally contradictory role in relation to education: on the one hand, social mobility generally requires that they be well-educated. Yet if they are to succeed in the education system they have to abandon certain features of their class background. They cease to be working class to some degree. Other oppressed or marginalised groups in education, do not lose their defining minority identity or status by being educated: an educated woman never ceases to be a woman, an educated black person never ceases to be black, and a physically disabled person who is educated never ceases to be disabled.

While the point being argued relates to the problematics of social mobility and identity, it is unfortunate to compare one oppressed group with another in this way. This type of explanation overlooks multiple subjectivities and the complex, unstable nature of identity. As Stanley (1997: 6) reminds us, 'People do not inhabit conveniently separated identities.' Setting social class against 'race' and disability undermines the struggles black people and disabled people encounter in the academy (Gibson, 1996; Mirza, 1995; Potts and Price, 1995; Rassool, 1995). Furthermore, it risks essentialising identity. As Sinfield (1994) has shown, members of subordinate groups have to work hard at ventriloquising established culture in academia, and this 'mimicry' can produce a self-division and painful lack of

convergence between the initial culture of family and neighbour-
hood, and the acquired culture. Lynch and O'Neill also made
repeated references to 'a working class perspective', suggesting an
enlightenment universality of experiences undifferentiated by 'race',
gender, sexualities, disabilities and age.

Stiver Lie et al. (1994: 211) draw attention to the need to consider
social class in comparative studies of women in higher education.
Using the high participation rate of women in Turkey as an example,
they suggest that:

> The relatively large proportion of university women ... were able to
> maximise their opportunities because of the availability of domes-
> tic help ... the sharp differentiation between classes helps to
> explain the small size of the gender gap in Turkey.

Social class privilege continues to influence equity initiatives in
Britain too. Recent isolated comments about the connection between
private education and social class privilege reportedly made by academics to students at interview stage in some British universities have
been met with outrage by the media and by the powerful public
schools themselves, who are protesting at what they see as discriminatory practices against them (Scott-Clark, Driscoll and Steiner,
1996). Just as men have learned to use equity legislation to further
their privilege, members of the ruling class are reinventing themselves
as victims, and calling upon equity to represent their interests.

SUMMARY

> For the past twenty years, feminists have been writing an academic
> success story – sort of. Armed with equal opportunity laws, we have
> forced departments to admit, graduate, and hire more women ...
> (Messer-Davidow, 1991: 281)

The above quotation from a feminist academic working in the USA
implies some qualified success for women in relation to application of
equity policies to employment and recruitment practices in the US
academy. Data from my study suggest that this has not been a universal trend. My questions on equity to European feminists revealed
significant dismissal of the effectiveness of public and organisational
policies in bringing about change. Some informants perceived power
as so deeply sedimented in organisational, social and interpersonal
relations, that policies for equality seem naive and based on a ratio-

nalist connection between intervention and outcome. While Eisenstein (1986, quoted in Franzway, Court and Connell, 1989: 95) described affirmative action programmes for women's equality as a form of 'feminist judo' – 'throwing with the weight of the state' – with the exception of one Swedish academic, nobody in my study felt 'armed' or empowered by equal opportunities. For the majority, equity was simply not affecting them in either material or discursive forms. It appeared that equity and feminism were operating on quite different trajectories.

Involvement in equity initiatives was often perceived by informants as the ultimate example of alienating work in so far as there is no control over outcomes and influence is fragmented, segmented and unstable. They maintained their agency, in a time when personal and financial resources are under pressure, by choosing to apply their feminism to knowledge production and curriculum development, rather than to the precarious process of policy implementation.

From discussions with feminists in three European countries, it was evident from their responses that current interventions and policies for equality appear to be contributing little to challenging cultural reproduction. Whereas MacGwire (1992: 23) asserted that the companies in which women thrive have well thought out equal opportunities policies, this does not appear to apply to the academy. It is questionable whether the ideological underpinnings of social relations, curriculum development, knowledge production and organisational culture are changing as a consequence of either social or organisational policies for equality in the academy. Ball (1994a: 15) defines two conceptualisations of policy: policy as text and policy as discourse. While 90 per cent of academic institutions in Britain now have equity policy texts of varying degrees of sophistication (Farish et al., 1995), few have equity as a dominant discourse in either employment or service delivery. The policies remain at a symbolic level, with limited attention to implementation and monitoring. From comments about the relationship between equity and feminism in all three countries, it seems as if equity discourses are not theoretically framed by feminism and are not sufficiently operating as resistance to dominant epistemologies and ideologies. Indeed, it would seem that equity policies merely enter existing patterns and practices of inequality in academic institutions.

4 Between the Lines: Gender and Organisation

GENDER, FEMINISM AND ORGANISATION THEORY

In chapter 3, organisational cultures were frequently cited as explanations for the failure of equity discourses in the academy. In this chapter, I examine theories of gender and organisation. Informants comment on organisational culture in the academy in terms of atmosphere and ethos, symbolism, networks, coalitions, women in senior positions and critical mass theory. Issues such as emotion, embodiment, motherhood, bureaucracy, creativity and the sociology of space are considered. Attention is also drawn to the micropolitics of coercive power relations such as harassment, bullying and spite as means of gendered regulation:

> Recent efforts to alleviate gender inequality have made it socially, and in some contexts legally, inappropriate to express overt gender prejudice … However, gender conflict in organizations is often unspoken or hidden 'between the lines' of what people say and do … Such suppressed conflict is easier to deny, harder to detect and combat, and more difficult to study. (Martin, 1990: 340)

As the above quotation suggests, gender inequality in organisations is both overt and ambiguous, resulting in complex and contradictory experiences for many women. Feminist analysis of micropolitics exposes the gaps and silences resulting from the exclusion of gender issues from mainstream organisation theories. Micropolitics discloses the subterranean conflicts and minutiae of social relations. It describes how power is relayed through seemingly trivial incidents and transactions. Micropolitical activity is engaged in from both ends of the organisational hierarchy, challenging reified notions of power. It is about relationships rather than structures, knowledge rather than information, skills rather than positions, talk rather than paper. Sparkes (1987: 42) claims that it is the stuff of tacit understandings and later denial, of informed sources and second-hand accounts, of rhetorical justification and proximal explanation.

As I mentioned in the Introduction, micropolitical awareness renders competition and domination more visible; revealing processes of stalling, sabotage, manipulation, power bargaining, bullying, harassment and spite. Micropolitical competence allows one to see how power is exercised, rather than simply possessed. That is, the examination of quotidian practices, relationships and emotions in organisations can reveal 'power operating in structures of thinking and behaviour that previously seemed devoid of power relations' (White, 1986: 421). All these nebulous phenomena contribute to the difficulty of effective application of policies for equality. As data in this chapter will indicate, the exercising of power in organisations can be overt and identifiable but also subtle, complex and confusing.

For decades, organisation and bureaucracy theory has been 'presented as if it were gender-neutral' (Rothschild and Davies, 1994: 583). When gender is considered as a variable, Calas and Smircich (1992) observe that only women appear to be gendered in traditional organisation studies, with gender an unmarked category for men. This separates gender issues from other organisational practices and processes and adds to the elusiveness of gender conflict. Whereas feminism has been an effective form of disruption to traditional academic disciplines, the process of inserting feminism into organisation studies has been problematic, with a strong line of argument showing that organisation theory and feminism are antithetical, as hierarchy and bureaucracy are inconsistent with feminist principles of collectivity and accountability (Ferguson, 1983, 1984). Iannello (1992: xi) explains how 'organization theory begins from the world as it is, a world in which hierarchies organize all aspects of life'. And she contrasts this with feminist theory which 'begins with the world as it ought to be, one in which gender hierarchies have been eliminated; thus, it assumes the possibility for fundamental social change.'

While the mainstream, dominant voices in organisation theory have been homogenised, it is worth questioning whether it would be possible to challenge theoretical marginalisation by developing feminist theories of organisation. This requires more than revisionist measures of 'just adding a "feminist paradigm"' (Calas and Smircich, 1992: 240). Rather, it involves engaging with the personal and political consequences of exclusions, domination and loss of opportunities.

There is an intertextuality between organisations and wider social structures, with organisations operating on the basis of existing power relations, such as racism, heterosexism and patriarchy. Organisations are created out of culturally available discourses, structures and practices. Mills (1988: 761) argues that 'organisational life exists in dialectical relationship to the broader societal value system, each is shaped and reshaped by the other.' This raises issues about how gender inequalities are reproduced and challenged in the micropolitics of organisations, if organisations are founded on gendered hierarchies.

SENIOR WOMEN – CRITICAL MASS AND INTEREST REPRESENTATION

Classic studies such as Kanter (1977) have been criticised for essentialising women's participation in organisational life, and considering women as a homogeneous group, without reference to social class, ethnicity, age, sexualities or disabilities (Morley, 1994; Morley and Walsh, 1996). For example, Kanter (1977) believes that entry into the informal system of an organisation, and hence across to power and opportunity, is determined by the relative numbers of men and women in the organisation. She suggests that a critical mass of women in the workforce is required to influence organisational change and remove women from their token status. Bagilhole (1993) applied Kanter's critical mass theory to her study of women academics, and predicted that by being in a small minority, women academics 'will encounter discrimination, performance pressures, and stereotyping due to their greater visibility and contrast with the majority' (Bagilhole, 1993: 263).

One criticism of the critical mass theory is that it suggests an essentialist, universalised construction of women by implying that, in seniority, they will function differently from men, and therefore change organisational culture. This is reminiscent of Gilligan's (1982) study, which argued that women occupy a different moral discourse, one that privileges empathy, compassion and relationship. These qualities, according to Loden (1986), mean that women are more effective in senior organisational positions. As informants in my study observed, the presence of women in senior positions is not an accurate measure of organisational development, as female cannot be unilaterally equated with feminism, nor are all feminists reflexive about their location in organisational power relations. Furthermore, a process of 'masculinisation' can occur for 'successful' women.

Superiority in organisations is often associated with masculinity. The more strongly a position/work area is associated with something 'typically' masculine, the more pronounced the dissonance when it is occupied by a woman. Considering gender symbolism, Alvesson and Billing (1992: 89) argue that 'a particular job stands for a particular gender, i.e. triggers off, or is associated with, meanings and understandings involving gendered connotations'. Marshall (1986: 205) discovered that over half the female managers she interviewed said they did not make a point of being female as they wished to be treated as 'people', rather than as women. They were concerned that their 'balanced perspective' on work issues would be disturbed if they identified as women. Davies (1995: 37) argued that while 'ignoring difference, acting as equal is often an important strategy for women ... it leaves patriarchal cultures intact.'

Early literature on women in organisations (Bernard, 1972) tended to essentialise women, idealising women's characteristics and culture, suggesting that their feminised interpersonal skills made them more effective in human relations. In relation to women's seniority in organisations, Ferguson (1983) argues that the solution does not rest with women becoming more like men, or vice versa, but in the abolition of a system that allocates human potential according to gender. Gherardi (1994: 598) exposed the paradox in the traditional polarised and hierarchicalised analysis of men and women in organisations:

> Yet ambiguity and paradox are the distinctive features of the symbolic order of gender which opposes male and female. Whenever we try to describe what is 'different' about women's positions in organizations, or when we attempt to set 'female values' against 'male organization' we fall into a ridiculous trap. We fail to realize, in fact, that we are celebrating the attributes of femininity as the second sex.

Many women resist coalitions formed on the basis of second sex identity, both from feminist and distinctly anti-feminist perspectives: the former because it essentialises women's socialised caring qualities, the latter because they want to identify with 'winners', i.e. men, rather than 'losers', i.e. women. My study produced several pieces of data suggesting that feminist students and academics expected advocacy and interest representation from senior women, and were surprised to find their personal and professional interests unsupported, or even attacked, by people they had seen as potential political allies. As a consequence of their disappointment there was considerable hostility, ambivalence and mistrust of senior women. One university lecturer commented:

> Although one of the pro-vice-chancellors is a woman, she is hardly

the sort of woman who helps other women along, so it's not really been much help to anyone. She is not into feminism *at all*. She's very much part of the male establishment.

A senior lecturer in a college of higher education noted:

I think probably one of the biggest things that happened was the arrival of the new director ... she was the only woman short-listed ... I began to feel at risk. More at risk than before she arrived ... I was told by a woman in her previous institution, 'she's actually the nastiest piece of work that you've ever come across'.

A postgraduate student in Sweden expressed disappointment with her female vice-chancellor and a sense of betrayal:

we have [a] woman vice-chancellor for the University and she is horrible, she is terrible ... she is a very elitist woman. She excludes working-class people. She excludes people who are not the same as everyone else. She is not a racist, you can't say she is a racist, because she doesn't say that you are black, you are not allowed to get in here. But there is structural racism, and she is underlining it with her politics. She could if she wanted to have pushed for the women's studies, she could have given them more money. She has been the vice-chancellor for two years now, she has not done anything. I don't like her, I was one of them who was really support-ing her because she was a woman two years ago. I made a mistake. She is terrible. She is definitely a terrible woman!

The energy in these women's denouncement of senior women raised complex questions for me. One reading could be further evidence of female lack; another interpretation suggests that it is through relations of conformity and resistance that power relations are reproduced and contested. These senior women were condemned for their failure to resist and change oppressive structures, and for the role they played in reproducing them. A British postgraduate student observed connections between seniority, sisterhood and constituency. She suggested that strategies for survival and accep-tance for senior women excluded the possibility of identification with oppositional standpoints. Ascending the hierarchy involves a tacit acceptance of organisational ideology:

the higher up you get, not just at this college, but at other places as well, the less likely perhaps you are to help other women. We found that you have to spend all your time and energies on keeping your place in the system so it's actually quite difficult to help other people ... The problems with actually being seen to help other women, we thought maybe it could jeopardise your career in some way, so we were slightly jaundiced about women in power and how they actually help other women.

A senior lecturer in a new university attributed responses like these to misogyny and the cultural devalorisation of women:

there're very few women in senior positions here, and unfortunately when there are they tend to alienate a huge number of individuals and then they become demonised as well: 'This is what happens when you get the women in,' you know. So everyone breathes a sigh of relief and I feel quite caught sometimes ... and say, 'Well ... yes, what I've heard about this woman doesn't sound marvellous, but equally I don't think that she quite warrants the demonising that she's getting, you know – she wouldn't get it if she was a bloke.' You know, it *is* the Margaret Thatcher syndrome.

These comments are reminiscent of McIntosh's (1985) suggestion that senior women are under unacceptable pressure to live up to unrealistic demands of perfection. McIntosh quotes a woman psychologist's contribution to a faculty debate on affirmative action:

I am hearing a lot of talk about excellence. But then I look around me and see a lot of mediocre men. For me the real test of affirmative action will be whether or not I can stand up here in 20 years and see equal numbers of mediocre women and mediocre men. (quoted in McIntosh, 1985: 4)

There also appears to be a powerful subtext, based on the patriarchal discourse of motherhood. As the family represents a major source of gender socialisation, gender can become a major psychic structure and organising principle. The woman in/with power symbolises the space where all needs are met. She is destined to outrage, frustrate and disappoint if she displays agentic rather than relational characteristics. Chodorow (1995: 539) observes that women are sometimes perceived by other women as 'withholding' because the cultural construction of motherhood mandates that they should 'give in to and give up to men and do not give to their daughters as they give to their sons and husbands'. Hence disappointment can relate to a sense of lack of maternal nurturance.

An unsympathetic interpretation implies that gender and feminism are commodities some women employ in the ascent to seniority, with no reflexive engagement with processes and the application of counter hegemonic discourses to practices. Gherardi (1995: 144) theorises this in terms of accusations of hypocrisy and observes that:

> The recurrent theme in the rhetoric of the female is the duplicity of women, their use of oblique methods to achieve their ends, their manipulative use of power, their indirectiveness in relationships …

In other words, women are so intrinsically flawed that they can never be trusted. Furthermore, exclusion from direct power suggests that women's influence can only be manipulative *à la* Lady Macbeth. There is an insider/outsider discourse too, implying that ascending the hierarchy bestows some kind of valorisation. To disrupt or challenge the system that has validated you seems like an act of bad faith and ingratitude.

Another reading could be that the disappointment of the 'junior' women essentialises women too, as it implies uniformity of subjectivities and political interests. Gherardi (1995) maintains that women are constantly expected to contribute to the power and status of others. While this usually applies to women's subordinate roles, it could be argued that women are expected to take responsibility for 'junior' women's career development too. This raises issues about how coalitions can be formed by women differently placed in organisational hierarchies. It also implies that all women should be helped to ascend the hierarchy many ostensibly reject, raising issues about quality and equality, with gendered interpretations of what constitutes academic quality. A Greek professor in my study noted that she supported feminist research when 'the method is all right, it's not a means to promote slogans'. On a more positive note, a senior lecturer acknowledged the part senior women had played in her career development:

> throughout I've had contact with very strong supportive women who served as role models, colleagues, friends and have provided a really important source of encouragement for me. I don't think I would ever have got to where I am basically without them. I know it sounds a bit trite.

The last sentence of this quotation seems to capture some of the ambiguities of women's sorority. The informant generously acknowledged her interconnection with other women in her career development, and then parodied herself for what felt like her sentimentality and use of cliché. By so doing, she symbolically moved away from those women who had helped her – an illustration of separation and connection, closeness and distance, identification and denial.

Recent scholarship on women in organisations (Acker, 1990, 1992; Mills and Tancred, 1992; Savage and Witz, 1992) has moved from simplistic notions of critical mass, with studies representing gender as a constitutive feature of organisational life, at the level of organisational rules and practices, the micropolitics of everyday interaction and at the symbolic level. In these studies, male power is perceived as rooted in gender differentiation, with patriarchal relations a resource for men to draw on in organisations. Davies (1995) conceptualised gender in organisations in relation to cultural codes of masculinity and femininity rather than to attributes of embodied women and men. She argues that organisations must be seen as 'social constructions that arise from a masculine view of the world and that call on masculinity for their legitimation and affirmation' (Davies, 1995: 44). These dominant cultural meanings are sustained and reproduced regardless of the gender of employees. One potent cultural code in the academy relates to the reason/emotion dualism.

EMOTION IN ORGANISATIONS

Weberian analysis of bureaucracies developed the notion of *sine ira et studio* (without anger or zeal), suggesting that bureaucracy develops more perfectly the more it is dehumanised (Albrow, 1992). Kantian and Hegelian concepts of rationality have also influenced theories on organisational development and change in the public services. Vince and Broussine (1996: 4) argue that this legacy means that

> Organizations give little space or opportunity for organizational members to access and understand their own and others' conscious and unconscious feelings ...

This takes a variety of forms. In my study, a women's studies MA student described the lengthy, frustrating process of trying to get sessions rescheduled:

> we were having a discussion the other day about whether there are feminist bureaucracies ... this department or course *is* – it has got a lot of bureaucracy involved in it. I suppose it's got to to a certain

extent to fit in amongst the university ... Some things that we want to do – the students, democratically – have been told, no ... On a Wednesday we have a lecture 9.30 to 11.00 and then another one 3.30 till 5.00, which means a 4½ hour wait ... We wanted to move the last option forward an hour and a half so ... because by the time you get in at half past three, when you've been sitting around all day, you're not as aware as you were, you're tired or you're bored ... And a lot of people find that it gets so dark so quickly that to get home they've got to walk a long way and they'd quite like to go back ... It took us three meetings to actually get it moved because [the course leader] was insistent that no way could it be moved.

As this student reveals, academic feminism frequently has to function within alien structures. As students and tutors are usually differentially located within the organisation, there are unequal opportunities to impose emotions and wishes. Democratic processes such as staff/student meetings were felt to operate at a symbolic level only, as concerns raised by students seemed to have secondary status to those of course managers. Conflict arose when bodily considerations, such as tiredness or fear of the dark, were introduced into an academic environment – a culture where rationality and emotionality are oppositional and gendered constructs. Martin (1990: 341) believed that women's interests in organisations often appear as 'contradictions, disjunctions, disruptions, silences'. The hidden ideology of an organisation is revealed at those points of disruption and disjunction, where a contradiction or inconsistency reveals the dominant culture. The students' interventions for change could have been perceived by tutors as manipulation, caprice – emotions which threaten to disrupt serious scholarship.

Organisations are a complex combination of political, social and emotional forces. The academy, by privileging propositional knowledge, de-emphasises the emotional world. An implicit aspect of organisational culture in the academy is the acceptance of disembodied knowledge. Failure to adhere to this rule is evidence of being insufficiently academic. Gherardi (1995: 153) theorised the origin of the emotions/reason dualism:

> The preoccupation of scholars with control over emotions originates from the manner in which the emotions symbolize an inner state of the subject which is closer to physiology than cognition ... The opposition between reason and emotion is based on the hypothesis that affect and cognition are independent processes.

The image currently associated with emotion is that of a disorganized response which interferes with the efficient functioning of reason and action.

Women's 'emotionality' and 'physicality' are placed in binary opposition to men's 'rationality'. Emotional maturity in the academy is often characterised by the absence of emotions, rather than in the skill of being able to recognise and use them effectively.

Informants in the UK and Sweden made the connection between the banishment of emotion (except fear and aggression) and the detrimental effect on creativity and change, suggesting limited opportunities for women's expression (Morley, 1995b). A Swedish university lecturer commented on the agentic, rather than communal work ethos which forces isolated productivity:

> It is a male climate ... totally. Absolutely ... Yes. It is. I couldn't say anything else ... it's the best description ... In the sense that ... formalist ... no emotions, you know? And I think in that sense it is also ... not creative ... It is not the way a woman would do her best in that, so to say, this career tradition ... To study ... you have to be quite anti-social ... You have to be egoistic. To make your own work. To finish with your own work, you shouldn't talk to others! ... You have to sit down, close your ears and just write ... And be very stubborn about that.

Menzies (1990) wrote that organisational cultures are often created as a defence against emotions, such as anxiety and desire. Jaques (1955) also maintained that collective defence mechanisms arise in organisations via the use of rules, procedures and formalities. A question arises as to what is the fear in the academy. What is so deeply distressing about emotions that they have to be so vigorously avoided and suppressed? Ironically, in the academy, emotions are often strenuously engaged to sustain the veneer of rationality.

Albrow (1992: 319) suggests that Weber's model of bureaucracy was not emotionally neutral, but involved 'timidity, defensiveness, harshness and resentment'. Ferguson (1983) explained how subordinate members of organisations have to dedicate considerable time and energy to impression management, paying attention to verbal and non-verbal subtleties in order to please superiors. Janeway (1971: 114) noted 'the powerful need not please. It is subordinates who must do so.' Pleasing people is a politically important skill and is often translated as an essentialised female quality. Coleman's study (1991) found that many women experienced a sense of dis-ease in their organisations:

> the major source of work difficulties for the women is how to appropriately and effectively express themselves in an organizational context ... It is almost as if women are searching for a different way of 'being' in their organizations; being themselves, as they are outside the workplace ... (Coleman, 1991: 7)

Marshall's (1995: 225) study of women managers, who were 'seeking fit between their inner and outer self-images and between themselves and organisational cultures' reached the same conclusion. This never-ending battle over self-presentation resulted in excessive tiredness and stress. In my study too, it appeared that many women were in disharmonious relationships with their institutions, a fact that raises questions about the high costs of attempting to negotiate and adapt to dominant organisational cultures.

ORGANISATIONAL CULTURE(S) IN THE ACADEMY

Rothschild and Davies (1994: 584) posed two important questions: what does it mean to say that organisations are gendered, and that gender can transform organisations? These questions can relate to organisational culture, as culture, gender and power are as inextricably linked in organisations as they are in wider society. Culture is a site where wider ideologies of homophobia, racism and sexism are lived out in organisational discourses and practices (Newman, 1995). Gherardi (1994) saw organisational culture as the production of meanings – the symbols, beliefs and patterns of behaviour learned, produced and created by people in organisations. She argued that it incorporates non-material domains such as values; symbolic messages, such as imagery and dress codes; and concrete practices and policies.

My study produced mixed responses to questions about organisational context and culture. It is often claimed that organisations are unpleasant for everyone, not just women, and that women have unrealistic expectations of organisational life (Marshall, 1995). In my study, discrimination and domination were taken for granted in what was perceived as the male-dominated ethos. This related to the sheer numbers of men in the academy, particularly in senior positions, and the predominance of cultures associated with the social construction of masculinities, that is, they tended to be competitive, aggressive and individualistic. This domination defined women. In some cases, there was a monolithic perception of power, with management blamed for perpetuating cultures hostile to women. A senior lecturer commented on the maleness of the management team in her new university:

> It's very macho ... very macho ... We've got a male vice-chancellor and then you've got his little threesome of deputies, you know – all men. And very, very macho. I mean we used to have a guy who was even more macho ... it's deeply male –

The term 'macho' implied management's unreflexive self-presentation and engagement with dominant constructions of masculinity. This was sometimes exemplified in the association of management's regulatory functions and with suppression of creativity, talent and potential. A retired senior lecturer expressed her frustration:

> I don't think it was an institution that had got its head round the idea of people as creative ... management, a number of key people at the top had a very *negative* way of responding to anything new. Any kind of change. They didn't seem to know how to encourage people ... in one sense you'd say sort of very conservative, or very fearful, bureaucratic, rigid, no sense of fun, except of course, their own jokes ... not very open, in that sense, not open to ideas.

A question remains as to how individual limitations, patterns, distresses, ambitions are transformed into the collectivity of organisational culture. Hargreaves (1994: 164) contended that:

> The postmodern organisation is characterised by networks, alliances, tasks and projects, rather than by relatively stable roles and responsibilities ...

These coalitions are highly gendered, with male-dominated patterns of networking and influence operating against women. Stanley (1997: 181) points out how

> Academic reproduction is in essence a homosocial one in which older men offer patronage to younger men who in return offer the appearance of homage.

This relationship, based on exchange, often underpins seemingly trivial social events. One senior lecturer commented on how homo-sociality excludes and therefore disadvantages women:

> The institutional culture works on the basis of who goes for a drink with whom and that's not changed. The people who go for drinks with each other naturally get on well … I think women fare very badly because they are not able to go down to the pub for a drink to talk about it for a start. I think there is definite undermining of women.

The observation about the pub as a power ritual recalls Ball's (1987: 221) finding that:

> in a micropolitical analysis, the informal assumes … significance … Social relations are frequently, by default, a vehicle for decision-making, amendments to rules and formal arrangements and information exchange.

Several informants, particularly those from humanities, faltered at my question on organisational culture, not associating the obvious patriarchy of their organisation with the concept of 'culture'. To some extent, this exemplified the slippery, taken-for-granted nature of culture, making it difficult to see, let alone challenge. As Clegg (1993: 158) indicated, 'structures of dominance articulate around more or less abstract cultural values …' A senior lecturer did not automatically understand the question on organisational culture, but had substantial data, once it was decoded:

A: Culture? I don't quite know what you mean by that?
LM: The ethos and the feeling and the atmosphere, the dominant values …
A: Gosh … Well in terms of the profile of the college of course it is hierarchically prominently male, and of course, you know, like most institutions … women are conscious that, you know, there are very few female PL's [principal lecturers]. There are very few female head of departments, there are no top managers who are women, and so on … And there is generally, I think, a sort of male-dominated sense in terms of research and promotion.

A lecturer in a new university highlighted hierarchy as a dominant feature and how differently placed individuals would have differing readings of the organisational culture. Equally, management was described as functioning coercively, via dictates and directives, exem-

Organising Feminisms

plifying a one-dimensional, behaviourist definition of power, i.e. that it consists of A making B do something B would not otherwise do (Lukes, 1974).

> I never thought about that before, it's strange. I think it depends who you're talking to and at which point they entered into the institution ... However, it has to be said that the institution is very much based on a pyramid of hierarchy that we get a lot of directives from above and we then jump when they say jump.

A senior lecturer commented on how the organisational culture of her college had been profoundly influenced by new managerialism and the imperative to focus on financial considerations. This was a more subtle form of power, as it involved workers regulating themselves to adapt to budgetary constraints:

> I feel very aware of ... worrying about money. I feel that is focused because it is high on my list and around. I feel it, I'm sensitive to it. I feel that is very much part of the culture, that kind of worry now, and there is of course any agenda I get has got money, income generation, so high on it all the time ... I can't help but feel that it's someone else's job to say how I fit into that and nobody is ... so it's trying to be quite macho in that sense, actually.

Once again, the term 'macho' was used to encapsulate the unacceptable face of management, with market values strongly associated with distorted masculinities.

Data from Britain, Greece and Sweden demonstrated that, in spite of state legislation and organisational policies for equality, a hierarchical division of labour exists in the academy. The notion of hierarchy as anti-women was expressed by an associate professor in Sweden:

> the University is one of the worst hierarchical, patriarchal structures that exists. So it's pretty awful for everybody, quite honestly, but given that women are at the bottom, it is even worse for them. So tenure is very difficult. Professors: I think it is even worse than in England, but there are very few professor positions altogether.

Swedish informants also commented on the macho, patriarchal nature of their universities, with one associate professor noting the difficulties for women, especially in terms of the damage hierarchies do to social relations. While the organisational culture was anachronistic, ultimately, she believed that neutrally constructed meritocracy would transcend gender:

> The University ... is very tough, you have to compete all the time and you have to compete with friends all the time ... I would not have constructed a system like this, if somebody asked me, but they didn't. They constructed the system in medieval times and it's a medieval system and it's very tough, very hard, very exclusive, but if you are clever, if you work hard, double hard for women, you will be accepted everywhere.

The notion of time-warp was also noted by a PhD student in Britain. She highlighted how dated the older, traditional universities are in comparison with other public service organisations, and how they reproduce gender, age and social class distinctions:

> The institution is very patriarchal ... I feel it's about twenty years behind. I mean, I don't suppose it's particularly true just of this university but compared to the world outside, and particularly to the public sector world it's about twenty years behind in terms of consciousness, and policy implementation and you know where women are at in the organisation and how women consumers are treated ... I mean my experience is that the university ... still thinks of itself as being where it was twenty years ago. There isn't this acknowledgement that half of it's full of mature students. There isn't this acknowledgement that half of it is women. There isn't this recognition that most of us didn't go to public school!

As this informant recognises, the demographic composition of the academy is changing, while organisational cultures appear to be lagging behind. Gherardi (1994: 608) suggests that 'organisational cultures express values and mark out places which belong to only one gender ...' Several informants commented on the gendering of disciplines, with certain subjects, such as engineering, medicine, economics and law, perceived as particularly hostile to women. While fragmentation and compartmentalisation mean there is not necessarily a single unitary culture in the academy, there often appears to be a dominant culture with defined norms and values, one that transcends disciplinary, national and temporal boundaries.

Dominant culture positions marginalised groups as intruders, outsiders, and this is actively, rather than accidentally, constructed. For example, the words 'gender' and 'organisation' are increasingly being used as verbs rather than nouns, as verbs imply action, purpose and social production. Gender is embedded in organisational culture, according to Gherardi (1994: 595), in terms of 'interactional and institutional behaviour (the gender we do)', and at the level of 'deep and trans-psychic symbolic structures (the gender we think)'. There are powerful sanctions and regulatory interventions to ensure that transgression of gendered cultural codes is minimised.

COERCIVE RELATIONS: HARASSMENT, BULLYING AND SPITE IN ORGANISATIONAL LIFE

My study produced several examples of harassment, both in terms of overt sexual harassment and bullying based on sabotage, undermining and spite. Many incidents which appear trivial in isolation acquire new significance when placed together, especially across institutional and national boundaries. Hearn (1994) reflects on how concepts that are regularly used in organisational analysis, such as domination, power, control, resistance and authority, are euphemisms for violence. In referring to violence in organisational life, Hearn (1994: 735) goes beyond literal descriptions to include discussion of 'that which violates or causes violation, and is usually performed by a violator upon the violated'. Connections between education and legitimated violence are well-established. Wellington's often quoted observation that the battle of Waterloo was won on the playing fields of Eton suggests that the ultimate goal of male education is leadership in times of war. Rehearsal for this role is embedded in academic processes. For example, academic 'debate' is often premised on the need to compete and cancel the other out. There have to be winners and losers. Loss implies failure, stupidity and lack. In my study, there were few reports of physical assault, but many accounts of spite and bullying as an everyday occurrence of organisational life, with elaborate rituals of resentment and retaliation. A Swedish postgraduate student described how subtle micropolitical interference undermined her professionalism and wore her down. She cited her minority status, as a woman, as a contributory factor:

> I had a really hard time ... I was the first woman that had ever been teaching in that field and I was working in a group with eight men. It did not work out ... There were many problems, practical problems, unlimited harassment, like when I came one day to teach suddenly there were no students because one of the male teachers

told them that they could have a day off … There were no books, suddenly they had forgotten to order books for the things I was going to teach. Once … I had a guest teacher, not a feminist, but still one of the other teachers suddenly cancelled this time she was coming to lecture and on the day I just got a message that it was cancelled. There was a lot of understated harassment, I think. So I stopped, I didn't have the energy to keep it up …

These examples testify to the quixotic nature of micropolitical domination. One can never be entirely sure if such events are the result of carelessness or incompetence, and to read them otherwise would be seen as evidence of paranoia. The violence of the events themselves combines with anxiety over the accuracy of the readings. The result is often exhaustion and a sense of defeat, as this informant observed.

A senior lecturer in Britain described how her institution sabotaged gender studies courses by telling students that they were no longer running:

I stumbled on this because … I was walking along, and a young man … said, 'Is the course still running?' In other words, was it still on offer? So, I said, 'Yes, of course.' And then I looked at him and said, 'Why do you ask?' And he'd been in to put his choices … he'd pretty well been told that the course wasn't running, that he must chose a second thing … I said to him, 'Well over my dead body, is it not running!' But, you know, I got this information incidentally. I got it from students all the time that they were in there, one-to-one, with the tutor that was doing this administration, and they were getting all sorts of stuff said to them which would destabilise … Either it would make them think, 'Oh this must be a crummy course, or whatever', or simply think, 'Oh, it's not running, Oh, I'd better look for something else'.

As most grievance procedures rely on written reports, it is difficult to capture the subtly nuanced intonation used conversationally to undermine and destabilise, as reported above. Equally, the meanings 'between the lines' are obscured. Micropolitical sabotage can be very successful in representation and interpretation functions, as the way in which something is interpreted can often influence how it is received. In the above quotation, those at the sales point for gender studies were able to sow doubts about the product. However, if this were pursued to the point of litigation, it could be perceived as a genuine mistake, or worse, as a result of lack of information from the course leader, and hence would rebound on the injured party.

In spite of the academic culture of disembodiment, a survey undertaken in one British university indicated that 55.4 per cent of female respondents had experienced sexual harassment (Butler and Landells, 1995). My study indicated that it was often left to feminists to confront and deal with the consequences of issues such as sexual harassment, and they then suffered the professional and interpersonal repercussions. As Hearn and Parkin (1987: 93) indicate:

> Men managers with female subordinates may use sexuality, sexual harassment, sexual joking and sexual abuse as a routine means of maintaining authority. This may be thoroughly embedded in the taken-for-granted culture of the organization.

A Greek associate professor described how confronting sexual harassment involved exposure to further bullying. Her story also exemplifies the extent to which dealing with sexual harassment is another form of emotional labour for women, as men often protect each other and are shielded from the distress it causes women:

> I had a student come in here, crying, because she had been, well, not assaulted but ... harassed, by a professor. She ... told this professor off. And when she did that ... he locked his door and kept her there for another half hour trying to convince her not to tell anybody else about it ... She came to me and, you know, I did what I could to, you know, calm her down because she was in hysterics almost. Then she went and told a professor who was then in a high position, and he laughed and he said, 'Oh yes, we know about him ... What could she [the student] do? ... I mean, if she were to file a complaint she would have to have witnesses. She had no witnesses. So it would be dismissed, I can tell you. Immediately.

As this illustrates, the burden of intervention was left to a feminist academic, whose confidence in her change agency abilities was undermined by confronting patriarchal complicity and collusion. This can often be a central paradox for feminist change agents. The more they attempt to confront and expose patriarchal oppression, the more they are damaged by it.

A lecturer in Sweden described the increasing number of incidents of sexual harassment reported by Swedish students:

> there is a certain frequency which is growing successively ... which

is sexual harassment, for instance. And it's quite a lot – it surrounds 8 to 10 per cent … it's been said that it's even more here.

Studies of sexual harassment often have to use measurement to convey the scale of the problem, as this account confirms. However, there are whole ranges of behaviour which are ambiguously classified. This inevitably distorts quantitative data. A senior lecturer in Britain described how applying her feminist analysis to a staff/student sexual relation disrupted other people's readings of the situation and revealed the dominant culture. By overtly challenging what she identified as misconduct, she was left feeling lonely and 'othered':

I feel very isolated … intellectually and in terms of perspective. There was a recent case with a member of staff who was involved with a student and it brought it all to a head because I realised that nobody else was going to see this from the perspective that I did, which was that it was completely unprofessional and it was an abuse of power. But everybody else saw it as consensual relations between two adults, you know. That kind of thing just makes me so angry and so isolated.

As this quotation delineates, feminists in the academy often offer different readings of pervasive heterosexual 'normality'. They often see the potential for abusive power relations and are frequently left to support female victims of these abuses. However, their marginalised status undermines their interpretations. Carter and Jeffs (1995: 16–17) offered an example of male worth set against female insignificance:

One Equal Opportunities Officer who spoke to a vice-chancellor about a professor who had been involved with a string of students was informed he [the male professor] was a leader in his field, an asset the university could not afford to lose. It was then made clear that she was employed to calm the students and not upset the professor in the process.

A senior lecturer in a new university described how an incident of sexual harassment elsewhere rapidly exposed colleagues limited understanding of gendered power relations:

there was an issue about sexual harassment where someone had made a comment to a woman about her chest size and she complained. That didn't happen here, that happened in another institution … It was a member of staff, senior member of staff said this to a member of the support staff and that she had taken it to a tribunal and had complained of sexual harassment and quite a large award had been awarded in her favour. And a note was sent round to heads of division here saying it was only one small comment and still it provoked this big tribunal, so be careful what you say. It was along those lines and it wasn't sort of saying you can see there is a problem with sexuality in our culture: it was saying be careful what you say because you might get caught.

This is a good example of how policies to challenge harassment, like those for equal opportunities, are often perceived as rooted in principles of coercion, rather than social justice. The skill exists in not getting caught, rather than in changing structures, consciousness and practices.

Harassment of women academics in my study often appeared more subtle than sexist comments about chest sizes. In many cases the harassment was designed to undermine them professionally and academically, and though not explicitly sexual, was enabled by gender inequalities. A Greek associate professor described how her career development was sabotaged because she crossed a powerful male professor:

If you were not in the favour of the professor who did exist in the past – as the one and only professor – it was almost impossible to come to the university, to be hired by that university, and this department in particular ... If you voiced a different opinion you had repercussions. Anything from delaying your promotion ... That's what happened to me for two years. Simply because I publicly said ... I opposed two candidates. They were both men, they were incompetent – they were *proved* to be incompetent and they therefore could not be hired ... But I paid for that, you know, with a two-year delay of my promotion.

Women's structural inferiority in academic hierarchies combines with social inferiority to make them particularly vulnerable. A Swedish lecturer described the taunts and threats she received in relation to her untenured position:

I don't have any support here ... On the contrary, I have always some male teachers who are saying that, 'you are going to lose your room very soon', and so on. If you don't get your TEMPUS project, you're out, and, you know, things like that.

A disabled PhD student in Britain who tackled her university for lack of basic facilities for the disabled maintained that she was penalised financially as a consequence:

> I was subsequently turned down for an access grant on hardship grounds and for a university grant on the grounds that I'd over-stepped the line by actually pushing for this [facility for disabled students], when all I'd done was thought, God, I can't cope, I should phone a person for help, that I'm told exists to supply it.

A senior lecturer described the spite she experienced as a result of her maternity/motherhood, exemplifying how women's embodiment and procreative powers are used as grounds for regulation, discrimination and, in this case, punishment:

> it was an absolute nightmare, I had just returned to work after maternity leave. On top of all this I had a baby four months old and they had moved all of my teaching into one semester so it was horrendous, it was, quite frankly, hard to cope. Everything that you could possibly imagine went wrong on that course, and then I had a group of four students who were particularly hostile in addition to all this. It was just a total and utter mess the whole thing. I've never never been through anything like that in my whole life, and I never want to go through it again. It was horrendous ... You know, it was sabotage from all sides. I know that I also equally was not able to give my best because of the pressure that was on me and I felt angry about that as well ... It was terrible! So as a result of that it is not surprising that I had a poor evaluation for that class, which for me I think was not easy to take because I'd never had one before. And it also looked like it was all my personal failure and that I got angry about too.

The informant was sabotaged by her organisation in order to demon-strate the incompatibility of motherhood with academic work. Structures were manipulated (putting her entire year's teaching into one semester) as a means of putting her under pressure and discred-iting her. The organisation punished and victimised by proxy, by making her so dysfunctional that the students attacked her via their hostile evaluations. Like many women, she attempted to absorb and contain the situation by working so hard that she then felt unable to cope. To admit to the stress she was under would simply have confirmed the original belief that motherhood and academic life are incompatible. As Martin (1990: 342) argues, 'the pregnancy of a female employee is seen as breaking organizational taboos concerning nurturance, sexuality, and emotion.' Maternity transgresses the public/private dichotomy, which Martin argues is 'an ideological assumption, not a social fact'. This public/private dichotomy is associated with gender and provides a rationale for a range of discriminatory practices.

SPATIAL REPRESENTATIONS OF POWER

Several informants raised the issue of space in their organisations, in terms of requiring separate women-only space, intersections between space and power and a sense of inhabiting different social and professional space. Observations about space provide useful data about the micropolitics of power in organisations, as the physical and symbolic ordering of space is a major form of social distinction. The metaphor of territory is frequently used to analyse and describe gender relations in organisations. Whenever women enter male domains, such as the academy, there is a subtext of trespassing (Gherardi, 1995). The gendered substructure of organisations is often apparent in the spatial arrangements of work (Acker, 1992). As Shilling (1991: 23) indicates:

> Space is no longer seen merely as an environment in which interaction takes place, but is itself deeply implicated in the production of individual identities and social inequalities.

Shilling (1991: 25) concluded:

> all social interaction takes place in space and it is impossible to conceive of social life outside of spatial contexts ... Space does not just provide opportunities to act ... it also constrains the possibilities of certain action.

A Swedish postgraduate research student cited her age, absence of deferential behaviour and location in an applied subject (social work) as explanations for the difficulties she encountered:

> I had some problems at my institution to get a room, it was a problem for me getting a room, some place to sit ... I came from a school with lower status ... and also I was a woman, so that combination made them want me not to take space, and I think maybe if I had been younger and more admiring of the big boys, of the big school and so on it would have worked out better ...

A Swedish lecturer, when asked about her position, juxtaposed her job title with her accommodation, evoking *cogito ergo sum*:

> I have a room, so I am a university teacher.

These observations are shot through with ambiguities. Space is symbolically associated with prosperity, and yet both Swedish informants captured the instability of the category, with interesting questions about space being given or taken (up).

A senior lecturer in Britain believed she was given a room of her own as a type of containment, to fence off a potentially dangerous feminist:

> I mean this wall was put up before I arrived because it used to be a big office and they didn't know what this feminist who arrived was going to be like ... so ... a bit of limitation in case I ... was sort of the embodiment of all of their nightmares, you know, rampaging with fire coming out of my mouth up and down the corridors and chastising them all for their sexist language.

This is evocative of the anthropological debate on menstrual huts – did menstruating women self-refer for sanctuary from the demands of everyday life, or were they sent as a pollution sanction? Messer-Davidow (1991: 283) believes that the 'purpose of partitioning is to locate and enclose individuals, to initiate or interrupt communications, to monitor and to judge'. The sanctuary/social (en)closure dilemma was evident in many informants' observations, with provision of separate space perceived as an indicator of an organisation's progressive attitudes to women's emotional and physical safety. A postgraduate student in Britain commented:

> I came over with my sister and we were trying to find somewhere to park and every carpark we went into we found signs saying *Women's Cars Only*, for say twelve places, which were closest to the building but under the lights ... And we were like ... Oh my God! It was amazing, because I've never seen that anywhere ... Even outside the Halls of Residences. And obviously they can't police it, but the fact that it's close to the building, underneath the lighting, it's really good.

While this feature had been a selling point for the student, it could also be argued that the concentration and advertisement of women's cars made women more vulnerable to attack. But space is seen as property and an indicator of worth. The boundary is an essential element in individual, group or organisational identity. As one post-graduate student commented:

> I like the way we have the room ... for two days just for women's studies.

A doctoral student in Britain described the difficulties she encountered in her university when trying to secure accommodation for a women's group:

> Well, it was quite difficult getting rooms organised ... and we had quite a lot of trouble with the Student Union because we started out initially saying that it was a women-only group and they said that that actually contravened their regulations about groups run by unions, and again we were quite shocked by that, we didn't realise that we were going to run into trouble on that.

A postgraduate student contrasted her experiences in the USA and the UK, exploring connections between affluence and privacy:

> ... the first place was where I did my undergraduate degree was in the States and a very wealthy University and in the States women's studies is much bigger and they had a women's studies Department and it was great. It was an old house that they occupied just the women's studies Department and it was a beautiful big old house ... They had a great big lounge with all sorts of reading materials where students could come in and sit and they organised things like take-back-the-night marches and stuff like that so they also tried to be activists and it was sort of like a refuge for women and that's ideal, it was perfect! [The British University] where I did my MA was completely the opposite ... there was nothing there for you that would make you feel like, 'Oh this is women's studies', no base, no centre, we had a really horrible campus, it was so depressing. You would go into the sort of tearoom and there were just ashtrays everywhere, litter dropping off the table. It was just a really dirty and smelly place ...

Another American student commented on the lack of spatial focus for her UK women's studies MA:

> I think the main problem is the organisation of this course within the university is that it ... doesn't really have its own physical space. I mean these rooms are fine but you leave and they're used by

someone else … it's very difficult to come into a space and just be there.

From these two accounts, it would appear that little has changed since Phoebe Sheavyn, the Senior Tutor to women students at the University of Manchester compiled a survey for the International Federation of University Women in 1924, in which she contrasted the poverty of provision for women in British universities with the dignified and spacious arrangements that she had seen in the United States (cited in Dyhouse, 1995: 11).

Space was also associated with emotional as well as material security. A lecturer emphasised the need for a safe space in a hostile environment:

> There needs to be some formal place where staff can go to if they are under that stress and pressure and someone that they can talk to and that that should be very well known and say yes there is a space for you, and somebody to listen to you.

SUMMARY

Feminists in this study, sensitised to power relations, offered gendered insights into organisational life in the academy. They analyse and feel the patriarchal structures and processes and yet are not made dysfunctional by them. Their overtly gendered location, as feminists, means that their experiences function as an audit, a litmus test of the organisation's political engagement with difference. Feminism is incorporated in part via women's studies courses and feminist scholarship, but the dominant values and practices of the organisation remain rooted in patriarchy. There is much ambiguity and instability, as various accounts demonstrate how power courses through social relations. These power-laden microprocesses are notoriously difficult to challenge through policies for equality. Feminists in the academy are organised within patriarchal power relations, but their particular body of knowledge means they can also stand outside those relations. These contradictory positionings mean that at times feminism is successful in destabilising organisational gender arrangements. At other times, the hostility that feminism provokes can result in dispersed practices of domination consolidating into a fortification of opposition. Some feminists decode and reject organisational norms and symbols in the academy, placing themselves in ambiguous relationship to hierarchies, female colleagues and organisational change. Gherardi (1995: 97) compared women in organisations with Alice in Wonderland:

> They must assume a role, and every role has its own inflexible etiquette, the principal rule of which – implicit, of course – is that questions must not be asked as to the etiquette's meaning.

Feminists in this study are, to a certain extent, transgressing this rule by interrogating through their scholarship, relationships and professional practices, the multiple meanings of power and difference in the academy.

5 Power, Pedagogy and Empowerment

As mentioned in previous chapters, feminists have often chosen to concentrate their efforts on knowledge production and pedagogical interventions, rather than on policy development in the academy. Pedagogy can represent a key message system and entail an alertness to the micropolitics of the classroom. This chapter explores the concepts of power, pedagogy and empowerment in relation to feminism in the academy. It critically examines empowerment discourses and raises questions about the contradictory role of feminist teachers and authority in dominant institutions of knowledge production. Issues of student resistance, group dynamics, difference and diversity in women-only groups are interrogated using the theoretical frameworks of critical and feminist pedagogy and postmodernism. The chapter draws on interviews with feminist academics who were asked how they applied feminism to their pedagogy/teaching methodologies, and students who identified as feminists were asked for their views on styles of classroom interaction.

Many feminist educators have seen the curriculum and teaching methodologies as sites of struggle, but also as potential areas for change (Mahony, 1988; Morley, 1991, 1992, 1993; Weiler, 1991; Weiner, 1994). As Mercer (1997: 33) observed:

> It struck me that all feminist endeavour, whether it involves working in a women's refuge or lecturing in women's studies, has a pedagogical component. Fundamentally, teaching is about change. If we're not changing, we're not learning. Feminism too is about learning and change. Our revolutions simply can't take place without them. The development of feminist pedagogies is absolutely vital then, a concern for all feminists, not just those who have traditionally been seen as teachers.

This vital connection between feminism, education and change is well established. Feminist theorists of pedagogy conjecture that women have been formed by coercive power relations, and that this influences how they engage with and generate knowledge (Bricker-Jenkins and Hooyman, 1987; Culley and Portuges, 1985; Nemiroff, 1989; Schniedewind, 1987; Shrewsbury, 1987). Feminist pedagogy is process-oriented and ambitious, implying transformations, consciousness-raising, healing even. hooks (1994: 59) identified how she came to feminist theory because 'I was hurting ... I wanted to make the hurt go away. I saw in theory then a location for healing.' Kenway and Modra (1992) remind us of the necessity of praxis and that consciousness-raising must lead to action for change. Feminist pedagogy for empowerment crystallises around a common purpose to change gender relations in a society characterised by power inequalities. Changes start in the micropolitics of the classroom. As I mentioned in the Introduction, the feminist movement has always insisted on juxtaposing the personal with the political. Griffiths (1995b: 1) believes that feelings are often 'deeply political'. Mechanisms for achieving feminist pedagogy's aims are the validation and sharing of women's experiences, democratised organisational arrangements and use of the group for support and development. Underpinning these approaches is the desire to counter women's internalised oppression and the recognition that confidence and self-esteem are gendered attributes (Shaw, 1995). As one women's studies lecturer in my study observed:

> I am very keen that the personal experience of ... mature students is validated and is used to increase their knowledge, to be able to theorise about their own experience ... We try to make assessment less threatening. We try to get the students, for example, to assess each other, listen to each other, criticise each other and talk about the process, not only learning lots of facts, but learning about the process of learning so that criticism becomes something that they can accept as something that is not necessarily threatening ... I think that is incredibly important for women who often have so little confidence in themselves and if you do criticise them you see them literally curl up.

A lecturer in women's studies and sociology had similar ideas:

> I guess I make every effort to incorporate aspects of both personal experience, everyday life and what it means to those in the classroom at any given time, with some kind of rigorous attempt to theorise and analyse these in terms of a broader structure of

society, I think that is an important balance … to bridge that sort of conventional chasm between personal experience and personal interpretation and subjectivity and more structural explanations, issues and analysis of problems.

'Bridging the chasm' between propositional and personal knowledges has been a traditional preoccupation for many feminist educators. Feminist pedagogy problematises the nature of knowledge itself, implying that it is partial, exclusionary and incomplete. It is considered erroneous that knowledge is fixed, certain and the property of teachers; rather it is produced in the process of the interaction of classroom engagement. Pedagogy is perceived as a political project. The macro is linked to the micropolitics of classroom interaction, in the belief that passivity required in traditional transmission pedagogy leads to a sense of political and social powerlessness.

Feminist pedagogy has also been developed in opposition to the traditional hierarchical relationship between teacher and taught. It acknowledges that social identity is constituted through hierarchical knowledges and power relations. In this construction, social relations are highlighted, in the belief that pedagogy is not something one does 'to' people, but rather, it is a complex interaction of at least three agencies – the teacher, the learner and the knowledge they produce together. One strategy used in the feminist classroom to promote interaction is disclosure. Some feminist teachers attempt to decentre authority, break down hierarchical barriers and encourage the sharing of experiences, as women. A women's studies lecturer in my study commented:

> I try to be quite up front about my own personal experience too, I don't see myself as the teacher … they know I am a returner, they know I went through University with a small child. They know that I understand what it is like to live on Income Support for years. So all those issues help us, I think to understand, and it also offers them some sort of opportunity that you can get through the other side of a degree. You can be a single mum with not much money and still get your degree, and it is not just because I am wonderfully clever or anything like that.

hooks (1994: 21) claimed that feminist educators need to self-disclose if they wish to generate openness in the classroom:

> it is often productive if professors take the first risk, linking confessional narratives to academic discussions so as to show how

experience can illuminate and enhance our understanding of academic material.

These ideas are open to a variety of readings. On the one hand, there appears to be a quasi-religious, confessional subtext, with the view that articulation is purifying in some way. There are psychoanalytic undercurrents which suggest semi-conscious material will surface with the support of group attention. This assumes that a transformation of consciousness will occur via the expression of one's voice. In either case, the need for self-awareness and reflexivity is important if teachers are not to abuse their positions by intruding and invading students' inner worlds, or indeed to use the group to meet their conscious or unconscious needs. hooks (1994: 5) observes how:

> The vast majority of our professors ... were not self-actualized, and they often used the classroom to enact rituals of control that were about domination and the unjust exercise of power.

Troyna (1994c) warns against the simplistic equation of empowerment and giving a voice, arguing that the former cannot be read off automatically from the latter. The concept of student voice has been strongly criticised by feminist poststructuralists such as Orner (1992: 75). She believes that it contains: 'realist and essentialist epistemological positions regarding subjectivity'. Feminist poststructuralists maintain that discourses on student voice are based on assumptions of the existence of a 'fully conscious, fully speaking, unique, fixed and coherent self' (Orner, 1992: 79). These discourses overlook unconscious processes of both students and teachers. As Shaw (1995: 92) indicated, teaching is about unconscious as much as conscious communication.

Mahony (1988: 105) asserted that feminist pedagogy can only succeed by disrupting traditional academic models and boundaries. Embracing the epistemological question that we all bring experiential knowledge to the classroom, she described a women's studies course she co-facilitated, using biographies as a starting point:

> We began the first term not with a pre-set syllabus, but instead each woman took a session, or part of it, to describe her own life ...

This practice attempts to confront the false binary between public and private, and mind and body by inviting the whole subject into the classroom. It also suggests that experience is a potent force of oppositional knowledge. However, this approach is dependent on teacher reflexivity, skill, commitment and self-actualisation necessary to deal with the emotions that inevitably surface. Furthermore, feminist post-structuralists challenge the notion of subjectivity as a fixed identity and reject the claim of single strategies for empowerment, emancipation and liberation (Luke and Gore, 1992). In this analysis, it is questionable what women choose to disclose about their lives. Griffiths (1995b: 14) believes that articulation of experience is dependent on language and what one says is not a transparent description of direct experience and direct descriptions of experience will change. Additionally, power differences, the organisational context and multiple social positions mean that many women will feel unsafe revealing their personal cultural histories in the classroom. It is debatable too whether there is a collective experience of oppression, as all experience is partial, situated and exclusionary. As Fuss (1989: 114) affirms '"female experience" is never as unified, as knowable, as universal, and as stable as we presume it to be.'

In much of the literature and discussions on feminist pedagogy there is a conflation of groupwork with empowerment. The importance of feminist process in group interaction and classroom organisation, as well as content, became centralised. This could be attributed to discussion in the 1980s, which problematised feminist ambivalence about using and accepting power within mainstream hierarchical structures that support relationships of domination and inequity (Moglen, 1983: 131). Collaboration and collectivity were perceived as more valuable than the competition that has traditionally underpinned education. The process of democratisation was thought to be enhanced by creating more opportunities for students to engage actively with their own learning and reflect critically on their gendered experiences (Bricker-Jenkins and Hooyman, 1987; Culley and Portuges, 1985; Nemiroff, 1989; Schniedewind, 1987; Shrewsbury, 1987). A common theme was the call to reconceptualise power in terms of agency, efficacy and effectiveness, rather than domination: the power 'to', rather than power 'over' discourse. Shrewsbury (1987: 8) commented that 'by focusing on empowerment, feminist pedagogy embodies a concept of power as energy, capacity, and potential rather than as domination.'

O'Brien and Whitmore (1989: 309) define feminist pedagogy for empowerment as:

An interactive process through which less powerful people experience personal and social change, enabling them to achieve influence over the organizations and institutions which affect their lives, and the communities in which they live.

The rationalist idea here is that by exposing people to appropriate educational interventions, they will gain the confidence to interweave self-efficacy with social change agency. The use of the term 'less powerful' is also controversial, implying lack, deficit and objectification. Shrewsbury (1987: 8) links personal efficacy to social change and claims that:

> To be empowered is to recognise our abilities to act to create a more humane social order. To be empowered is to be able to engage in significant learning. To be empowered is to be able to connect with others in mutually productive ways.

This interpretation constructs empowerment as inherently benign, automatically translating into positive social change. As Deem (1992b) states, who becomes empowered and what they do with those powers is more crucial than an abstract notion of empowerment regarded as a 'good thing' in itself. Equally, the micropolitics of empowerment needs to be set against a wider political backdrop. For example, Blase and Anderson (1995: 135) comment that:

> at the same time that US workers are being 'empowered' in the workplace through participatory, site-based management, their unions are being systematically weakened, their salaries and benefits are being rolled back, their companies are being 'downsized' and their jobs are being moved overseas.

However, women's studies and feminist pedagogy frequently name empowerment as a goal, in line with their connections to critical and liberatory education. This is often conceptually linked to teaching methods. A senior lecturer in women's studies and education indicated:

> we say in some of our documentation about the academic front and being woman-centred in terms of looking into theories and so on ... I think we actually used the word empowering ... What we say in our policy documents ... we make some statements about participative methods ... We do a lot of group and co-operative work.

One women's studies lecturer in this study defined empowerment in terms of 'power to':

> it's around enabling women to do things that they might never have

dreamt they were capable of, or had the confidence to do, without taking over their lives and sort of saying this is how you must do this ... I see empowerment as enabling women to be able to make changes in their life, make choices, even if I might not agree with those choices later on. So I don't say that everybody comes out of a women's studies class as a right-on feminist, because some of them don't and they are not interested in that, but at least feminism has allowed them to do whatever it is they want to do.

The notion of power as energy was echoed by Robinson (1994: 7) who maintained that:

Empowerment is a personal and social process, a liberatory sense of one's own strengths, competence, creativity and freedom of action; to be empowered is to feel power surging into one from other people and from inside, specifically the power to act and grow.

Gore (1992: 56) is less evangelical and counsels caution in relation to the need for reflexivity and humility on the part of feminist educators. Whereas early thinking on feminist pedagogy sought to challenge difference in the academy, more recently, the debate has shifted to call the feminist teacher to account for her role in perpetuating power inequalities. Gore deconstructs empowerment and suggests it first presupposes an agent of empowerment (teacher, youth worker, therapist, manager); second, it holds a notion of power as property; and third, it has some kind of vision or desirable end-state. There is also some criticism of feminist teachers who position themselves as empowerers of 'others' (Luke and Gore, 1992). The question is whether feminist discourses of empowerment are 'instruments of domination'. Gore (1992) asks if the teacher is the agent, does this imply that students are mere objects to be worked on? In other words, empowerment discourses disguise power differentials between teachers and learners.

This aspect was explored by Ellsworth (1989: 306), who described her attempts at progressive pedagogy across differences of 'race', ethnicity, class, sexuality in a progressive university course. She concluded that 'strategies such as student empowerment and dialogue give the illusion of equality while in fact leaving the authoritarian nature of the student/teacher relationship intact.' She questions how a teacher 'makes' students autonomous without directing them. Gore (1992) suggests that feminist teachers should pay more attention to contexts as this would help shift the problem of empowerment from dualisms of power/powerlessness, and domination/subordination, 'that is from a purely oppositional stance, to a problem of multiplicity and contradiction' (Gore, 1992: 61). Weiler (1991) argues that empowerment rhetoric based on Freire's concept of critical pedagogy is reductive, overdetermined and neglectful of the contingent nature of identities. It essentialises identity and suggests a fixed relationship. In certain circumstances the disempowered may become powerful, or vice versa.

Lather (1991) explores the question of what constitutes an empowering approach to generating knowledge and claims that empowerment is 'not something done to or for someone, but instead is a process one undertakes for oneself' (Lather, 1991: 4). She defines empowerment as:

> analysing ideas about the causes of powerlessness, recognising systematic oppressive forces, and acting both individually and collectively to change the conditions of our lives. (Lather, 1991: 4)

Largely as a result of the interventions of black feminists about the ethnocentrism and class bias of much of feminist theory, notions of systems of domination among women and differences within sexual difference have become an important topic of debate within feminist pedagogy (Amos and Parmar, 1984; Hill Collins, 1990; hooks, 1989, 1994; Lorde, 1984). The question of empowerment was raised in the context of the systematic and continued disempowerment of black women. Lorde (1984: 123) believes an essential stage in empowerment is to root out internalised oppressions and develop 'new definitions of power and new patterns of relating across difference'. hooks (1994: 111) identifies how black students often bring 'a positive sense of challenge, of rigorous inquiry to feminist studies'. This feature was always very noticeable in the time I spent teaching women's studies to black and white women. By constantly challenging homogenising definitions of women, many black students' interventions repositioned everyone's thinking about difference. The pedagogical challenge was to ensure that all students stayed open to new information about 'race', sexualities and disabilities, without collapsing under the weight of internalised narratives of guilt and lack (Morley, 1992).

Theorising feminist pedagogy has traditionally been characterised as Anglo-American-Australian. This has excluded more global perspectives. Whereas French feminism is well known for its theories on psychoanalysis and language, gender and power, more recently a school of Italian feminism has contributed to the idea of empowerment. At the heart of this work lies the practice of *affidamento* (entrustment): a relationship in which one woman entrusts herself, symbolically, to another woman, while acknowledging the disparities of class, age, status. The belief is that an authoritative female interlocutor is necessary 'if one wants to articulate one's own life according to a project of freedom and thus make sense of one's being a woman. Without a symbolic placement, the female mind is afraid; exposed to unpredictable events' (Milan Women's Bookstore Collective, 1990: 31).

This practice is often referred to in Britain in terms of mentorship, particularly in relation to women in organisations. It could be said that the role of the feminist teacher parallels the idea of the interlocutor. By giving good attention to women's experiences and operating as a female anchor in an otherwise male environment, she is the *madre simbolica* (the symbolic mother), a figure that represents female values and that enables *affidamento*. Psychoanalytically, this can be translated into the need to identify before one can separate and is reminiscent of the processes of transference and counter transference. Criticisms of the *madre simbolica* perspective are that it essentialises women teachers and places the locus for change on women themselves. Furthermore, it institutionalises socially constructed female patterns of nurturing and caregiving.

Walkerdine (1986) points out how progressive, school-based education was based on women teachers' emotional labour and aspects of female sexuality:

> It is love which will win the day and it is the benevolent gaze of the teacher which will secure freedom from a cruel authority ... Through the figure of the maternal teacher the harsh power of the authoritarian father will be converted into the soft benevolence of the bourgeois mother. (Walkerdine, 1986: 34)

One women's studies lecturer in my study stressed her rejection of the maternal role and the importance of separation as well as connection for women students and teachers:

> I try incredibly hard not to take on the mother role and I know a lot of women teachers who do take on the mother role and I try to resist that as much as possible. I don't mind being in the sort of friendship role but I don't want to be their mothers because then I

don't think you are empowering them. You are just sort of saying this is what I do – you must do what I do. I'd rather they criticise me and challenge me about some of the ways I teach and some of the things that I do, and feel that they can do that rather than having to agree with me all the time, and follow my particular path.

As many feminist teachers point out, dealing with sexism both against themselves and other women represents an additional workload (Pearce, 1992). Walkerdine (1986) was one of the first to recognise that liberatory education does not liberate women teachers, and that there is a 'psychic economy' in progressivism (Walkerdine, 1986: 58). Part of the patriarchal ideal of motherhood is the fantasy of overaccommodation (Young-Eisendrath and Wiedemann, 1987). This suggests that however unsupported and under-resourced feminist teachers may be, they need to be constantly available to meet others' needs. As Mercer (1997: 42) warns feminist pedagogy can reinforce the cultural construction of women as 'all-sacrificing, all-nurturing' mothers. She points out how:

This mother has no desires of her own, no needs, no problems, no will of her own except to nourish and empower all her students/ children, whom she loves equally and without reservation!

This characterised my experiences of feminist pedagogy in women's studies. The sessions themselves were often intense, demanding and emotionally unpredictable. We had to work with conflict, hurt, rage, fear, euphoria, hostility, prejudice and domination. Students would frequently follow me out of sessions when I was already feeling tired, depleted and in need of a short break before the next teaching session. They would often be angry, upset or very stimulated, either from the potency of memories and experiences of gendered oppression, or from their reactions to other students in the group. They wanted to talk, or secure some attention to help them discharge or make sense of what they were experiencing. Sometimes, they simply wanted to continue the intellectual discussion. Frequently, they would have started to make connections between the theoretical input and their lived experiences and they wanted to talk.

For years I responded, thrilled that I was so needed and trusted. I was also terrified at times, when students felt safe enough to attack me for discrepancies between the democratic ideals of women's studies and what they perceived as autocratic, dominating academic practices, such as assessment. On occasions, they would call me to account. For example, I was frequently asked what I intended to do, both pedagogically and managerially, about individual students' retrogressive views on sexualities or 'race'. There was a powerful subtext of good/bad mother, which often left me in emotional agony. I soon realised that I was connected to students in a way that colleagues didactically teaching social policy, engineering, etc., were not, and that I was insufficiently protected from the turmoil of emotions surrounding me. Equally, I was expected to operate quasi-therapeutically in an environment where there was no emotional support whatsoever for me.

Shaw (1995: 54) discussed the feminisation of pedagogy, with the slippage from 'good teacher' to 'good parent' to 'good mother' increasing the scope for anxiety about teaching.

> Though the ideal of the good teacher has got closer to the ideal of the good mother, it is no easier to achieve for much the same reasons – namely that at the unconscious level part of being a good mother means letting oneself be 'used up'. (Shaw, 1994: 54)

The extent to which 'mothering' is considered empowering is controversial. It can reinforce dependency and powerlessness in students and guilt and depletion in teachers. Feminist teachers could also inadvertently fulfil a malestream micropolitical function, containing female distress and gender differences and ensuring they do not disrupt dominant organisational cultures.

EMPOWERMENT: THE ANTI-DISCOURSE

The part pedagogy plays in reproducing and/or challenging power relations, in addition to its connections with social change, has produced an emerging rhetoric of empowerment. Empowerment is an abstract concept, but it has entered the discourses of education, management, development studies and the public services. As Clarke and Stewart (1992) suggest, empowerment is a theme for the 1990s. Whilst the use of the term is proliferating, it remains ill-defined and scantily theorised. Troyna (1994c: 4) argues that in the context of the New Right, it ostensibly means 'enfranchisement, consultation, involvement, partnership, participation and choice'. However, this construction masks an insidious move towards authoritarianism (Morley, 1995a). Ball (1990: 158) warns that 'psychoanalytic or psychological analyses are frequently mobilised in response to resistance'. By focusing attention on individual agency, rather than on structures, empowerment could be perceived as an extension of the New Right's commitment to self-sufficiency, efficiency, cost-effectiveness, quality and standards, employed to disguise government intervention. To understand empowerment requires an analysis of power. How and who constructs power determines whether there will be an alertness to its full implications in pedagogical relations. Conger (1989: 18) defines empowerment as 'the act of strengthening an individual's beliefs in his or her sense of effectiveness'. Conger also believes that individuals are empowered when they feel they can cope with environmental demands. In this reading, there is no suggestion that the environment needs to change. The emphasis is on cognitive restructuring of the individual. A second question that has to be asked about the process is: empowerment for what end? For some it is a cognitive exercise, with an objective of promoting psychological benefits, for others the aim is socio-political, with material implications and changes to substantive social reality. Often, it is reduced to simplistic behaviourism, seeking socially decontextualised personal change. Kreisberg (1992: 19) cautions that the term empowerment is '... used as rhetorical device without being carefully defined by its wielders'. He also noted that 'it has begun to be drained of its critical edge' (Kreisberg, 1992: 21).

In education, empowerment was traditionally associated with liberal and Marxist positions (Giroux, 1983, 1985, 1988; Dewey, 1933, 1966; Freire, 1973, 1985; Shor, 1980). Critical pedagogy suggested a more interactive exchange, with an emphasis on dialogue and knowledge production, rather than transmission and the 'banking' of 'facts'. Freire's early thinking (1973) stressed the importance of 'conscientisation' and the importance of the illiterate poor developing a radical consciousness. Power, in critical pedagogy, is represented as 'something that is negatively imposed on students, or given to them as a gift of emancipation' (Yates, 1994: 431). Pedagogy became synonymous with redemption of the oppressed. The notion of empowering students by teaching in a non-hierarchical way implies that power is property and can be shared and redistributed through pedagogical interventions. In this analysis, there is a modernist rationality embedded in the idea of empowerment, suggesting that outcomes rationally follow interventions.

In the wider context of citizenship, empowerment was traditionally linked to Enlightenment values of universalism and rights, such as franchise, the rise of the trade union movement, housing initiatives, employment contracts and access to education. The transference of micro-practices and achievements in the classroom to macro social change remains a problematic in the empowerment discourse. Shor and Freire (1987: 111) refer to 'social class empowerment':

> if you are not able to use your *recent* freedom to help others to be free by transforming the totality of society, then you are exercising only an individualist attitude towards empowerment or freedom. (Shor and Freire, 1987: 109)

Shor and Freire emphasise that:

> this feeling of being free ... is still not enough for the transformation of society even though it is absolutely necessary for the process of social transformation. (Shor and Freire, 1987: 110)

Giroux (1988) spoke of self- and social empowerment, distinguishing between and connecting the empowerment of individuals and social positions. Giroux (1985: 379) also linked empowerment to transformation, by uniting the language of critique with the language of possibility.

Empowerment can also be perceived as a manipulative strategy. Habermas (1984) theorised that welfare bureaucracies and 'therapeutocracies' disempower clients by pre-empting their capacities to interpret their own needs, experiences and life problems. This is often referred to as the therapeutic, or 'nanny', state, colloquially exemplified in the 'we know what is best for you' syndrome (Polsky, 1991). This suggests that individuals or groups with more cultural capital, in terms of educational qualifications and professional status, can have power over those denied access to such capital. A postmodern view could articulate how higher education is part of this manipulative network of power, in so far as it provides a constant surveillance of the individual and legitimates what counts as cultural capital. Empowerment can imply lack and a deviant passivity which must be worked on through new forms of disciplinary regimes such as watching, listening, knowing.

While appearing emancipatory, pedagogy for empowerment could be behaviourist, intrusive and provide opportunities to invade and colonise inner worlds. It moves the relationship into a psychological subtext with quasi-therapeutic interventions. The issue of boundaries and their transgression is paramount. In the empowerment discourse, it is questionable if there is any realm of personal life outside the pedagogical relationship. Empowerment contains the danger of promoting models of social pathology by implying that the group to be empowered is reduced to the status of raw material to be worked and moulded by experts who have decoded the mysteries of power. Interpersonal relations can be considered as carriers, relays or micro-cosms of external power relations.

Troyna (1994c) challenges the idea that certain pedagogical inter-ventions and interactions are self-evidently 'empowering', and criticises the empowerment discourse for dealing in absolutes – for example, disempowered or powerlessness at one end of the contin-uum, with a linear progression towards empowerment at the other end. Gore (1993) believes that there are no inherently liberatory practices or discourses, and that power must be analysed as a micro-process of social life. Her fear is that empowerment has become yet another regime of truth, and thus she attempts to unravel the connec-tions between authority and power. In so doing, she exposes an inherent paradox in the argument: authority is a necessary attribute in order to empower, and yet authority itself is frequently acknowledged as problematic within liberatory discourses.

Jeffs and Smith (1994) concludes that there is a control culture and a new authoritarianism masquerading in the language and philosophy of progressivism. The rhetoric of empowerment is aimed at refash-ioning marginalised members of communities. For example, students are deemed to be in need of empowerment if they display behavioural or attitudinal traits that distinguish them from the 'empowered' main-stream. Whereas empowerment ostensibly appears client-centred and liberatory, it could well be a normalising discourse, or part of the ideology about the powerful bearing the social, economic and emotional burden of the less powerful. In other words, there is a strong social class element embedded in the concept. Empowerment could be part of the gaze of the new moral technology, aiming to regu-late and survey.

Feminist pedagogues would be right to contest these readings, emphasising their agency. The perception of empowerment as 'power to', that is, confidence and self-efficacy to take responsibility for stating and achieving personal goals, is dependent on a psychody-namic formulation which offers the central notion that our personal histories, expectations of the future and present interpretations inter-act. Anna Freud (1937) suggested that subordinate and oppressed parties tend to introject, or internalise, the negative characteristics that their oppressors have projected on to them. This interpretation acknowledges the extent to which misinformation as a result of

racism, sexism, classism, heterosexism and disablism has been internalised by subordinate groups (Morley, 1991, 1992, 1993).
Empowerment, by this definition, involves oppressed groups over-
coming the internalised barriers created by the dominant group's
negative evaluations and challenging subjectivities founded on victimhood and powerlessness. A question remains as to how this process is
achieved pedagogically.

Kitzinger and Perkins (1993) urge members of subordinate groups
to stop seeking solace in the 'psychobabble' of white, male-dominated
humanistic cults, such as therapeutic interventions informed by theories of Co-counselling, Transactional Analysis and Gestalt. They
suggest we should campaign politically for an end to the conditions
that create the hurt, distress and dis-ease in the first place. There can
be no theory of empowerment, they argue, apart from the social and
political, and it is vital to consider and change the social context of
power relations. Kitzinger and Perkins' thesis, while refreshingly challenging, could be perceived as a form of dichotomous rationalism,
implying that personal development and political action are mutually
exclusive. Political activity can often be marred by unreflexive social
relations, with unconscious processes impeding solidarity and collective actions for change.

POWER AND AUTHORITY

In my study, several feminist lecturers expressed concern that they
could manipulate their authority or overpower students. Shaw (1995:
146) believed that the 'muddling' of teaching and parenting in liberatory pedagogy is most evident in the unconscious links made
between teaching and feeding. A senior lecturer used the feeding
metaphor to describe the interdisciplinarity of her women's studies
course:

> So they have this one opportunity, this one seminar evening a week.
> I always describe it as a chance for us to get together to discuss
> things, to share ideas, and that we are in a way giving them plates
> of beautiful dishes of food that they can taste.

Feminist teachers often struggle to maintain a delicate balance in
pedagogy between over-/under-feeding students. A challenge is how
to facilitate student development, without assuming the role of surro-
gate mother. An associate professor in Greece commented:

I think that young women in Greece ... start sort of being conscious of various things that, you know, never crossed their mother's mind ... so they need somebody to raise the questions and point out several things. Of course, there's always the problem of authority involved, OK? ... I make an effort not to be overpowering, although unfortunately as a person I'm not, you know, the meekest person in the world. However, I try to raise issues and let them talk, just ... on a very first phase, you know?

A lecturer in Britain found that, paradoxically, by attempting to divest herself of authority, she increased it. She highlighted the role strain embedded in ostensible power-sharing, and how we are all inscribed in institutional discourses as either teachers or students. Her attempts to decentre her authority resulted in her being perceived as 'with-holding' by her students:

In the MA I have tried to explicitly introduce feminist pedagogy, with amusing results! ... I tried very much ... to divest myself of the authority of being the one who knew, and so I wouldn't say very much because I thought that if I kept out of the discussion that would minimise my kind of dominant role. But, of course, all it did was magnify it, so I became this kind of silent sphinx figure who knew all the answers but just wasn't going to tell anybody! And by the end – it was too late before I realised this was happening. But on the feedback sheets there was a lot of, you know, we wanted to hear more from you ... So this year I sort of was more upfront about it ... about not wanting to dominate, wanting them to think, but also being the teacher. And I found it – so we would work in groups and I would always be in one of the groups, and ... some of them go, 'Oh no, we've got [the lecturer] in our group this week!' ... they still did very much see me as the teacher, and I just sort of accepted that more I suppose, because however friendly we were I was marking ... their work ... So I think I've concluded for the moment that you can't divest yourself of your authority. You just can't. Because you work within a system where the system sees you as the tutor and the one who's going to mark their work ... So within the system as I am, I'm accepting that I have to acknowledge, you know, power.

This example testifies to the complex, contradictory and uncertain role of the feminist teacher, constantly seeking to balance authority on, with, over. Inscribed in a discourse as impossible as motherhood, the gaze is always on her because students imagine her gaze to be on them. Her embodied classroom presence cues students' socially constructed deference to authority.

The issue of feminist pedagogy as a learning tool was raised by the director of a women's studies centre in Sweden, in relation to assessment and quality enhancement:

> it's [the women's studies course] influenced very much by feminist pedagogy. So the methods are different both in terms of the actual teaching and also in examination. Examination has been take-home papers, they have really done excellent papers.

A Greek associate professor observed the complex interaction between authority, participation and responsibility. She also highlighted the pleasure involved in social interaction (discussion) in opposition to the dullness of a monologue (lecture) (see McWilliam, 1996):

> I think that one cannot deny the fact that the relationship is given, this cannot be ignored ... I would say from my part I think it is very dull just to lecture, I mean I find it very dull and very frustrating also. So what I try to do is involve the students in discussions. On the other hand, this discussing process requires necessarily that the students have followed some of the reading that is required of the specific course and this is not always the case. So what it always comes down to is to combine the two. I think it is inevitable to lecture in a sense.

Feminist pedagogy is only successful if students take responsibility, but the performative dimension of pedagogy can leave some lecturers feeling they have abdicated theirs. Once again, there are concerns about balance and judgement. There are anxieties that groupwork wastes time as it offers the preconditions for anecdotal interventions, commonsense knowledge and trivia. Additionally, it allows opportunities for normalising discourses such as heterosexuality to dominate. As one women's studies lecturer commented:

> you have to subvert this idea that you are the mentor, the person with all the answers and that they are there to soak up everything you have got to say ... I'm not trying to shirk my responsibility to be somebody that guides them and takes responsibility for teaching people but I think you have to instil in the students some responsibility for themselves and it is difficult with some of the students

that come up through their 'A' levels to do that, there tend to be consistently a small proportion of them critical of groupwork. They say groupwork is a waste of time, and all they do is talk about what they are going to do tonight or talk about their boyfriends or whatever.

One MA women's studies student expressed frustration at the lack of student commitment to utilising space made available:

I liked student seminars, when students would prepare a paper and the tutor would make an input too … But there were problems sometimes, as students wouldn't turn up, or they would turn up and say, 'Oh, I haven't done the reading.'

Age was cited as a factor determining responses to feminist pedagogy, with differing interpretations. A senior lecturer in women's studies and social policy noticed:

older students like groupwork. Younger students – if they do reading and preparation – the groupwork works well.

An MA women's studies student polarised theory and experience, linking the latter negatively with older students:

I was really interested in theory and a lot of the students just wanted to talk about themselves – they were not interested in theory … They talked about their husbands and families. A lot of them were older students with a lot of experience, but I wasn't interested … I got really pissed off and complained.

A lecturer in women's studies observed:

older women who remember school as somewhere where you did sit in rows and have somebody up at the front, and they don't like it when you say 'I'm not a fount of knowledge, but I might not know the answers but I can probably find out for you or show you where you can find the answer', and some people find that very threatening because they want you to be that fount of all knowledge.

In the new consumer-oriented market economy of the academy, some students are very conscious of wanting to get value for money from course fees. One group of women's studies senior lecturers reported how:

We were horrified when the MA students accused us of 'skiving', because we preferred participatory, student-led seminars … they said we weren't earning our money, making them do all the work ... they felt that if they were paying fees, they should get lectures, not student-led sessions.

In this reading, it appeared that students interpreted feminist pedagogy as no pedagogy at all – something that happens by default, rather than design, to disguise teacher inadequacy and laziness, rather than promote student empowerment. The teachers, therefore, were perceived as bad mothers, as they were not giving enough. Elsewhere, teachers are accused of giving too much, leaving students feeling dominated and overpowered. Discourses of feminist pedagogy appear as impossible and unattainable as patriarchal discourses of motherhood.

POSTMODERN PEDAGOGIES

Discourses on power frequently include references to Marxist and postmodern positions. In Marxism, power operating in society is ultimately grounded in the economic power of the dominant class. In a postmodern analysis power is no longer seen as a reified possession. Postmodernism rejects the notion that power is concentrated exclusively in monolithic structures such as the academy. Rather, it is also perceived as capillary, that is, exercised in every moment of social life – in inter- and intra-personal relations. Furthermore, as postmodern subjects, the belief is that we internalise power relations and monitor ourselves. According to Bartky (1988), disciplinary power is dispersed and anonymous, invested in everyone and no one in particular. Postmodernism also conceptualises power as a generative, productive, paradoxical phenomenon, as well as repressive. Gore (1993: 120) argues that:

> It is this productive conception of power that undergirds notions of empowerment and notions of emancipatory or liberatory authority, authority-*with* rather than *over* others.

Postmodern pedagogy is characterised by a suspicion of grand narratives that promise 'truth' or 'liberation'. It challenges assumptions of fixed identity and unified, rational subjectivity. There is also interest in historical, social and political contexts. Its concern with difference suggests that regulation occurs via embodiment and discourses of 'race', class, sexuality and gender, and that these cannot be overcome simply by a teacher's good will (Yates, 1994). Furthermore, it cannot be assumed that teachers have escaped any regulation themselves. McWilliam (1996: 313) thinks that radical pedagogy overlooks teachers' self-interests and desires as they become '"no/bodies" in the discursive construction of good educational practice'. Gore (1993) examines feminist and critical pedagogies through the lens of postmodernism, and questions whether they represent new regimes of truth, with new regulatory practices discursively constructed. Sensitive to the issue of reflexivity on the part of educators, she draws attention to the pedagogy argued for and the pedagogy of the argument. For example, educators speak from a discursive location, with a degree of hegemonic certainty. One such certainty of critical and feminist pedagogy has resulted in the cliché of the physical arrangement of the classroom, with circles perceived as more egalitarian than rows. Orner (1992) argues that in Foucauldian terms the circle can replicate the panopticon, with students visible to an all-seeing eye.

Postmodernism suggests that every form of knowledge is an effect of power, and disqualified knowledges have no more claim to revolutionary status than any other discourses (McNay, 1992: 137). A postmodern idea is that in so far as every counter-power moves within the horizon of the power it fights, 'it is transformed, as soon as it is victorious, into a power complex that provokes a new counterpower' (Habermas, 1987: 281). If this argument is applied to feminist pedagogy, it would appear that its oppositional status and women's 'disqualified knowledges' have no greater claim to truth or reality than dominant discourses. Feminist pedagogy is only desirable because there is so much to be against, and this oppositional stance is framed by patriarchy.

THE MICROPOLITICS OF THE GROUP

Feminist pedagogical practices rapidly expose and reflect personal and organisational values and belief systems. Pedagogy which departs from the didactic mode and aims for participative group interaction privileges the student voice. By paying attention to difference, diversity and power inequalities and letting the subject into the classroom, feelings and attitudes surface which remain unseen in other subjects (Hanmer, 1991). This also means allowing oppressive student voices an opportunity for expression. This places feminism in a double bind.

By theorising and naming difference in relation to gender, 'race', class, sexuality, disability, age and ethnicity, feminism can be accused of creating discord where there had previously been harmony.

The dynamics of women-only teaching groups have been an area of interest for many feminists (Holloway, 1994; Morley, 1992, 1993; Weiler, 1991). Experience and analysis of one form of oppression does not necessarily sensitise one to other forms. Describing the dynamic in her women's studies course, hooks (1994: 111) observes:

> Suddenly, the feminist classroom is no longer a safe haven ... but is instead a site of conflict, tensions, and sometimes ongoing hostility.

Hardy Aitken et al. (1987: 263) noted that their women's studies seminars functioned simultaneously on

> at least two levels: an intellectual, consciously rational discourse set in tension with dynamics approaching those of an encounter group.

As one women's studies lecturer in this study commented on the pedagogical complexities of dealing with difference:

> there has been a lot of theory around how it is better for women to work in women-only groups and how it's safe and it's empowering ... I don't think that just because you are all women together that it is necessarily an empowering, safe situation to be in. Sometimes when we have had problems occasionally with women who are very anti-single mums, lesbians, are racist and they are all things that you have to deal with within that group and it's incredibly difficult because you don't want to threaten that person, but you want to challenge them, confront them with their prejudices. So I don't think it is all loving and caring and wonderful in women-only groups.

The issue of classroom dynamics has provided challenges for feminist educators, who, as Weiler (1991: 450) indicated:

> want to retain a vision of social justice and transformation that underlies liberatory pedagogies, but they find that their claims to universal truths and their assumptions of a collective experience of oppression do not adequately address the realities of their own confusing and often tension-filled classrooms.

Lusted (1986: 10) points out that in so-called progressive pedagogy, 'the learner can only accept/reject the terms offered'. Exposure to feminism can disrupt and dislocate students' lives as they re-evaluate experiences and lifestyles (Lewis, 1990). This process produces strong emotions, which can often get transferred on to feminist teachers. Feminist teachers attempt to offer an education which is critical of and proclaims its difference from the institutional mainstream/ malestream. This necessitates sensitivity to any gaps between the two. As far as more radical students are concerned, the feminist teacher is often seen to represent the same class interests as middle-class, white, male academics. In spite of liberatory pretensions, she is implicated in course management and design and is therefore a contributor to oppressive structures. Less radical students can feel dominated by their teachers' feminism, and experience it as another coercive discourse in their lives. One women's studies lecturer commented on dissonance as a consequence of personal change:

> you get some [students] that have this political resistance too, who get to that point, when they've done 18 months or so of women's studies and they suddenly feel very hostile because the knowledge is disruptive personally and quite challenging and you can get quite a bit of political hostility.

This observation is reminiscent of Said's belief that intellectuals should fulfil an abrasive function, challenging certainties and rigidities of thought. As he suggested:

> Least of all should an intellectual be there to make his/her audiences feel good: the whole point is to be embarrassing, contrary, even unpleasant. (1994: 9)

Said's intellectuals tend not to be gendered and being unpleasant, or so highly visible as to cause embarrassment, is not part of female socialisation. Working with student resistance and hostility can cause considerable anxiety for feminist academics. A women's studies lecturer described student feedback on what they perceived as the proselytising aspects of women's studies:

> A lot of students felt that we were thrusting feminism down their throats which I thought was kind of interesting considering they had opted for a feminist degree, but I'm not sure that they had really taken that on board or understood the consequences of that. By the end of the year however, they were much happier with having feminism thrust down their throats as it were.

Hostility in women-only groups appears to surface very rapidly around the exploration of difference, particularly in relation to social class, sexuality and 'race'. Women often feel disappointed, isolated and angry when they discover oppressive belief systems in people they want to consider as allies, sisters. This situation was described by one women's studies lecturer:

> groupwork has been difficult, really difficult because of student assumptions, breaking down this barrier that often exists that we are all sort of sisters. It's hard and we have had some bad times with the group ... Hostility, politically, between students. Conflict between lesbian women, heterosexual women, black and white women and class, those have been the key areas of conflict. On the women's studies course that we taught last year we did have some problems with one student who felt very isolated, as a lesbian woman, from most women, who was in a group with women who were, well they weren't actually all, mostly middle class heterosexual women – there were quite a few black women who identified themselves as working-class – she had big problems and she felt very angry and she said she found it disempowering working in that group and basically we tried to confront it and tried to get the group to hear what she was saying. She didn't feel they were hearing what she was saying and basically the way that we resolved it was to allow her not to be involved in groupwork. Although we did think would it be better for her to work in a group with just lesbian women, maybe she would feel better that way, but in actual fact we talked about it and some people felt that that would not help at all as she had a particular view of what women's studies was about ... she was not open to hearing other people's arguments at all.

The issue of isolation and further exposure to oppression for lesbian students has contributed to Lesbian Studies as a new disciplinary area. The 'othering' of lesbians, even in women's studies courses, often means that lesbian students are contained and frustrated in a discourse of opposition (Corrin, 1994; Garber, 1994; Wilton, 1995). Lesbian knowledges and experiences can sometimes be perceived as disruptive and destructive, rather than as positive challenges to heterosexism. The theoretical exploration of sexualities can also leave lesbians feeling tokenised and vulnerable when deeply embedded heterosexual assumptions are expressed and explored (Morley, 1993). Student diversity can produce wide variations of consciousness and experience. Contingency of identity means that while women share gender oppression, they are differently oppressed on the basis of 'race', sexuality or social class. Strategies employed in feminist pedagogy for empowerment, such as democratised, interactive processes mean that paradoxically some students feel disempowered by exposure to what they perceive as unaware, oppressive attitudes. This can be particularly noticeable for students with activist backgrounds in the women's movement who see academic feminism as a slow and lukewarm substitute for radical action for social change. A women's studies lecturer outlined one student's disappointment with women's studies in the light of a discursive opposition between activism and academia:

> She had been involved in quite a lot of women's activities so she had a lot of experience from the activist side and she found it frustrating when she had to spend time talking with other students who didn't have that background ...

The question arises whether students should be subdivided into groups according to their identity, e.g. lesbian or black feminist studies, or whether this represents fragmentation of the women's movement. As women have been divided by patriarchy, the counterpoint can be to work across differences. However, power relations between women can often mean that important aspects of identity become marginalised in large, heterogeneous groups. In my experience, I have noticed that it is invariably women advantaged by differentiation who want to stay as a group, using the rhetoric of difference to justify their thinking. They realise they have much to learn from other women's subjugated knowledges. However, for black women, disabled women, lesbians, working with white, heterosexual, non-disabled, middle-class women can represent more of the same. A PhD student theorised how feminist pedagogy involved working through conflicts that could be walked away from in other spheres of life.

> I think for a feminist pedagogy to really work well there has to be a lot of interaction between students and sometimes I'm sure it doesn't work, I've been in situations where it doesn't ... It's finding out sometimes what other people are thinking, and realising that if they have a completely different perspective from you, it's just *having* to deal with that different perspective, I mean in your regular life you can choose to drop people. And I find that [working through difference] incredibly empowering in the long run ...

Student expectations of feminism and women's studies vary, with some welcoming these opportunities to theorise experience. A lecturer in women's studies and education commented:

> some students come with a clear agenda that this is going to be all about their experience almost, or their experience is going to be the only thing, and of course that is not how it is. Others come thinking maybe it's a subject like any other and then they are quite pleased to find that they can relate perhaps more to this than to some others, or more immediately anyway.

In many cases, feminist academics reported student appreciation of feminist pedagogy, particularly because it was distinctive from other methodologies they had experienced. hooks (1994: 7) observes that 'neither Freire's work nor feminist pedagogy examined the notion of pleasure in the classroom'. The enjoyment factor was commented on by one senior lecturer in women's studies and communication studies:

> when they actually got an opportunity to do something, about women ... it really meant a lot and they put a lot into it. At the same time, I could see their hesitancy – the feeling that, am I allowed to do this? About women? ... a tremendous amount of guilt ... I think that they got the message from the institution, and probably every other institution which they'd been into, that they were indulging themselves. This was not academic work, paper work ... was it the puritan thing as well, you know, if you're enjoying it, it can't be work?

Students interviewed in my study had a range of responses to feminist pedagogy. One PhD student recalled her MA women's studies experiences and highlighted the considerable skill required for students and teachers to implement feminist pedagogy:

> Some of the lecturers just really were not that good. They were awful! Sometimes the sessions just really seemed to be going nowhere fast, and they were not able to get the discussions going and sometimes it just didn't really work and you would go away thinking what was that all about. Everybody sitting there in complete silence, looking around trying to think of something to say and some of the lecturers were not very good at keeping the discussions going, or generating enthusiasm, they just did not seem able to do it. If nobody was really responding then there was not really much of an effort to really get it going.

The issue of gaps, silences and passivity was particularly noticeable for an American MA women's studies student in Britain.

the worst thing about the course is … I guess it's the difference between the US and the UK in that American students are encouraged and encouraged and encouraged to always be asking questions in the States, and I mean we will drown out our lecturer all the time … I thought it was one of the best things about women's studies because, I mean, my seminar at the end turned into real discussion groups, and it was free-ranging and covered a huge amount of material. And here, there's silence.

Silence and inertia in groups can often be the result of unprocessed conflict, anger, resistance and hurt. The group goes dead as it can feel powerless or insecure to resolve differences. Silence can also be a time for reflection and processing. In the case of part-time students, it can also be linked to fatigue. Another American student expressed her disappointment at student dependency and inertia.

I liked small group discussions but I was in a minority, most of the women – and this I found really disappointing – when they were given the choice, they said, 'Would you just lecture to us?' They didn't want to do anything. They wanted to come in and sit down and be completely passive … sometimes we would come in and the lecturer would say, 'OK we can start discussing now. I've got topics if you want to get into groups.' And they would say, 'No, could you just run through a lecture for us?'

Elsewhere, a women's studies MA student protested at imposed passivity by transmission pedagogy:

We do have one lecturer that is very sort of 'on the blackboard' and 'I'm going to dictate and write on the board for you' … We are just not coming to terms with it at all … I like to think that they respect you even though you, obviously, you may not have done anywhere near what they have done, or written or whatever. But to tell you their experience and what they have read and certain things about the subject, but then to offer it out to people, to … not to contradict but to add to or take up the point.

A PhD student commented on the value of working through painful experiences, rather than suppressing them:

I think of the things that have empowered me the most are the things that have challenged me and at the time in a really weird paradoxical way things that sort of confront you the most and made me feel incredibly disempowered at the time. Sometimes that can be the most empowering in the long run, those things have really shocked me, jolted me.

FEMINIST PEDAGOGY FOR EMPOWERMENT AS EMOTIONAL LABOUR

Working through conflict requires process skills, energy and commitment. In this context, the empowerment directive can sometimes represent exploitation of feminist educators. Fineman (1993: 3) described emotional labour as employees being paid to smile, laugh, be polite or 'be caring'. He believes that this can be stressful and alienating as it involves the suppression of workers' own needs and feelings, as they are paid for their skills in emotion management. Early thinking, encapsulated in the work of the organisational psychologist Bandura (1977), identified four means of empowering others: (1) through positive emotional support during experiences associated with stress and anxiety, (2) through words of encouragement and positive persuasion, (3) by providing opportunities to observe others' effectiveness, and (4) by enabling the mastering of a task with success. All these interventions, while open to criticism for being behaviourist and mechanistic, are also highly labour intensive.

In terms of feminist educators, it is pertinent to ask who empowers them? Feminist educators often provide services without resources to replenish them. Ferguson (1984: 53) explains that:

> emotional labourers are required to take the arts of emotional management and control that characterise the intimate relations of family and friends ... and package them according to the feeling rules laid down by the organization.

Van Maanan and Kunda (1989) note that emotional numbness and burnout frequently accompany the incongruence of felt and displayed emotions. So, it is not simply a question of the volume of emotional demands, but the gap between demand and capacity that causes the stress and exhaustion (Fisher, 1994). The empowerment discourse attributes a great deal of agency and responsibility to feminist educators, and overlooks the constraints imposed by location in underfunded, patriarchal and hierarchical organisations.

In my study, several academics commented on feminism as emotional labour. One lecturer contrasts her experiences of teaching women's studies with teaching social policy:

> Teaching women's studies has been an interesting experience but also a very painful one. It's got a lot to do with the nature of the subject and people's expectations of what women's studies should be, the type of students we get, the impact that studying women's studies will have on the students. We get to Year 2 and something happens to a lot of the women on the courses that we teach. Suddenly women's studies has a very profound impact on their lives. Things happen in their lives, they start reassessing their sexuality or their relationships start changing. Everything seems to happen in Year 2 and they also have very high expectations too of the people that teach them. The boundaries are always difficult so I think it is emotionally draining ... So, I actually do think that social policy is a lot less complicated, a lot less emotion involved in it.

A Finnish student contrasted pedagogical aims and processes in Britain and Finland:

> I feel that it's ... more politically oriented here ... there is some kind of policy in people's minds that they want to make a change in the society ... In Finland ... we just study academic discussion and it has little to do with your personal feelings. In Britain, I feel pulled into some kind of emotional atmosphere and that has been a surprise.

It is interesting to note the informant's equation of politics with emotion, discursively located in opposition to academic discussion.

A Greek associate professor described how, in spite of delivering disembodied, transmission-style mass lectures, women students still identified her as a possible source of emotional support:

> I feel great responsibility because they come here to the office, they talk about their personal lives especially, you know ... And they ask me to tell them what to do in their life but you know I have no idea what I'm doing in my life, you know? ... It is, it's an emotional burden as well ... Huge emotional burden. It strains you emotionally.

The feminist imperative to link the personal with the political has been extended to links with the educational in feminist pedagogy. The transgressive nature of feminism in the academy, means that boundaries are being tested and broken. This has strong implications for balance and self-care for both students and teachers who often appear locked in a very pleasurable and painful dyad.

SUMMARY

Pedagogy for empowerment can be born of a desire to democratise and decentre authority by encouraging active participation, with a view to socio-political as well as personal change. It has been criticised as both simplistic and sinister. It is evident that no pedagogical intervention is innocent, and there are no formulae for effective pedagogies. Postmodernist analyses of power locate critical and feminist pedagogies in coercive and rationalist discourses, representing new regimes of truth and forms of domination. In this reading, pedagogy for empowerment is intrusive, colonising and naive. As Orner (1992: 87) asked: 'How do the micropolitics of the "emancipatory" classroom differ from the macropolitics of imperialism?'

Pedagogies for empowerment can also be perceived as part of the manipulative, victim-blaming ideology suggesting that oppressed groups have the power to change their material circumstances through psychological restructuring. In this case, pedagogy for empowerment is superficially conceived and borders on simplistic behaviourist notions of change. Feminist educators are discursively and materially located in the interstices of theoretical hegemonies, trying to negotiate a commitment to women's liberation, while acknowledging their authority and suspicion of grand narratives with liberatory pretensions. Equally, there is a tension for feminist educators between location in a quasi-therapeutic discourse of pedagogy for empowerment, and location in institutions dedicated to the life of the mind and the banishment of emotion. Feminist students vary in their responses, with some appreciating process-oriented approaches and others believing these represent poor value, or coercive, intrusive interventions. In the new market economy of the academy in Britain, students have mixed responses to participative approaches, sometimes preferring 'value for money' information-as-commodity, teacher-led lectures. Feminist pedagogy, while often effective in terms of student support, can also be seen to fulfil a micropolitical function. This means that issues of oppression and difference can be contained and dealt with via the emotional labour of feminist academics, leaving the rest of the academy untouched.

6 Feminist Students: Radicalism, Rights and Resistance

READING DIVERSITY

As I indicated in the previous chapter, feminist students have a variety of expectations and experiences. This chapter considers student experiences of academic feminism and focuses on student diversity, feminism's transformative potential, negative popular images of feminism, hostility and resistance, post-feminism, men in feminism and academic support. The latter is explored in relation to the tension between the emergence of an entitlement culture and depleted institutional resources. Students and tutors respond to questions on student evaluations, capturing both consumers' and providers' knowledge of feminist courses. Diversity is considered in relation to age, social class, sexuality, disability, ethnicity, with examples of how the academy has 'othered' or accommodated aspects of student identity forged in marginality, such as disability.

During its early history, the university represented a forbidden place for women: 'those who attempted to enter experienced a wide variety of discriminatory practices' (Stiver Lie and Malik, 1994: 205). In 1833 Oberlin College in the United States was the first university globally to admit women on an official basis. In Britain, the University of London was, in 1878, the first to admit women to its degrees (with the exception of medicine). From around 1900 the number of women students rose steadily, especially in arts departments, all over Britain. Figures from the University Grants Committee (UGC) show that women represented 16 per cent of the student population in 1900: this proportion rose to 24 per cent in 1920 and 27 per cent in 1930, falling back to 23 per cent on the eve of the second world war (Dyhouse, 1995). The success of the initial campaign for access to universities in Britain was followed by a long period of stagnation. Women made up only about 25 per cent of university students until the mid-1960s. It was not until 1991 that they were 45.1 per cent of all UK university students (Sutherland, 1994). Halsey (1992: 66) indicates how women have always been in a minority in elite institutions. For example, in the 1920s, while women took over 20 per cent of university places, in Oxford men outnumbered women by 5 to 1 and in Cambridge by 10 to 1. (As with many statistics on gender, they are rarely controlled for social class, 'race' and age, so diversity among women students is infrequently explored.)

In my study, feminist postgraduate students were black, white, lesbian, heterosexual, many were from working-class backgrounds, one was disabled and their ages varied from the twenties to fifties. They were from urban, rural and suburban areas. The majority had first degrees in social sciences. Their backgrounds led to different expectations of academic feminism. For example, some had been involved in the women's movement, trade unions, women's aid, rape crisis. Some were post-experience professionals, with successful careers in social work, teaching or community work. Some younger students were hoping to apply women's studies degrees to careers in international agencies, equal opportunities work or research.

While several of the feminist academics I interviewed commented on student diversity as a feature of women's studies, many of the students highlighted privilege and heterogeneity as problems on courses that have still to be addressed. A postgraduate student in Sweden drew attention to the under-representation of working-class students in her university:

> only 14 per cent of the students have a working-class background, that's not speaking about immigrants – that's another story. So what we get here is a very privileged group of young people and that was very different in the 1970s because there were other ways to get into the universities, so what we get is very young women from privileged homes.

Another Swedish postgraduate student felt that, in spite of decades of liberal democracy, social class was a critical factor in terms of access to the academy:

> about the working class, you need to change the structures of getting into University. That's one of the main problems both for foreigners and working-class people ... They [the state] renamed class during the 1970s, they call them social categories. I think that is why very few people in Sweden talk about class. They say social category 1, 2 and 3. 3 is the lowest, working class, 1 is ruling class,

professional ... We don't actually have a very big underclass, we don't, but we are actually producing them right now.

The use of measurable indices suggests stable, structured economic inequalities. However, research suggests that in both Britain and Sweden class inequalities widened during the 1980s (*Guardian*, 10 February 1995: 7). The Rowntree Inquiry into Wealth and Income (1995) revealed that since 1977 the proportion of the population in Britain with less than half the average income has trebled. Sweden is understandably anxious about following suit. In Greece too, social class was identified as an issue. A Greek professor noted how, while there was an overt declaration of open access for all to universities, material differences influenced young people's life chances:

> Yet recent studies have shown that discrepancies [exist] ... and according to which social strata one belongs, plays still a great role ... Still because you see the problem is that we have a limited number of students which can enter the universities. And we have the severe system for allowing those who compete to enter. So in order to have the knowledge ... you have to be prepared with private professors and private teachers. And these costs are very high, extremely high.

A senior lecturer in Britain noticed how feminist students in her university were attacked from all sides when they attempted to set up a women's group – on the one hand for being separatist, and on the other for discursively eclipsing other forms of difference, such as social class:

> They've had a huge amount of stick from other students for being separatist, you know, a women-only group – that's against the constitution of the union, etc. They have had to fight very hard to even feel comfortable with calling themselves feminists, so I think it is in the institution but I think that reflects the hostility towards feminism. And it's been amazingly successfully lambasted as lesbians-in-dungarees, you know – on the one hand, and on the other hand as being exclusively concerned with women ... as being sort of blind [*sic*] to issues of 'race' or ethnicity or class or difference, you know ... And that's one of the things I find so hard is that when people talk about feminism they obviously are just talking about sex difference, whereas my understanding of feminism is that, you know, it has grappled with all of these differences.

This is a good example of how the hierarchy of oppressions functions to silence women. Equally, the use of homophobic (and dated) imagery of 'lesbians in dungarees' is a means of regulating women and manipulating them into their prescribed roles. The idea of feminism as a discredited politics was discussed by Ramazanoglu (1995: 31):

> Most women reject any kind of feminist identity ... feminism has such a negative popular image that many young women associate it with a man-hating older generation that has nothing to offer them, or an able-bodied, white ethnicity that excludes them.

Many British informants chose age, rather than social class, sexuality or ethnicity, as a signifier to communicate student diversity on women's studies courses. A lecturer in a new university commented:

> I don't think there is a particular profile, a particular background, the age range of students [here] is enormous anyway and in Sociology and in other disciplines as well, we have a lot of mature students and so they are any age from 18 to fifties ... I don't think I could sum them up.

Age and political consciousness were noted as signifiers of difference by a Swedish postgraduate student describing the student composition of women's studies courses:

> Different kinds of people actually. It's very radical women, it is women who are a bit interested in women's questions and women's politics but they are not active in this society so to speak. They are not active in any political party or demonstrations, or anything like that, but they are interested. And it's all kinds of ages. When I went, there was a woman who was 73 years old and the youngest who was about 19 years old.

A senior lecturer in a college also highlighted the age and political expectations of her women's studies students:

> They are very mixed in age group so we have people straight from school and we have people post-retirement ... They do come with different ideas about what women's studies is so there are things to clear early on which I find I just don't have in other areas of teaching ... Also I think the agendas can be unpredictable and sometimes that has given us difficulties. We have found such a range of expectations in a class ... Some come with a very clear political agenda and they want a degree but they also want to study

women's studies very much and explore their own experience and put it into context and theorise it. Others come really with very little idea about what it might be at all. We would include in that some students who don't want to use words like 'feminism' or are a bit wary shall we say?

Fear of feminism was noted by several informants. It comprised another major strand of difference. A Swedish postgraduate student theorised this in relation to radical and liberal politics:

> I think that there are two kinds of women [students]. In Sociology, on the one side you have this kind of new feminist, and they are very political and radical, their sexual identity is very important to them, and anti-pornography. We have that group then we have a kind of humanist young woman that are terrified of course by this terrible radical feminism, so that could be the two groups that I think we get.

This description implies that women's political stances and social identities are fixed. Whereas exposure to academic feminism courses can sometimes have a transformative effect (Morley, 1993).

A senior lecturer in Britain described the strategies she had to employ to allay students' fears of feminism in her women's writing courses:

> I mean the MA course Contemporary Women Writers and Feminist Theory is deliberately trying to keep the word 'feminist' away from the word 'writers' ... And in my undergraduate teaching I've been even more careful not to let them link the two terms because I just think it's unhelpful ... I don't advertise the courses as being feminist ... in the same way that in my personal presentation I do describe myself as a feminist, but ... only if asked. It isn't the first thing I say when I go in to do a lecture about feminism, and I've sometimes played it, you know, in wearing feminine clothes when I'm giving that lecture, or whatever ... I wouldn't say it was disguise, I'd say it was ... wooing them really ... Because I get the feeling that the atmosphere has changed a lot and, well I mean, you know, I'm sure you know the hostility towards feminism.

This measured presentation of self and course content is evocative of feminist observations of 'doing gender' or gender as performance (Butler, 1993). The concept of identity as 'schizophrenia' is well rehearsed in feminist theory. Braidotti (1986: 51) referred to the double interaction – on the one hand, between women and masculine institutions of discourse and, on the other hand, between each woman involved in the process. Walkerdine (1990: 47) maintains that success depends on

> splitting – the negotiation of an impossible array of identifications in which women, becoming what the academy wants, can no longer be what they want and *vice versa.*

However, for the senior lecturer quoted above, the binary of feminism and dominant organisations is not the issue; rather, her caution is in relation to hostility from students. As she mentioned, 'the atmosphere has changed a lot', suggesting there has been a deradicalisation of the student body. Some academics reported evidence of forceful beliefs in post-feminism, particularly among younger students, that is they feel that the battles have been fought and won. A senior lecturer remarked:

> And most of the students will say it's all changed now – you know, we're not discriminated against. And of course, you get the position, always, that it's the mature students who say, no it hasn't changed and what about this? And it's the young 20 year olds who think that everything's equal now.

The myth of post-feminism has gained international currency (Coppock, Haydon and Richter, 1995). A Swedish student attributed this complacency in Sweden to decades of welfare liberalism:

> I think if you look at Sweden, it is a bit different from other countries, just because of the welfare state. I think that many … students, the reason that they are saying that there are no gender issues, no inequality, no class, whatever, of course they are wrong, they will notice when they go out, no doubt about that. But if you put those people in the context where you are actually socialised into a quite fractional society where you get money when you are pregnant, where you get your child care when you go out, where the women have problems but they are invisible because of the equality politics.

This example suggests that women have been pacified by equality measures – lulled into docility via basic welfare provisions. Conversely, in Greece, a professor believed that the New Right, with its emphasis on individualism, had eroded decades of socialist radicalism:

I think that the younger generation do not understand what the problems are with women and their careers and their family lives and their social status – they cannot understand it. They think that living in a civilization in which everyone is free to follow its own ambitions then there is no problem. And this is what makes me sad because I think that the dangers do exist ... They cannot perceive the dangers.

Both in Sweden and Greece, some women students' failure to engage with feminism was seen as a type of false consciousness or fools' paradise. In Britain, the notion of danger and frontier crossing was emphasised by a women's studies course leader:

It seems to me still that for very young women to opt to do women's studies is still quite a brave thing to do. Because I still get comments from them about friends of theirs – male friends, female friends – laughing at them for doing women's studies. The perception is that it's somehow not an academic subject, or that it is, you know, viragos talking nonsense about, you know, sort of anti-men or something like this. And I think that a lot of these young women find it very difficult, they've got to be very strong and very sure to opt to do women's studies at all. And some even drop out after the first year and I think because of this reason that they're feeling this pressure that the subject has been denigrated. I also have students who come to me saying, 'Oh I've been told that I won't get a job if I do women's studies'. So there's this perception that women's studies will actually prevent them from, you know, getting a job in the outside world, rather than facilitate it, which I find is very worrying.

The fears described in this account appear to spring from a variety of hegemonic views. The political economy instigated by the New Right means that young people are anxious about the currency of their university courses in a depressed graduate labour market. A black MA student in my study felt that this deterred many young black women from opting for women's studies. She noted that 'racism means they have enough problems getting jobs, even with degrees in law or medicine.' Another critical factor in young women's fear of feminism was the dominant discourse of heterosexuality which made them reluctant to follow courses which run the risk of courting male disapproval. A women's studies MA student in Britain described how these factors influenced her decision-making process:

I worked for a couple of years with the intention of doing a post-grad. course, but not quite sure what in. And I'd always obviously been interested in feminist issues … But I wanted to do this a few years ago and people were saying to me, 'Oh no, don't do it because of the stigma' … People said, 'You don't want to be seen as like a burn your bra, lesbian feminist, do you?'

This account, similar to the observations made in an earlier account of 'lesbians in dungarees', indicates how hostility to feminism is fuelled by misogyny and homophobia. The implication is that the most undesirable identity for women is lesbianism. In this analysis, radical feminists rather than patriarchy itself, are perceived as the negative reference group. These types of retrogressive attitudes meant that a young lesbian student in my study felt she could not come out, even on her women's studies course: 'All the other women talked about husbands and boyfriends all the time – there was no space or understanding for me to feel good talking about my sexuality.' However, as a women's studies course leader noted, fears and differences are to be worked through. As changes in perception occur over time, it would be erroneous to classify these utterances as immutable forms of closure:

We have a very wide-ranging group of students who come on the course. So we have some who can be radical feminists, have been steeped in feminist theory for 10–15 years, and come on the course at what one might say is a very high level of knowledge – about the issues and wish to explore those in more detail, more depth … And then we have all grades of students to those who come on the course and say, 'I'm not a feminist!', and feel quite nervous. They are obviously interested in the course but they're quite nervous about it. They're nervous often with the other students, if there are radical feminists or whatever in the group. They may be very tentative about their own feelings and their own knowledge, although of course most of them have a first degree in a specialism they often have, you know, quite low self-esteem in relation to this material and what they're doing … And so often those students will get from the course – sometimes will be a transformation. I mean some students come on the course at the beginning and saying, 'I'm not a feminist', and end the course saying, 'This has changed my life.'

As Lewis (1994: 101) implies:

the transformative power and social significance of feminism lies in the coherence of a process that articulates a politic out of the personal.

For some students, this process was too terrifying, and their defensive reaction was to demonise radical feminists. Others may have already decided to open their lives to change and discovered feminist courses in higher education as a powerful starting point.

EVALUATING WOMEN'S STUDIES: IMAGERY OF IMPACT

Many students evaluate feminist courses in terms of quasi-religious conversion (Morley, 1993). Raymond (1985: 53) identified the 'profound religious dimension' to women's studies and recognised that many 'see women's knowledge as having revelatory power'. This evangelical zeal can be countered by the sinister side of religions, with many viewing feminism as a dangerous cult (Patai and Koertge, 1994). This negative discourse has been effectively facilitated by the dominance of the New Right notion of political correctness – something that delegitimises movements of the Left by framing them as coercive and regulatory. Patai and Koertge's study contains numerous examples of women students who claim to have been terrorised and permanently disempowered by their exposure to radical feminists in women's studies courses. These accounts are not deconstructed, however, to reveal dominant anti-Left values and the demonisation of women who challenge patriarchy. They are left at face value.

In contrast, my study produced many positive, yet constructively critical evaluations of feminist courses. There was a strong thread of the transformative potential of feminism. An American postgraduate student commented on how it influenced her identity and represented a type of Lawrentian exposure to the metropolitan other:

> When I first went to university I had just come from a small town in Ohio. My whole family are Republican voters. I never really questioned anything, you know. I was very, very, very naive and I went to university and started doing women's studies courses and I wouldn't even really call myself a feminist before I went to university.

Feminist scholarship was also described as 'rescuing' women from mundane occupations, as it encouraged them to be more critical and not to settle for second-class citizenship, as a postgraduate student expressed:

> Well, it completely revolutionised my life. I had been stuck in dead-end jobs for a number of years and ... As soon as I started getting these booklists and started reading for a purpose, it just completely changed my way of thinking and me as a person. It made me start thinking much more about life. I was very accepting when I was younger of what I had been taught and I didn't really challenge anything at all, but when I came back as a mature student I really started wondering why I had been taught certain writers and not others and thinking much more clearly for myself, so it completely changed me ... I have just come to question absolutely everything about the education system really and what I was taught and why I was taught it.

As this account suggests, exposure to academic feminism resulted in a commitment to recovery of women's lost knowledges, reconstruction of what constitutes literature and reflexivity about the validation and production of social knowledge. De Groot and Maynard (1993: 4) argued that: 'Recuperation, reconstruction and reflexivity all remain constituent elements of women's studies practice.' While it can be argued that reconstruction and reflexivity are important elements of all disciplinary knowledge, some students in my study felt that the recuperation side of women's studies was particularly powerful. As one student exclaimed:

> And it really, really changed my life. It's changed it just sort of totally. One's centre shifted and ... I would use the word 'healing', absolutely, healing.

Congruent with consciousness-raising processes in the 1970s, several students commented on the power of group experiences. A postgraduate women's studies student phrased this in terms of the normalising discourse of polarised madness/sanity:

> I wasn't very sure of what to expect really, just that a lot of women would be there who felt quite frustrated, the way that I did ... Usually, if you try to figure out what's wrong with the institutions or whatever, people would look at you as if you're paranoid. And I think it was to get together and share the frustration... then you realise that, okay, you're not going mad, you know, it's not just you.

The terms 'paranoid' and 'mad' resonate with ideas about the disqualified knowledges of those deemed to be outsiders in the system. Cain
(1993: 85) believes that an important question to pose, particularly
for 'those who have sometimes felt they are going mad', is whether it
is 'possible to have an experience without a knowledge (let alone a
discourse) to have it in?' In the extract above, the student seemed to
suggest that she sensed her otherness precognitively, and women's
studies provided the theoretical framework in which to analyse this
feeling. Cain (1993: 89) considers that: 'A recognition that a formulation is apt brings immense relief and gratitude that something
unsayable can now be said and shared.' However, the student's
account assumed a degree of shared feelings and homogeneity among
feminist students which is not always in evidence. A women's studies
lecturer felt that the notion of a unified group was highly suspect, as
students engaged with course content from partial and situated positions, meaning that there were always multiple readings of any
session:

> In terms of teaching as in the actual interacting with the students, I
> think, one of the things that I think is very difficult is how differ-
> ently different students feel about the issues when they are being
> discussed, so that what may seem to some a very sort of benign
> discussion about the politics around child sexual abuse, for
> example, may seem on the one hand to some completely uninter-
> esting, and they may even say, 'Well, child sexual abuse is not really
> a women's issue is it? As mostly men do it' ... So there's that end of
> the spectrum and then there's the other end which is students who
> have experiences of sexual abuse maybe or are just more highly
> sensitised to the issue and may actually find it very uncomfortable
> and upsetting, and so to try to keep any idea that women's experi-
> ences are unified – this is obviously not at work in that sort of
> scenario.

Group dynamics were believed, by a senior lecturer, to be an important motivating factor, and success was based not on commonality,
but connection:

> They were highly motivated. I think the way that they prepared for
> their seminars ... demonstrated that. What they actually say in
> their evaluations is that it changed their life ... Now this was ... to
> do with the transformation that took place as they explored, as they
> read, as they talked, as they engaged. I think the culture of the

group as well, and the fact that they shared and interacted such a lot.

As this account implies, power-sensitive discourses support a subordinated and excluded group in their work to make sense of the gendered social world. In some cases, feminist courses appeared to provide important theoretical, political and emotional functions by facilitating those deemed as 'other' to analyse their own histories and voices. This links with comments made about the aims of feminist pedagogy in chapter 5. A university lecturer described how initial resistance transformed into situated engagement as students began to identify with the course content:

> they are all women at crossroads in their lives. Some of them at first are rather resistant … Not all of them, some of them have got quite a feminist background … but with the resisters it can be more difficult with them, but you usually find, especially when I am teaching women's history, that within a few weeks they are so engaged by the whole issue of women's history, all these ideas are coming up that they never thought about. They never thought about women as having a history … that some of them turn out to be … strong feminists from being the resisters to being really strong. They really flip from one thing to another I find … they suddenly realise there's a pattern to women's oppression then … It's a good exercise in consciousness-raising.

The idea of intertextuality between past and present can be a powerful constituent to positive identity formation. A women's studies lecturer noted how the androcentric bias of knowledge production means that many women feel that their personal and collective histories are excluded from academic work:

> One thing that a student said once in the evaluations, which I valued greatly … she was a white mature student … And one of the things she'd said was, she didn't have to … deny all of her past. She felt that she'd been rubbished and now she was OK. It seems to be very damaging if people are put in a position where they have to deny a previous life, rather than actually being able to draw on that as material for moving forward.

Success was conceptualised by many students in terms of movement. Instead of feeling that they had to expend energy explaining and justifying their feminism, some feminist students appreciated associating with those who assisted them to consolidate and progress. An MA women's studies student articulated feminism's challenge to hegemonies, and how that enabled her to move forward:

> people don't realise that it's [patriarchy] there. It's just tradition, it's just normal, you know. When you try and – people think that I just pick at things deliberately, but when you start realising you do want to pick everything apart, don't you? ... it is nice to get into this sort of scenario – where people understand really. And then you start from there and you go on and you learn more than you thought was actually happening.

Student resistance can often be the result of the emotional need to stay attached to certainties. Attachment is a powerful psychic structure and it requires a robust sense of ontological security to permit psychic and social disorientation. A postgraduate student described how a women's studies course left her feeling initially adrift, but subsequently intellectually and emotionally developed:

> I value things that really make me think and challenge my own perception of the world. This one particular class really shook the foundations of what I never really thought about, about myself and I think it did for a lot of people ... it really moves you forward in weird ways, all of a sudden. It's like having the foundations come out from underneath you and you think WOW where am I now? I have never thought about this I have never examined this aspect of myself or whatever.

Not all students wanted such a profound emotional experience. The uncovering of deeply submerged social practices of domination and interrogation of accepted norms can leave many students feeling destabilised. A women's studies lecturer believed that there were varying levels of engagement with the subject, with some students remaining detached, while others reported significant personal disruption as a result of their certainties being challenged:

> they found it very difficult, very emotionally upsetting quite often – students get very upset sometimes because it ... makes them question how they've conducted their lives or how friends of theirs perhaps are conducting their lives and so on. So they can find it emotionally quite upsetting and disturbing in a way that perhaps, you know, doing a Biology MA or doing the Eng. Lit MA they wouldn't. Others will come and will say, 'I'm not a feminist'; will do

the reading, will be interested, will participate, will be a voice, will perhaps do something about, you know, women in society, women in history, but will perhaps not have radically changed their positions by the end of it ... Because you can tell from their thesis that they're doing it in a fairly, what one might say, a straight academic way ... they remain more cautious about ... the perhaps more radical elements that are present in the course, or that ... they don't take advantage perhaps of those more radical elements. They feel they don't want to.

The idea that for some students, women's studies is just another option rather than the 'hard fought for political and institutional spaces that were generated through years of commitment and struggle' (Skeggs, 1995: 477) can be a painful reminder of the individualistic consumer ethos and commodification of knowledge fostered by decades of New Right influence on education.

A senior lecturer was particularly interested in some of the imagery students employed in their evaluations to illustrate their personal change processes:

evaluation comments on the whole for everything have been good, very good, some of them have been really inspiring and brilliant, and say things like, 'I really enjoyed this course'. One that sticks in my mind is this woman that said that she felt it was 'stretching her brain'. You get some lovely comments like 'really mind-blowing stuff'. That sort of comment, I think, is really good is when the students say that you have made them feel secure too and comfortable and been approachable and understanding. That's really nice too. Occasionally you get comments that say it was thought-provoking ... it was uncomfortable and personally challenging but they felt it was worthwhile ... you have the odd comment that says not very interested. But very, very rare. The evaluations, on the whole are generally quite good.

Many of the images reported depicted expansion, impact and security – 'stretching', 'blowing my mind', and the comfort/discomfort dichotomy. This could suggest a degree of invisible pedagogical skill involved in creating a sufficiently secure environment for challenges to be experienced positively. A senior lecturer connected enthusiasm for women's studies with academic success:

We have a number of students, incredibly varied, quite a few mature students, quite a few returners, so-called, who make tremendous achievements through women's studies. I think I see more change and more positive energy from them than I do in any other group and that tremendously feeds back to the staff in general I would say, well certainly to me, so that's a great thing. I find energy in the students when I am lacking in it myself. There they are going on and wanting to know – the thirst for knowledge which I don't meet in any other area. So students are keen, different agendas or not, pretty keen on the whole, so that is an absolute delight.

These observations about energy and thirst for knowledge imply a connection between the significance of course content and academic success. This raises important questions as to the extent that alienated, disembodied knowledges, by positioning women as outsiders, may have stifled women's academic potential for decades.

SUPPORTING WOMEN

Unfunded expansion in higher education has resulted, in many cases, in a production-line approach to student support. The number of mature students entering higher education in Britain more than doubled between 1982 and 1992. As Skeggs (1995: 475) indicates:

> because [women's studies] places did not come with adequate resourcing ... the demands from students far outweigh what can be provided.

The Higher Education Quality Council (HEQC) Report (1994: 329) also noted some of the complexities of mass participation:

> Indeed, for others, democratic participation in higher education is a contradiction in terms. Universities cannot function effectively as centres of intellectual production if they are overrun by students. Some colleagues draw parallels with the effects of mass tourism on National Parks and similar amenities. For them, increased student numbers and the pursuit of diverse income sources are leading to the *industrialisation of education,* where the mass production of graduates and credentials is replacing the carefully hand-crafted scholar of a former era.

Many students in my study felt strongly that they were not being 'hand-crafted', and that this situation promised possibilities for intellectual autonomy as well as frustrations over lack of support. While many feminist academics spoke of the exhaustion they experienced as a consequence of their commitment to students, several students complained of their tutors' inaccessibility. Commitment to students appears to both motivate and consume many women in the academy. Women academics are often perceived as more approachable than men. As Pearce (1992: 2) wrote:

> what has become the most stressful part of our [women staff's] jobs is coping with the demands of so many extra students on a one-to-one basis ... In our predominantly male-staffed arts and social science departments it was to be expected that the (predominantly female) students would seek us out.

Jackson (1989) discovered evidence that male students may also confide more readily in women academics. This sense of tutor exhaustion and student need was theorised by Skeggs (1995: 482) who, speaking as a beleagued feminist academic, traced the contradictory relationship between the 1990s entitlement culture and unfunded expansion. She highlighted how:

> we are dissatisfied, the students are dissatisfied. We all want more, we all want it to be better. We don't want to be the physical embodiment of un-met student demands but we do want to do women's studies.

A postgraduate student substantiated these ideas in her account:

> I'm not sure whether we've got what we want. Because they all seem to be so busy, because none of them are actually women's studies lecturers ... We've got so many of the lecturers here involved in research, so it is quite difficult actually pinning people down, and I know that my tutor ... before Christmas I asked to make an appointment with her and she couldn't fit me in for three weeks. Which I didn't find very good at all. We do feel like there's a little bit more perhaps support needed, but I don't think it's intentional, and the course leader doesn't ever seem to be around because she's got so much to do.

Some important factors were contained in this description: first, lecturers are teaching women's studies in addition to their disciplinary responsibilities. Second, in the new political economy of higher education, research has to be prioritised over teaching in order to ensure continued funding of posts and courses. Third, there is an expectation on the part of the student of immediate access to a tutor. The last point is a good example of tension between consumer-oriented, rights cultures without adequate resourcing. A postgraduate student in Sweden identified how feminist academics, because they were so few in relation to the numbers of students wishing to academically explore feminism, were always in demand:

> We have two professors who are women, out of four. They are not feminists and they are quite aggressive to feminism, I think so anyway. We have two readers who are feminists, which is good but everyone who wants to write about women choose those two readers. So they are overloaded with work because there are many students, especially undergraduates who want to write about women.

Another postgraduate student identified these problems and, in the spirit of the 1970s and 1980s women's movement, opted for self-help strategies, in the form of a women's group:

> Well I have been lucky with support from my supervisor, I have found her very good, I know other people who have not been quite so lucky … I think a lot of things that have gone on we have actually had to set up, hence the women's group … I think it happened because there is a critical theory group that is held every few weeks in the department in the evening and we had been to one of those and it always seemed to me that the men tended to dominate, or that the women felt slightly uneasy about saying things out loud and partly because it was run by the department, so you always felt that you were having to perform really. But also we felt there was a slightly patronising behaviour on the part of one or two people, male students, and really we wanted a more secure, informal group which was just women where we could feel free to exchange views and not just to do with literature but to do with a whole range of women's issues. So we started that up and initially it was very successful, for one of the first meetings we got something like 30 women together, from a wide variety of departments. We talked about various things like women and madness, women in education, issues around feminism, current ideas and pornography, things like that.

Objections to male-dominated sessions and the perceived need for performance provided the energy and momentum to initiate a feminist alternative. However, this soon became dogged with the problems of voluntarism. The student went on to say:

> For a while it was very successful and there was obviously a need for it … it actually took a lot of organising and I had to do the posters and the mail-outs and organise rooms and just simply deciding what to do next, although we tried to get as many people involved in that as possible, it nearly always came down to the four of us and then me alone, and so I found that quite difficult to carry that on, so once I said I wasn't going to do it, it really kind of fell apart.

As this account implies, feminism has become associated for many as a complex combination of hard work and emotional and intellectual stimulation. While some feminist students invest considerable energy in extra-curricular support activities, others resent the demands placed on them. This reinforces Edwards' (1993) observations that mature women students get caught between two 'greedy institutions' – the academy and the family. As I mentioned earlier, the academy still functions with the notion of a student as a 'bachelor boy', that is academic studies are the sole focus, and there are no other, competing responsibilities.

However, for many women students, fragmentation and multiple role requirements were the norm, echoing Burrell's (1993: 79) question: 'Might it not be that the student body inhabits the postmodern world whilst staff inhabit a modern world?' A women's studies MA student identified some of these discontinuities of perception:

> I know there is some form of ivory tower thinking … that is a left-over from the 1960s – where women students, or students *per se*, came into university, had nothing else to think about – you know, were there to just study and have a good time and that was a great three years or whatever they were doing … all of them do have to understand, not just some – that women, particularly of my age, have all sorts of other things going on and it's very difficult to balance it all up. Just to find the time to come in and spend time here, and go and earn wages, and get to Tesco's, and – not for me but for a lot – get the kids out of school, and do all those things too … And that it is a balancing act and there's a lot of pressure, and finances are often uppermost in people's minds when they're on these courses. And sadly we would all love to say, 'Oh yes, we'll spend as many hours as possible here and all have a wonderful

time', but ... as one of them said, 'to sit around philosophising all day – it's nice!'

The comment about preoccupation with survival issues, such as finance, is indicative of the high price students now pay for postgraduate education. As postgraduate grants are not readily available, many self-fund, condemning themselves to years of debt. This situation is about to be exacerbated in Britain, with New Labour's policy to introduce university fees. These preoccupations with material considerations were summarised by Luke (1994: 213), who placed them on a continuum of difficulties that pursue women throughout their entire education:

> Much of the 'women and education' literature has documented the significant and multiple difficulties women encounter throughout their educational careers: first, as girls in public school classrooms and later, as women in university settings ... and, finally, of the emotional and financial strain many women encounter in attempts to fulfil multiple roles such as students, wives, mothers and, often, part-time workers.

However, this statement contains a heterosexist normalising undercurrent, suggesting that all women live in traditional nuclear families. My study, and indeed my experience as a feminist academic, demonstrates that even when women are single, childfree and dedicated to the academy, they still experience considerable professional difficulties. A young Swedish postgraduate student in education described how her feminism was provoking hostility to her:

> I've got my best support from the Forum of Women's Studies... but not from my supervisor ... I do think that is because he does not understand me really ... He wants to force me into another direction, really to focus on other things ... forcing me to other things. Maybe I am saying too much.

It is interesting to note from this account the amount of remedial work and troubleshooting the Forum for Women's Studies had to undertake to compensate for lack of feminist support in disciplines. This young student turned to them because she felt pressure from her supervisor to deny her feminism and focus on his interests instead. This potentially dangerous situation left her feeling angry yet hesitant to express her anger for fear of repercussions on her career. Luke (1994) pointed out that women students cannot afford to risk antagonistic relations with male supervisors as they are dependent on them for academic sponsorship:

> For the most part, women students still rely on male approval of research topics, the distribution of research funds, promotion, tenure, or appointment. How well a woman's research project or term paper fares has much to do with how well she has learned to read the hidden curriculum and is able to cite and reproduce the master discourses in a given discipline. (Luke, 1994: 216)

MEN IN FEMINISM

The issue of whether women's studies courses should include men is highly contentious. Legally, and in line with universities' charters, courses cannot exclude students by virtue of their sex. In practice, in Britain, women's studies attracts a majority of women students. The women-only space is often highly appreciated by women students and there are fears that opening up the space to male students represents a major form of deradicalisation and appropriation of discursive and physical space. Luke (1994), like many feminist educationalists (Spender, 1980; Tannen, 1992), defines male dominance in classrooms in terms of verbal interactions:

> research on the gendered differences in classroom interaction has shown that boys tend to out-talk girls by 3:1, that girls' contributions to classroom talk do not receive the same amount or quality of teacher praise as boys do, and that girls by and large tend to 'underplay' their knowledge ... In short, girls do in fact receive 'less' direct pedagogy than boys. (Luke, 1994: 215)

But male domination takes many forms, as an American MA student described the contrasting atmosphere in women's studies courses in Britain and the United States:

> There are no men on the courses here ... there are in the States ... and it was hell ... Having the men there ... In my first women's studies course I had two football players in our class who sat there and didn't say a word for ten weeks ... And, I mean, I found out later one of them assaulted a friend of mine. I mean, and this is a guy who took a women's studies course! ... And there was nothing we could do to stop them ... I mean a lot of time was spent with the other men in the class saying, 'I don't want to talk about this

anymore', or 'I'm not interested in your experience, I want to talk about –' you know, like, what we're *really* talking about … Well we spent a lot more time than we should have on their problems … It's a much better environment here.

This account raises disturbing questions about women's sense of safety when men self-select on to women's studies courses. In this case, there was a sinister incongruence between the footballer's interest in women's studies and the allegations of his violence against a woman. This raised uncertainty about his motives for participation, with discomforting suspicions of women's studies fulfilling a type of pornographic function for some men. This was hinted at in the reference to his silence and one-way gaze, which was experienced as a form of voyeurism. Conversely, the non-footballer men managed to centralise themselves by constantly rehearsing their problems, using the attention of women as a support group for their discomforts with masculinity.

A Swedish education lecturer expressed a controversial view that male students need to be exposed to feminist challenges too, in order to counter hegemonic notions of masculinities:

I think that it is a good way, you know, for all … I mean to have both sexes. And as an educationalist I think that you have to address both sexes. In education it's very important.

A Greek professor shared this view, expounding the idea that women's studies preaches to the converted:

And the people that switch off are the most important to reach, because the others are aware of the issue anyway. Perhaps they are too sympathetic, or in a way that is not very functional, so you could change that but what is, I feel, much more important is to have access to the top levels of student population including men students.

These beliefs have led to some advocacy for gender, rather than women's studies. But many feminists have contested this relabelling as, once again, it decentralises women (Evans, 1991). Delphy (1996: 33) argues that the 'use of the singular ("gender" as opposed to "genders") allowed the accent to be moved from the two divided parts to the principle of partition itself.' While many feminists would agree that both sexes need to be involved in anti-oppression work, the issue is whether this should occur simultaneously in the same group. Not only does this imply a symmetry of experiences of sexism, but it also raises issues about power in groups. As Luke (1994: 216) argues:

> Women who wish to critique the unifocal vision of masculine worldviews, the contradictions, omissions, and misogynist fictions, find themselves quickly silenced by the more authoritative voice of logic and reason emanating from male students or the male professor in charge ... For many but certainly not all women, the university classroom can be a demeaning experience which contributes to her sense of intellectual inadequacy, and which perpetuates (indeed, rewards) her continuing silence.

Lewis (1994: 55) believes that the presence of women, or absence of men, in academic settings should not be taken as proof 'that we partake of social relations free of the male-dominated phallocentric discursive forms which pertain in society at large'. Male domination is an ever-present feature in terms of discourses, language, competitive interpersonal relations. However, there are strong feelings that as women have been so deeply discriminated against for centuries in higher education, epistemologically and interpersonally they have the right to a new discursive space. Fears abound about the way in which hegemonic masculinities always appear to colonise resources. A Swedish postgraduate student commented on how resources were being invested in men and masculinities, similar to the preoccupation with boys' educational under-achievement in Britain:

> We have some men also [in women's studies], also we have discussions, about the masculinity, many of our researchers have discovered masculinity, and we have a masculinity group here in the institution, and a lot of money is put into masculinity just now.

But what becomes of the reconstructed, sensitive new male who would also like access to the considerable benefits of women's studies courses? A Swedish lecturer described how the positive experiences male students had on women's studies courses often made them dissatisfied with the way in which other university courses were taught:

> There was a young man who was here yesterday. He said to me, 'I don't know if I am going to continue with my studies at the university.' So I asked why, and then he said, 'Well, I don't think they are really suited to my way of working and thinking.' He said, 'The course I have done here, is actually the best course I have ever

done.' So I said, 'Explain to me why you think this course is better,' and he said, 'Well, the pedagogics'. And it's because it's influenced very much by feminist pedagogy.

As this anecdote suggests, men stand to receive substantial benefits from participation in women's studies courses. However, this needs to be related to collective benefit as well as individual advantages. It is debatable what women students gain, or indeed lose, from men's presence. I share Smyth's (1992: 334) concern: 'Why bother fighting so hard for space if we're just going to hand it back again ...?'

THE DISCOMFORT OF DISABILITY

Disability is often a hidden discourse in the rhetoric of difference. One of the postgraduate students I interviewed had a particularly distressing story to tell about her university's engagement with the issue of disability. Hearn and Parkin (1993: 158) describes how able-bodism means that disability is not recognised in organisations.

> We are increasingly recognizing that fundamental to organisations and the way they oppress is an unquestioned assumption around possession of abilities, particularly the possession of intact senses and mobility... in most organizations the 'fit' and 'able-bodied' dominate the workplace, and hence disability becomes the most prevailing form of oppression in terms of numerical over-representation and lack of research and recognition.

Potts and Price (1995) explore how engagement with the life of the mind takes for granted that a healthy body will facilitate mobility to libraries, academic conferences, etc. While the body is often ignored in academia, its relevance soon becomes evident when it malfunctions. The postgraduate student in an 'old' university, with a career background in trade unions, traced how subtly discrimination against disabled people is produced and reproduced by organisational arrangements and attitudes in the academy:

> probably about a year ago ... I was getting very concerned that my back was very bad, I was kind of more disabled, rather than less disabled ... I didn't feel that I was coping very well, so I thought, well there must be some kind of formal support where you can go at the university and was told by the master of the college ... that same day that he would get the disability advisor to phone me. Two

weeks later this woman phones up and says 'I'm the advisor to the handicapped', and I said, 'well if you don't mind me saying so, it's not really a very good expression to use … talk about the disabled if you must, or people with disabilities, but you know, this is really offensive.' She immediately got very, very upset and ratty and didn't have a clue what I was talking about … She said there was information about, but she hadn't got any of it in front of her, so even when she'd got round to phoning me, she hadn't bothered to actually get the information to hand before she spoke to me.

I said I'd got two particular concerns in the college, one was the fact that women's lockers hadn't been operable all year, and it's this system where you've got to queue up with a tray in the dining room for lunch, and of course it's very difficult for me to stand with the tray, but it's impossible for me to stand with the tray and a bag under my arm. So without locker facilities I was absolutely stuck … And the other issue I raised was the fact [the university] charges £20 a year to hire a locker in the library and I thought this was discriminatory because the disabled students have got no choice but to have a locker, which is the only way you could physically get round the library … so she ended up putting the phone down on me.

As this account shows, disability is a profound stigma and taboo area. Shilling (1993: 86) comments: 'People with stigmas … confront problems in social interaction with "normals" which can have especially damaging consequences for their identity.' The social model of disability (Lloyd, 1995) articulates that it is the prejudices rather than the disability itself that disempower. Not only did a student in considerable distress have to offer in-service training in language, power and labelling to someone who was supposed to support her, but she had also to attempt to explain how discriminatory practices were embedded, and hence normalised in the quotidian practices of the academy. The use of the retrogressive term 'handicapped' demonstrated how oppression is not just material, but is enacted linguistically in definitions of the oppressed. The advisor demonstrated her limitations and the extent to which she valued the student by the hostile act of putting the phone down on her. This raised numerous questions about interpersonal skills and public relations in the context of quality assurance.

The student related the labour-intensive process of attempting to draw attention to these issues in a large bureaucracy, supporting

Weber's view (1948: 231) that bureaucracy *is* a form of domination. Her experiences contributed to her physical disability, once again revealing the negative effects of power relations on the body. It also exposed the ineffectiveness of the organisation's policy and practices for equality, in so far as equity principles did not seem to have permeated basic services such as student support:

> I think I then wrote ... to the Equal Opportunities Officer. I then got a very abusive letter back and this went on where I was then writing to the University Senate saying, 'Well, I've got these complaints but what you're saying I'm saying is wrong' ... but every time it was like, well this is your fault, you didn't tell us when you decided to come to the university, and I said, 'Well, actually, I was interviewed by somebody who was disabled and spent at least half an hour talking about it,' and on my medical form it's got 'chronic back problem which is long standing and permanent' and then it was kind of, 'Oh, you haven't done this, you haven't done that, you didn't do this, you didn't do that'. It was ridiculous, I spent hours and hours writing letters.

The last comments relate to the bureaucratic structures of the academy and the familiar pattern of blaming victims if they protest about oppression. They also provide further evidence of the ineffectiveness of equality measures in the academy. As Morris (1993: 68) identified:

> To experience disability is to experience the frailty of the human body. If we deny this we will find that our personal experience of disability will remain an isolated one; we will experience our differences as something peculiar to us as individuals – and we will commonly feel a sense of blame and responsibility.

Almost as if working to the script identified by Morris, the disability advisor tried to make the disabled student individually responsible for her predicament by suggesting she organised a self-help campaign:

> So not only did I never get any help ... [I was told] that if I was unhappy about the disability provision, I should run a campaign. But I said, 'Well, I'm coming to you because I can't cope with a private and a personal problem, and you're telling me to run a campaign about it, I mean, why aren't you running a campaign about it, you're getting paid?' ... But I just couldn't believe that I

was being told that to get an equal opportunities policy implemented I should run a campaign about it. You know, not that this
policy exists and you're being paid to do this, you know I'm just
coming to you asking for some help. I mean I was sent out-of-date
information, which I then followed up and discovered I was never
entitled to in the first place, so that was more waste of time. You
know, the Equal Opportunities Officer actually eventually got back
to me and said she was one hundred per cent on my side but there
was very little she could do. The Student Union came back and
said, well they quite agreed, but there was nothing they could do.

The Pro-Vice-Chancellor, which is where it got to, came back to
me eventually and said, 'Yes, I do agree with your version of events,
I'll pass your name on to the Welfare Committee.' I never heard
another word. I finally, in December, you know eight months later,
had a letter from Welfare Committee, saying they have registered
that I was disabled, could I give them some details. I wrote back
with copies of all this correspondence saying, 'You were supposed
to get this eight months ago, I presume you haven't', and of course
I haven't heard another word since then. So I went through so much
stress and upset and of course every time I go through that kind of
stress and upset, it's having a really negative impact on my whole
body, and certainly eating into hours and hours that I could be
researching.

The juxtaposition of the student's politicised engagement with
equity issues and feminism contradicted the popular stereotype of
disabled people as powerless. Her refusal to separate her mind from
her body made her antithetical to the dominant academic culture of
cogito ergo sum. Furthermore, her entitlement culture consciousness
('you're getting paid') served to alienate the disability advisor and
distance the student even further from appropriate support services.
This case study not only represents the failure of equity in relation to
disability in this particular university, but also indicates how differences are not just theoretical or discursive, but are material and
embodied.

SUMMARY

Feminist courses continue to attract a wide range of students in
Britain, Greece and Sweden. Many students have high expectations of

potentially life-changing experiences and intellectual repositioning. For others, their engagement is less impassioned, as they keep an emotional distance from the subject. Differing political backgrounds means that courses such as women's studies can be perceived as just another option for some, and for others as a major commitment to personal and social change, with quasi-redemptive powers. The entitlement culture set against a political backdrop of unfunded expansion and the preoccupation with individual rights, rather than collective action, means that feminist academics often struggle to meet the needs of a rapidly expanding diverse student group. Many feminist students are particularly alert to the micropolitics of power in their institutions, and have serious concerns about how the academy accommodates their differences. The success of academic feminism means that more students, including men, would like a share of the action. I asked the only man on a women's studies MA why he chose the subject, and he replied, 'Because it's so deliciously subversive!' In the same way that white people have always flocked to black areas such as Harlem, as these represent the exotic other, women's studies intrigue some men and women who have no background or interest in feminism. This echoes Smyth's (1992: 333) anxieties about lost connections between politics and feminist scholarship: 'There is, for me, a loss of politics in women's studies ... I do want to know what is de-radicalising women's studies.' There are no easy answers to her questions.

7 Feminist Academics: Disruption, Development and Disciplines

BECOMING FEMINIST ACADEMICS: ROUTES, ROADBLOCKS AND REWARDS

In this chapter, feminist academics apply political understanding to teaching, research and writing in the academy. They consider knowledge production, career development, voluntarism, isolation, networks and feminist research. Academic feminism is problematised particularly in relation to the linkage of the two terms. For many, academic feminism is a contradiction in terms, an oxymoron, selling out feminism's commitment to everyday praxis. Yet, on the other hand, academic feminism is also frequently viewed by the establishment as insufficiently academic (Morley and Walsh, 1995).

The academic/activist divide is a popular binary, with shifting weight attached to each polarity (Warwick and Auchmuty, 1995). Women's studies has been described as the intellectual arm of the Women's Liberation Movement (De Groot and Maynard, 1993), yet activists outside the academy question whether the struggle against gender-based oppression can be effectively mounted in academic provision, where elitist, class-bound traditions of white male abstract logic threaten to dilute or co-opt radicalism (Morley, 1995d). Currie and Kazi (1987: 77) asked whether academic feminism is the graveyard of radical ideas. Equally, while feminist theory has become increasingly sophisticated since the early days of second-wave feminism, levels of abstraction and academic rigour have not always necessarily been matched with women's social and political advancement (Faludi, 1992; hooks, 1993). It is hard to have this debate without adopting a judgemental position and imposing hierarchical binaries of what constitutes effective feminism. Rose (1994: 55) argues that:

to speak of feminist activists and feminist theorists is not to create

155

an antagonism, but to acknowledge that over time, because of the shifts in the movement's structure and to some extent as the price of feminism's success in entering the academy, a division of labour has developed between feminists.

But McNeil (1993: 166) wondered if there has been a 'hermetic sealing of intellectual labour'. She believed that the 'relationship between our production (critical knowledge) and feminism outside the academy is not clear'. Much of the debate implies that the central division is between feminists inside and those outside the academy.

However, my study and feminist theory in the wider sense is full of diversity among feminists *inside* the academy. Warwick and Auchmuty (1995: 184) describe how feminists were motivated to enter and change the academy and how they encountered tensions and paradoxes between their political commitment and organisational structures:

> we wanted to challenge the patriarchal curriculum and provide the current generation of students with less alienating courses than we ourselves had experienced as undergraduates and postgraduates. But our victory – and it was a victory with practically all British universities offering women's studies by the mid 1990s – was won at a cost. In entering the patriarchal structure of higher education, we lost some of our control over what, how and whom we taught.

As the above quotation illustrates, some women enter the academy after a history of involvement in the women's movement, and find themselves ambiguously located in hierarchical organisations. This group, like Gramsci's organic intellectuals, often views academic feminism as an expression and extension of their political commitment. But the situation is changing as women enter feminist scholarship who have not been exposed either to organising principles or campaigns of political movements on the left. This group may become politicised via academic studies. The following two accounts, both from university lecturers in my study, exemplify different routes into women's studies lecturing:

> I've been a feminist for a long time and I went back to university as a returner when I was 30 and took history as my subject and was appalled all the way through my degree how little of the staff were women, and how I always had to construct my own courses around women so ... I got together a Women in Society-type course and really learnt from that way, from my own personal

experience, the problems finding books in the mid-1980s for women's history and realising there were a lot of women out there who wanted to do women's issues too, and I didn't really know what women's studies was then. It was just something I knew that was missing that women wanted and it started off like that and I got more and more involved in women's studies ... my teaching has got more and more feminist as time goes on as well, as I've learnt more about academic feminism.

In response to my question on how she became involved in academic feminism, a young lecturer in a new university explained how she had acquired her women's studies post:

It almost wasn't really a conscious decision, an active decision on my part, it was almost by default because, going back to my undergraduate career in my third year I took a course on gender and politics for the first time, and it was the first time I had ever thought about gender as politics and sexuality and distribution of resources as having a gendered and political dimension. It concurred with a time when I was involved in a long-term relationship that was breaking up and I don't exactly know what the causality was there but they actually were related in various ways in my choosing the course and also the relationship being called in to question a bit more ... So when I was applying for this job I hadn't finished my thesis and I didn't intend to really start teaching in any sort of full-time way but this job came up ... and it was in sociology and women's studies ... So I couldn't really pass the opportunity just to apply, if only for practice. And I got the job ...

The first quotation exemplifies how feminists have been forced to evolve courses in response to patriarchal omissions, while the second quotation suggests that some women have learned to use the tools of academic feminism to examine discomforts and uncertainties in their own lives.

The second quotation also hints of feminism as a career advantage, opening up employment spaces. As feminist scholarship has entered into conventional reward systems and power networks, it has evolved its own micropolitics, with its own opportunities and inequalities. As Smyth (1992: 334) states: 'In the race for jobs, sadly, feminist elbows perform the same function as any other kind.' If career development is a micropolitical function or byproduct of women's studies for some, at the same time scarcity of opportunities will create competition and opportunism that cut across feminist principles of collectivity and collaboration. If feminism is a counter-discourse, which produces new knowledges, it could follow that it also constitutes new powers and new regimes of truth (Morley, 1995d).

A Greek lecturer, with a long history of political involvement, was very critical of commodity feminism, that is women who perceive individual career advantages in feminism, but who have never been involved in collective struggles of the women's movement:

> (There is not a very developed reflection on these issues and because women's studies is a new issue and it is easy to get European networks on that, and it is easy to make contacts, a lot of women have been involved in this. In my view without the necessary background or analysis ...) It is very difficult to define feminist perspective. One thing that one can say is these women have never taken part in the feminist movement, but I cannot question their sincerity as far as feminism is concerned. Who can? But having met feminism through books more than through action, they have a lot of issues not very well elaborated ... but we are not talking about activism *per se*, I would say that feminism cannot separate the two. Feminism is both theory and practice as well, but one can do more or less one or two at the time ... but I think one has to have quite an idea of what feminism is, politically speaking, not only to be able to study – one can study very well without having any political involvement. But in order to do more than that ... it is quite embarrassing to speak like this sometimes ... but I think there is also a lot of opportunism in women's studies.

She implied that this situation is being created, in part, by opportunities for international work and the tokenistic inclusion of women from southern Europe. This raises numerous questions about the delicate balance between consciousness and colonisation. A Greek professor described how she had felt angry and ashamed that it had been left to foreigners to politicise her about gender in her own country. She explained how her exposure to international research foundations encouraged her to focus on women's issues in Greece. This provided both opportunity and a sense of further subordination:

> I had to ... struggle to get to the university, after many years graduated from high school, and all this, the working in the university, did not allow me to think about women's issues. Although I knew how hard things had been for me and for my generation but still I

was involved in issues of Constitutional Law, Constitutional History, but not on women's issues. And then it was in a conference which was organised by the Ford Foundation and the Italian Social Consulate ... I had a paper on Political Evolutions in Greece – constitutional and political too ... And at the end of the conference the supervisor of the Ford Foundation advised the Fellows of Southern Europe not to turn always to what other European countries did or what their problems are but to study their own problems. And he said – it was March 1982 – and he said one of the main issues of your area is the status of women ... You can't believe that I was ashamed that a foreigner – had told me that here is a problem you have: how can you be blind [*sic*] over this issue? And when I came back, immediately, I published an article ... This was my first contact with women's issues.

By extending her network of influence the professor was given permission by a foreign male to pay attention to women in her research. The inference being that academic work could contribute to social change (and that southern Europe was less evolved on gender issues!).

The role of the intellectual in change processes has been problematised in postmodernist thought. Foucault suggested a facilitative role for the intellectual – 'not so much a creative place in the discursive vanguard as the job of clearing the roadblocks' (quoted in Cain, 1993: 88). While not identifying as a postmodernist in any way, the Greek professor described how older women had also cleared the roadblocks for younger women in the academy. She believed that the anger and frustration older women felt as a consequence of exclusion from the academy fuelled their political struggle. She repeatedly used expressions to illustrate how the body responds to power relations, and it is these memories, inscribed on the body, that provide energy for change. Younger women who had not experienced this were able to engage with feminism as an academic, cerebral process, rather than from 'their flesh':

You know, X, my friend, is in your generation. Her family sent her abroad to study. And *so she hasn't felt it in her flesh.* ... what patriarchy means and what to do when someone says, no, you cannot study ... the only possibility you have [is] to get married and that will solve all your problems ... she hasn't experienced that frustration ... You see it's very disadvantageous to be a woman of [the] older generation!

While the Greek professor cited age and intergenerational conflicts as major signifiers of differing power relations, a senior lecturer in a British new university identified 'race' as an issue in her women's studies team:

> We're a very, very white team of teachers and on the whole our students are white. But we have had other ethnic groups and so on been involved as students and we're very conscious of this – what can one say – disparity in our team ... It's partly geographical ... But we have had black students who have been, of course, critical of the all-white teaching team and ... what they would say is the sort of tokenism in inclusion of those issues on the course ... At the beginning we really did try and address that, as well as lesbianism, sexuality, and so on, and make sure that these things were addressed all the way through. At every possible opportunity. But we are very conscious that we are this all-white team ...

These comments explain Currie and Kazi's (1987: 88) observation that 'merely adding women to the academy will not radicalize knowledge as power relations extend beyond the power of men over women'. Black people are significantly under-represented as academics in higher education, and while the percentage of black students is slowly increasing, particularly in new metropolitan universities, students are likely to be taught by all-white staff, even in power-sensitive subjects like women's studies. So, when references are made to women entering the academy, it is important to ask, which women?

FEMINISM AS ADDITIONAL WORKLOAD

Discussions about whether feminism is best located in academic disciplines or constellated in subject areas, such as women's studies, have been taking place since women's studies first appeared in British higher education at the University of Kent in 1981. In a sense, the debate replicates another binary which has troubled feminists, many of whom resent the closure involved in either/or choices. Luke (1994: 218) identified the no-win politics of location for feminist academics:

> Women often find that once they publicly identify with a feminist politics, conservative male colleagues ignore or avoid them, and

liberal colleagues consult or debate with them primarily on matters of gender. In other words, her professed feminist orientation can suddenly erase any disciplinary theoretical knowledge she may have.

Feminists located in their disciplines in my study were often wary of having a mono-dimensional identity imposed on them. A senior lecturer located in an English department felt her professional identity was reduced to the one who 'banged on' about feminism. She had to keep reminding herself that this was a distorted view:

> But something I find really difficult is that I ... because I only teach in my own areas, I lose perspective on the fact that most of what they're learning is still the old canon, you know, it is still dead-white-men. But because I never teach dead-white-men really, or only on the compulsories ... I kind of feel as though I'm just banging on about the same old thing again, you know? And it gets ... it gets *boring* ... I feel embarrassed, I feel like.' Oh God, you know, here I go again, talking about feminism or about gender and language.' They must have heard so much about this; and I have to keep kicking myself and remembering, no they haven't actually, you know, there isn't really anybody else ... who's telling them this in this way.

As this quotation illustrates, responsibility for providing counter-hegemonic interventions can make one vulnerable and visible. A senior lecturer identified how once you situate yourself outside your discipline and become associated with new knowledges, you lose the security of your institutional home:

> Women's studies is vulnerable in the institution ... I am possibly the most vulnerable person in the institution.

There are also issues about time and gender-based inequality. An AUT survey (1994) showed that female professors work an average of 65 hours a week compared to the 55 worked by their male counterparts. Many feminists straddle women's studies and their traditional disciplines. This situation can contribute to overload, as the following quotations demonstrate:

> I'm a hybrid actually, I'm a senior lecturer, but I'm a quarter – .25 to women's studies and .75 to Social Policy and that has definite drawbacks because if obviously you're working across two departments you have double the number of meetings, double the number

of exam boards you're involved in and basically double the amount of frustration, double the number of projects.

Women's studies, as a new area, is frequently developed in conditions of deficit expansion, that is expansion must have taken place before resources can be provided (Skeggs, 1995). A women's studies course leader in Britain described how her organisation refused to create a women's studies post, opting instead to staff the programme on the basis of voluntary work:

> And for all of us women's studies is placed on top of our full-time lecturing course. We've been arguing since the very beginning that we should have a women's studies appointment, that we should even, you know, just have *one person* who is called a women's studies lecturer and which there could be some sort of focus within the university. It still hasn't come through ... we're all doing women's studies and have done women's studies on the backs of our already existing full-time commitments in our particular disciplines.

In addition to extra teaching, the interdisciplinary ideals of women's studies necessitates keeping abreast of a wide range of academic areas. As Skeggs (1995: 481) indicated: 'We have to develop analytical tools to be able to understand different disciplinary methods, and we have to understand increasingly abstract theory.' I have noticed from both my scholarship and from my praxis that feminists have to be acquainted with the traditional male canon. We have to cite key male theorists and constantly interweave feminist theory with a whole range of other social theories. However, successful and influential mainstream academics can proceed without ever having to read, reference or acknowledge feminist scholarship. A Swedish postgraduate student commented that the additional workload imposed by feminism was a deterrent for young women:

> I think that one of the structural problems of feminists is that you have to be engaged in feminist theory discussions, which is actually very complicated and then you have to know all the other theory if you want to stay here ... That's one of the things which I think has consequences, especially for the young students. I feel that well, if they choose to be feminists, they choose to double work.

Sexism represents an additional workload for feminists. The additional workload is both material and emotional. Skeggs (1995: 482) mentions 'the heightened expectations of the increased number of students who experience emotional fall-out generated by feminist courses'. Feminist academics are often perceived as counsellors. To deny women students support is perceived as unsisterly. But this process can operate to define feminist academics out of academia and into an undifferentiated group of nurturing women (Morley, 1995d). Laurence (1991: 54) felt that acceptance of an empathetic and nurturing role 'has helped to confine women to specific sites within education'. The assumption of responsibility for other women's political, academic and emotional development seemed to burden several informants. This reminded me of Chodorow's (1978) feminist interpretation of object-relations theory. She argued that women frequently experience another's emotions as their own. In practice, this can translate into an emotional predisposition to fulfil the needs of the other. This can also be displaced into a sense of political responsibility too. A senior lecturer based in an English department described how she experienced

> a feeling of huge responsibility ... I feel like, well if I don't do it nobody will! And this is a challenge – you know, I've got this very kind of over-inflated version of my own importance, I'm sure. But I do have this feeling of, you know, well this is their chance to start thinking about how monstrously big the system is and how subtly it marginalises and silences women, you know. And if I don't – if I can't get this across to them then they might never see it. And it must be very different if you're teaching Renaissance Literature and you're telling them about plays. I mean you know my heart is in it, it's there, it's sort of ... it's something I believe in passionately and that has advantages and disadvantages, but I think the major disadvantages affect me rather than the students or the institution ... I think I'm tired.

As this account suggests, political work in the academy or passionate scholarship, as it is sometimes known, can be draining because the struggle has to be sustained by so few. Haug (1992: 84) theorises this overdeveloped sense of responsibility in many women as female masochism. She reflects that:

> Women are positioned at the meeting point of individual lives and the exorbitant claims of society, and acquiesce without flinching. They would rather be torn apart than give up or enlarge this unreasonable responsibility. They experience this state of being torn

apart as guilt. They take this guilt upon themselves. The humanity which thereby enters their actions covers up the inhumanity of society at large.

Feelings of exhaustion, emotional depletion and the notion of utilising vital energy reserves were widespread among feminist academics in my study. However, there were also feelings of elation and exhilaration at the interaction with feminist students, as a senior lecturer indicated:

> Oh the sheer pleasure of working with students, and feeling that you're all getting an enormous amount out of it. The feeling of warmth, the feeling of friendship and affection. The feeling that you're all in something together and actually making changes, achieving, doing things, the excitement, the pleasure in each other's work.

A key question continues to be whether the pleasure of passionate scholarship remains at an individualistic level, or translates into energy for social change, or both. Haug (1989) believed that while the women's movement has pushed its way into the academic mainstream, this had been accompanied by a reduction in political activity outside. A Greek assistant professor felt that academic feminism was even more important now, in the absence of widespread grassroots political movements, as for some students it represented the only contact with critical discourses:

> But my priority is my students because I mean in Greece the lack of alternative organisations on a grassroots level, let's say, I think that we've got huge responsibility when it comes to our female students.

While the overt declaration is politically motivated, there is an emotional subtext of assumed responsibility for others' development. This process is sometimes described as 'sex role spillover' (Nicolson, 1996), in that women have expectations of themselves in organisational settings which correspond with the traditional roles of females and mothers. This corresponds with my findings on feminist pedagogy discussed in chapter 5. Nicolson (1996: 80) states that:

> Women have to teach themselves not to be responsible for their students' potential misery or failures, which is not the same as the negligence of student needs operationalised by some colleagues.

I have observed that this spillover is held together in the academy by a complex cocktail of guilt, social positioning and feminist engagement with sisterhood. Self-care and boundary-setting can seem like right-wing individualism.

According to Fox-Keller and Moglen (1987: 500), identification with others has two faces. 'In the traditional writings, it is seen as interfering with the development of ego boundaries, while in the feminist literature, it is seen as fostering relational abilities.' This complex combination can mean that feminists are using energies which adversely affect their well-being and academic standing (Jackson, 1990: 313). It could be argued that while women are spending time emotionally supporting students, they are not making strategic interventions in the political life of their organisations. The Carnegie Foundation (1990) researched women academics in the USA. They discovered that while women make good 'campus citizens', and spend more time in service to their university than men, they still form a minority voice on important decision-making committees. As a consequence of under-representation in senior positions, the Carnegie Foundation highlighted the lack of opportunities for women to shape educational policies.

Feminist curriculum development in my study was often viewed in the same way as voluntary political work. Because political, personal and academic boundaries can become blurred in the case of feminism, it is easy for it to be viewed as a personal interest or hobby, rather than work. In Britain, much of women's studies is organised in the same way as a cottage industry, as a women's studies senior lecturer indicated:

> Our goodwill has been exploited because, you know, in order to get the MA up we were prepared to, you know, work evenings, weekends, whatever in order to do it, even if we weren't going to be given any time. So I think the managers have taken advantage of the fact that we're hard working and we do more than is necessary.

With the disempowerment of trade unions and degenerating employment conditions in British public services, it is rare to hear mention of terms like 'exploitation' these days. But the possibilities for co-option of socialised gendered patterns of caring into the educational workplace was predicted by socialist feminists in the 1970s:

> With training for docility, teaching becomes an extension of women's maternal role as capitalism's 'soft cops', serving the dual

function of both presenting the capitalist patriarchy's human face and providing social and political containment. (Rowbotham, 1973: 91)

Overwork and 'presenteeism' are examples of both changing economic and organisational cultures and the internalisation of coercive power relations. Overwork is also a potent source of political containment as we drive and discipline ourselves in response to powerful, punishing psychic narratives telling us we must do better. The situation is reminiscent of Boxer, the workhorse in Orwell's *Animal Farm* (1945), whose response to growing political oppression was simply to work harder. Fox Keller and Moglen (1987: 495) comment:

As universities are presently constituted, influence and power are by definition in limited supply; in accordance with larger social assumptions, its entire motivational structure is organized around these limitations.

The myth of meritocracy means it is easier to blame oneself if one fails to be promoted than take on a discriminatory system. An associate professor in Sweden commented on how she has become caught up in the compulsive, research-driven culture:

I work harder and harder ... I have to fight harder and harder to get new research money too and I have an ambition to do good things and to further my career, although I say why further your career, I have a tenured position. I can enjoy it, but I don't, this is my personality maybe. Somehow you want to go up in a way ... and it's also built into the culture of the University to do that, you are supposed to do that, maybe that is the problem, that you feel all the time that you have to be better and better, and use the knowledge you have because it's old in two years ... I am never free when I am at home or on holiday. I always work actually evenings, Saturdays, Sundays, holidays, all the time I do something.

As this suggests, the emphasis on research productivity can lead to intensification and a compliance culture. Morris (1988: 22) notes that 'Most female intellectuals one can unearth tend to be discreet writers, but raving workaholics.' It is questionable whether the widespread overwork that was highlighted in my study was in response to policy changes, management or potent internalised narratives of women who, having been positioned as representing lack and deficit, had to work hard to disprove their secondary status. Overwork can also lead to the increased docility of employees. Miller (1987: 27) identifies an internalised narrative in those who feel at risk:

I must always be good and measure up to the norm, then there is no risk; I constantly feel that the demands are too great, but I cannot change that, I must always achieve more than others.

However, feminist overwork in the academy has resulted in a significant development of cultural capital. The HMI Report (1993) commented on the high productivity rate of women's studies in universities. Zmroczek and Duchen's survey (1991) indicated the existence of an impressive range of feminist research in the UK, with sociology leading the way. This is reminiscent of Foucault's point that power relations can be productive as well as oppressive. Feminist publication has flourished in the 1990s too, as publishers realised that feminist journals and books were highly marketable. Rose (1994: 56) commented:

Even in the depths of nineties recession, feminist lists have remained strong, so that the market remains a complex ally in the task of disseminating the new ideas.

As Deem (1996: 15) noted: 'Marginality can result in exclusion but it can also be responsible for considerable creativity and innovation.' Said (1994: 44) also observed that:

While you are neither winning prizes nor being welcomed into all those self-congratulatory honor societies that routinely exclude embarrassing troublemakers who do not toe the party line, you are at the same time deriving some positive things from exile and marginality.

I would agree that there is a paradoxical engagement with exile and marginality, and that outsider status can enhance creative critical knowledges. But I would also argue that the costs of marginality to women are high.

SOMEONE TO WATCH OVER ME: SUPPORT, SORORITY AND SELF-CARE

Many feminist academics in my study had had to evolve elaborate support systems and mechanisms for confirming their self-worth in the absence of external reassurance. A Swedish associate professor commented:

> I very much like to work in the university but it has been very very hard, since I am from a working-class background, a single mother, with three children ... What is so difficult is that you have to build up your self-esteem only by yourself. You get no support, no good words, no good advice and that is something I should like to change, more co-operation, not that much competition in the University ... you never get any feedback actually, only from the students, and once semester is over, this is wonderful, the next group say 'Oh this is terrible', you never know ... Yes, and to get that self- esteem is very hard, I have got it now ...

As this quotation suggests, a powerful part of class oppression is to negate the intelligence of working-class people (Morley, 1997). To struggle from that position to one of authority in elitist, competitive organisations requires powerful strategies of self-care.

It is difficult to give attention to others' needs when one's own needs are unmet. Women cannot always be allies for each other when they are struggling to survive themselves. A senior lecturer working in a department of women's studies described her disappointment at the lack of sorority, as a result of pressure and fragmentation rather than malice:

> I don't think there is any [support] ... it was impossible to support one another because we were so overstretched too and so spread about, and we just physically did not have the time ... So I don't think we supported each other well at all, and I feel bad about that. I actually can't see any way out of it at the moment, which is also depressing because you always think that if you are working as a group of women teaching women's studies that perhaps it will be supportive, you will do things differently, but that's not been my experience unfortunately.

This observation indicates one of the many ways in which feminism is compromised by its entry into segmented, boundaried disciplinary structures of the academy. It is hard for sisterhood and collectivity to flourish. A senior lecturer in a college of higher education noted that management offered her no support either, particularly for her career development, as they had a vested interest in her overwork – at a low grade:

My Brilliant Career-wise, I don't feel they are offering me things or persuading me or necessarily helping me, no. The culture is that you can work yourself to death, at your own expense.

Responses varied from neglect, indifference, to outright hostility from colleagues and superiors. A Greek professor commented on the antagonism she had received from a female colleague in response to her feminism:

And while I wrote this paper and I was correcting it, a fellow of mine ... we share the same office, said, 'What are you writing?' I told her I'm writing a paper on women's studies. And she was so scornful and she said, 'Oh let's have now Men's Studies separate' ... Out of – I don't know many women are now in this university – it is only two of us that involved not only in writing about women's issues, but also being involved in women's organisations, only two.

In contrast, a senior lecturer in Britain described how women in her new university had created their own community which combined serious political issues, campaigns and fun:

In terms of support ... we run – myself and another person – coordinate a Women's Staff Forum ... we broadened it out for all women employees and it became quite a powerful campaigning force ... We get people to come and talk about Women and Science or Childcare, is it a Management or a Personal Issue? – you know, those kinds of things; we have those sorts of talk – Is Feminism Sexist?, and on International Women's Day we had a wonderful belly dancing demonstration and workshop because a couple of the women said, you know, they'd be very happy to do it because they'd discovered this thing. So we had a brilliant session and there were about 50 women who turned up from across the Institution, you know. And they were all having a go! So that ... I think, that helps; well it helps me and I think it probably helps other women, it's sort of networking.

Networking via celebratory events rather than just on the basis of oppression proved to be an effective means of relationship-building, as the above illustrates. An assistant professor in Greece expressed her regret that networking opportunities seemed difficult for Greek women. She commented on how patriarchy had cut across the establishment of networks, and the successful application of the divide-and-rule principle had kept women locked in competition:

We've been brought up on a very antagonistic basis. I mean we're being raised on the principle that we have to fight other women for the man ... I mean until very recently this has been a very traditional society ... I think that perhaps one of the reasons that Greek women are so strong, relatively speaking of course, you know, are they have to stand up for themselves, have to deal with the fact that patriarchy here is quite obvious and quite threatening and oppressive, especially the family ... when you have to face patriarchy in your brothers, in your father, in your male friends, you've got, you know, to demarcate your own position. So you come across very strong women here. But the trouble with Greece – and this is my problem, my sort of political problem I mean – is that there is no way of us getting together.

The idea of adversity producing strength has long been a way for oppressed groups to compensate themselves for the material and psychic consequences of their struggles. In postmodern terms, it can be theorised as the power/resistance dyad. However, resistance is in relation to domination and is therefore defined and constrained by it. Engaging with organisations and the social world from an oppositional location demands sophisticated strategies for self-care, which were not always evident in my study.

FEMINISM AND CAREER DEVELOPMENT

The faces of many respondents in my study clouded over at the term 'career development'. This appeared to be an area of profound hurt for a lot of women. Careers have patterns that progress according to our socialised understandings of age-appropriate behaviour. They are also inextricably linked with notions of self-worth, self-esteem, as well as social status. In her autobiographical account of her ascent to the professoriat, Deem (1996: 6) stated:

It is important to emphasise that the career as outlined here is neither a unified entity nor a series of carefully planned, rational, measured steps. What has occurred has frequently been contingent, rarely linear, sometimes accidental and often serendipitous.

It is difficult for many women to follow age-related linear career expectations. This can mean that older women sometimes feel as if they have 'missed the boat' if they have not achieved senior ranks at certain ages. In her research, Park (1992: 230) found that 'in both universities and polytechnics the key age at which the chances of being a professor improve dramatically is 40'. Presumably, this applied to both men and women, with differing implications. I have observed a collective sense of hurt in the academy too, with women constantly forced to witness talented women being overlooked, while mediocre men are promoted. This can demotivate and discourage attempts to enter the lottery of promotions procedures.

Brown Packer (1995) asked women academics in three research universities in the USA the extent to which association with women's issues had impeded or enhanced women's careers. Her findings were mixed, as in my study. For some women in my study, feminism had been a significant career advantage, as it identified their expert power, structured their research interests and provided them with an endless source of sophisticated theory to stimulate creativity. It enabled them to theorise personal and professional hurts and develop a gendered sociological imagination which relieved them of the view that micropolitical oppression and their low organisational status was their fault. Feminism also enabled some women to move out of disciplines they felt to be constraining and androcentric. Feminism, like postmodernism, has been very critical of the way in which social sciences have participated in modern forms of domination, with disciplinary knowledge, such as psychology and sociology, linked to the emergence of subtle mechanisms of social control, and 'the elision of other forms of knowledge and experience' (Sawicki, 1988: 161).

Many feminists descry the notion of mono-dimensional identity imposed by disciplinary location. Speaking more generally, Lorde (1984: 120) remarked: 'I find I am constantly being encouraged to pluck out some one aspect of myself and present this as a meaningful whole, eclipsing other parts of self.' This is exacerbated in the academy by the practice of dividing the world into disciplines and licensing individuals to speak about specific areas only. Discipline can mean closure, rigidity, control. The process is similar to marriage vows. You make a commitment, usually at a young age, and are expected to stay faithful. A transdisciplinary or interdisciplinary approach is transgressive, akin to promiscuity, and is seen as evidence of instability. As Messer-Davidow (1991: 289) stated: 'Paradoxically, we may have escaped from our domestic enclosures only to find ourselves two decades later ensconced in disciplinary ones.'

A senior lecturer described how her decision to move out of her initial discipline and into women's studies was seen as a type of betrayal. While her feminism increased horizontal options, it had not necessarily enhanced vertical career opportunities:

> It's [feminism] ... been helpful in terms of I had a position which I didn't like and didn't want to stay in ... and I decided to move out of it ... culturally, it is not easy to move out of a position without being seen to let down the side ... I was able to use the fact that I was going to move into women's studies ... in terms of getting me up ladders or finding me jobs elsewhere, I'm not so sure ... moving up ladders is not so much a concern but moving around into other areas I could certainly sell it as an experience, but that is not the same as saying, has it actually helped me? As a label, I don't always know how much it is regarded and I think that will be quite interesting to know what are people reading when they read that on your CV ... I wouldn't think it is something that gets you up ladders. On the other hand, the tenacity and personal qualities that develop *might*. I think you have got to have both before you go in, don't you?

The ambiguity expressed in this account replicates the ambiguity of her position and her shifting identity. She left an established disciplinary area to enter one which is often regarded as maverick. However, this act in itself could represent evidence of risk-taking and innovation. Deem (1996: 16) argued that:

> Living in border territory, belonging neither to one camp nor the other, can enhance the willingness to take intellectual risks and permits an open-ness to new ideas that may be less characteristic of those who live within more defined and more central academic areas.

This raises questions about who feminist academics are trying to please – themselves, the women's movement, or some invisible jury of mainstream academics who will always find them wanting? As Griffiths (1993: 306) suggested: 'Accommodating to the wishes of others can lead to feelings of inauthenticity.' A Greek professor described her shifting perspectives on what should be the focus of her attention:

> I think that it [feminism] has been disadvantageous. Yes. Because if I spent the time I spend writing papers on women's issues, if I spent this time writing on more strictly constitutional problems then – I would achieve much more ... it was so bad in Greece that

when, four years ago, I told myself, enough of the women's issues, now I will only write papers which will enable me to attain the higher positions. But when I went to the States for three months, and I had participated in the National Conference of the Law Society Association, then I realised, because I'm very sensitive myself in women's issues, they are part of my heart ... but I realised there that women's issues are highly appreciated among academic circles. And this gave me more courage to go on writing papers on women's issues. And when I came back I had changed my attitude: No, I will write even more.

The observation that women's issues are 'part of her heart' summarises the dilemmas for many feminists who emotionally feel drawn to directing their intellectual skills to making sense of and exposing women's subordinate status. In this sense, the emotional involvement transgresses the academic rule of disembodiment, thus sometimes delegitimising feminist research. However, the emotional charge can spark creativity. Von Franz, a Jungian analyst, is clear that the artist's emotional life feeds creativity:

To be cut off from one's emotional basis always means complete sterilisation. Whoever cannot connect with his [*sic*] emotions feels, and is, sterile. (1972: 138)

The desire for authenticity and connection with their interests, emotions and creativity often meant that women would opt for feminist pathways, while also believing this could be disadvantageous for their careers. There is a powerful myth that women will be more successful if they remain in their disciplines. The implication is that career development is a rational procedure to be decoded and strategically operationalised. It also implies that feminist academics can ventriloquise dominant discourses while ignoring their own interests and experiences. Straying into women's studies was seen as self-sabotage. A university lecturer explored this notion diachronically:

I've been told by women academics, where I took this part-time job as a women's studies convenor, 'Oh what do you want to get yourself into that for? That's the death of your career!' And I said 'I don't think it is because that is what I want to do and I don't want to get into that again, doing the right sort of academic work.' But I do think that that is a real danger that women do face ... I do worry about imitating men because that is exactly what happened in the nineteenth-century women's movements as far as I am concerned.

They took on board male hierarchies and therefore a lot of women didn't have a voice at all.

This is an interesting point about competition between women. The belief being that if some women ascend hierarchies, this automatically silences other women lower down the scale. It is evocative of Legge's (1987: 55) observation: 'If some women succeed, the illusion of equal opportunities is maintained as the unsuccessful may be portrayed as inadequate, rather than discriminated against.'

Connections between seniority and having a voice have become hackneyed observations in anti-oppression work. A Swedish associate professor described how she used her seniority to voice equity concerns. Once she gained her academic credentials through research and publications, she could take more risks:

> I'm tougher, I dare to stand up for my opinions and to take it through and to go against the mainstream opinions, and when I sit on these boards for the appointment committee at the university, I just try to raise equality questions all the time and they listen to me now, so I dare.

Her observation that she is listened to more now she is senior merely confirms the previous informant's comments. It also raises issues about gendered change processes. As so many women are constellated in lower grades, often with short-term contracts, opportunities for influence are poor. A Swedish lecturer believed her feminist interventions were constrained in the academy as a consequence of her insecure contractual position, illustrating how degenerating employment conditions were silencing many women:

> This issue of tenure, it's a very important one here in Sweden ... who gets it and who doesn't – why ... so I can have courses ... But I am not invited to the discussions, plannings and so on because I'm not tenured. So there are differences in the way – I mean I couldn't make a career without being tenured, you see.

Feminists were also perceived as useful signifiers of progress, or mascots, in some universities, wheeled out for display purposes at appropriate moments, but ultimately without a significant locus of power, as a senior lecturer in a new university commented:

> I wouldn't even be here if I hadn't eventually discovered feminism, you know ... I don't think it's stood in my way; I mean I think that

the institution has been ... is very grateful to have people like me in it because it sees us as energetic, we look good on ... you know, when it invites X or whatever for its Honorary Degree, it can invite me to the tea party ... they've given me a very easy time in terms of letting me do my little thing. But in terms of actually effecting any change where the power is, you know, they wouldn't –

The intimation here is that feminism is acceptable so long as it remains at a low level. Like little girls who are cutely allowed to be 'proper little madams', feminists are fine if they stay within the boundaries of acceptable feminine behaviour, that is, are not too ambitious, disruptive or obstreperous.

However, a Swedish associate lecturer believed that not only had her feminism promoted and defined her career, but her specialised knowledge had facilitated her entry into decision-making structures:

Without that [feminism] I would not have a career, I think so, it has really promoted my career, because I suddenly had knowledge nobody else had and I have also worked very hard within all the boards of the university and I still do and I work for equality, to promote equality. They know me and they always call me and ask me to participate in that and that and that, so if you are known to be a good feminist then you will be asked, and it will help you.

A Greek professor observed how women's outsider status in the academy was part of their long struggle to participate in public life:

You see in Greece the problem is that women were excluded from university studies till the beginning of the first decade of our century. They could become only teachers in the primary schools ... Because although our constitution declared that all Greeks are equal before the law – yet due to traditions of patriarchy and other conservative traditions they interpreted it as: the people who could get to public positions would have the right to vote – and women have not the right to vote. They acquired it in 1952 ... So you see there is a great ... discrepancy between the careers that men followed and women. And you can't make it up in twenty years ... So there is a problem that you can find many women – it's about, I think, 20 per cent, if I'm sure, of women in the university staff, teaching staff of the universities, but women in the higher positions like mine are very few.

Time-lag factors need to be taken into account. The historic location of women as latecomers and outsiders leaves a collective sense of lost time to recover. This historically deterministic view also suggests that women today are paying the price for centuries of exclusion – a type of academic version of Eve's original sin. However, Bourdieu (1988) reminds us that any of the most influential male theorists of both structuralism and poststructuralism had rather tenuous relations, if any, with the academy.

The idea that women are always in deficit, regardless of material, performative evidence to the contrary was explored by Walkerdine (1990). A senior lecturer in Britain in my study commented that her work in women's studies was ignored for promotion purposes. She indicated that she had gained her promotion for long service rather than innovation in curriculum development and course management. This is redolent of Walkerdine's observation (1990: 134) from her research with girls and women that 'the discursive production of femininity as antithetical to masculine rationality' results in 'femininity' being 'equated with poor performance, even when the girl or woman in question is performing well'. If girls and women do succeed, it is a consequence of hard work and sustained 'plodding', rather than brilliance, innovation or ability, as the following quotation from a senior lecturer in my study indicates:

Because I was taken on as an Art History lecturer many, many years ago, and only just been made a senior lecturer (and should have been, you know, long since), and that I don't think was anything to do with women's studies ... I haven't had any, you know, career development effectively. I mean the SL is simply through long years of service, so to speak, rather than anything else. I think the perception of colleagues of me might have changed because they associate me with this rather strange and peculiar thing called feminism ... But I think it hasn't affected my career in any way. It hasn't changed.

Elsewhere, some women believed that feminism had changed their career paths. A university lecturer believed her feminism had helped her career development, as it endowed her with expert power:

I think it has helped, because whenever there is anyone needed to do something around feminism, guess who they come to? ... I'm a good teacher, so I get the work, but again having said that feminism is still very marginal, there is not that much in my university ... it's certainly not a pathway to promotion. In fact, you could almost see it as the opposite. And I think as well when you do interdisciplinary work.

It is worth noting that the lecturer highlighted that it was her teaching orientation that was sought out, rather than her research or management skills. She suggested too that interdisciplinary work is identified as some kind of pollution, or evidence of superficiality. So, while she is called on by many sources to provide 'the feminist perspective', she is also condemned for being too flexible. Her flexibility allows others to keep their pure disciplinary locations intact. In many respects, women's studies teachers become part of a service industry. Fears about the vulnerability of feminists who stray from their disciplines have led to attempts to define women's studies itself as a disciplinary area. For Boetcher-Joeres (quoted in McDermott, 1994: 162), this is a retrogressive move:

> If feminism is to be inside the academy, it goes without saying that it will take on the characteristics of that institution. It will begin to define itself as a discipline, for example, it will want to lessen its reputation as being made up of magpies and nomads who, after all, really don't belong.

While the 'not belonging' can be a refusal to accept patriarchal paradigms, concepts and knowledge boundaries, I am reminded of another type of non-belonging. In my previous job, I attempted to initiate an inter-faculty MA in women's studies, and the planning meetings attracted the most unlikely selection of women. Many of them disclosed that their primary interest was to make up their teaching hours, gain full-time posts, or, if they were researchers, to gain some postgraduate teaching experience. Very few expressed a commitment to the ideals of academic feminism. I was left feeling very frustrated, but also very sad that women who had been so spectacularly shut out of the academy felt that women's studies would be a benign means of entry and something they were automatically qualified to do as they were women.

Toren (1993) indicated that there are subtle temporal dimensions to gender inequalities, with women frequently disadvantaged by age-related career development measures. A Greek professor mentioned that Greece, unlike Britain, had quantifiable criteria for promotion, but these had normalising undercurrents as it related career development to chronological factors.

Our law says that in three years you have a right and an obligation to demand a higher position. But this three years' period is not sufficient for women with family obligations to compete on equal terms.

Statistics frequently reveal low numbers of academic women in senior positions. In July 1996, statistics from institutions with more than 40 professors in Britain revealed that South Bank University had the highest percentage of female professors (32.6 per cent [14 out of 43], whereas University of Manchester Institute of Science and Technology failed to have even one woman out of 94 professorships. Nationally, only 7.3 per cent of professors are women, though women comprise 30 per cent of academics. New universities come top of the league table, but in engineering and technology the proportion of women professors is below 1 per cent (Ince, 1996: 16). There are now five female vice-chancellors in Britain. However, Park (1992: 228) states that 'simply observing a correlation between sex and rank does not capture the complexity of the specific mechanisms through which being female influences, for example, the chances of promotion to a professorial post'. As research is such an important signifier for academic promotions in Britain, Greece and Sweden, it is important to untangle gendered processes and opportunities for research productivity.

RESEARCH: CLAIMING CREATIVITY

The gendered micropolitics of research was commented on by many interviewees, in terms of who gains access to resources, that is funding and time for creative work. Additionally, some felt that feminist research was delegitimised. This can mean feminist academics have to produce more research outputs and pay more for promotion, i.e. staying longer on each grade (Toren, 1993). Park (1992: 232) observes that: 'An individual expressing interest in research ... is ten times more likely to occupy a chair than is their counterpart who expresses a greater interest in teaching.' However, the matter is not as simple as a research/teaching binary. Research also appears to be stratified, with feminist work frequently delegitimised. A Greek professor identified this process:

> And then I continually write on women's issues. But the problem is
> that in Greece women's studies ... have not acquired the status that
> they have in foreign countries. And I ... am obliged to consider that

my studies on women's issues are second-rate studies and papers in comparison with what I have to write on other constitutional issues. Although I consider that women's problems are constitutional problems and social problems.

This account is reminiscent of Carroll's (1990: 158) argument that judgements of academic worth are 'mysterious, serving a political, not an intellectual purpose'. Studies on the sociology of knowledge outline the gendered roots of scholarship and demonstrate how the powerful have traditionally assessed the quality of ideas (Fuchs Epstein, 1988).

Some feminist academics saw research as a type of crucifix to Dracula, so long as it resulted in publications, the academy was indifferent to the political standpoint. A senior lecturer in a college of higher education observed:

I don't think people in this institution would know what feminist research is! They wanted to get some people that they thought would do some good stuff on criminology so they brought me into this meeting where they had this bloke who wanted to look at whether or not violence was caused by people's genetics and excess drinking. They brought us together thinking that we may have something we could decently say to one another. They haven't got a clue whatsoever!

In addition to a gender binary concerning allocation of research opportunities, there is also a hierarchical relationship between old and new universities in Britain. There has been an 'academic drift', in that many new universities have tried to emulate the research focus of older universities, but without the resources. For example, the new sector received £30 million for research in 1988–90 compared to £800 million for universities (Kogan, 1993). In my study, women in Britain's new universities noted how teaching and research were antagonistically related. Many British informants comments on how they had to use their spare time in which to undertake research, as their official working week was taken up with teaching and administration. Rose (1994: 66) comments on how Nordic countries have seen women's studies research as part of a general 'equality' project', whereas in Britain it proceeds largely through self-help. A senior lecturer in a college of higher education identified how the academic drift translated into micropolitical tensions and an intrapersonal sense of inadequacy:

> On the one hand there is a body of thought that it's a teaching insti-
> tution. On the other hand there is a body of thought ... that
> research is very important and you have got to do it, so you are
> pulled in two directions really. Whatever you do you are failing I
> think.

Fisher (1994: 64) notes how 'time-sharing between tasks implies
constant interruption, which is ... stressful'. A senior lecturer in a new
university described how staff were still expected to undertake vast
amounts of teaching, whilst also required to produce research in
response to changes in higher education funding policies.

> Some people have had a lot of support for research I think,
> although others have complained that they were taken on with the
> understanding that they would have time for research and then
> were given enormous teaching loads and couldn't do any research.
> I think that our institution anyway has been extremely ambivalent
> about research. On the one hand it's been over the years saying, no
> we're a teaching institution, we're not a research establishment –
> and have been often quite reluctant to support research – and on
> the other, and particularly recently because of the funding business,
> it's now suddenly turned round and said, 'You must all research.'
> And so, you know, my response to that is, 'OK I'll research if I'm
> given some time.' So I think it's quite uneven ... And there is gener-
> ally I think a sort of male-dominated sense in terms of research and
> promotion. For me personally I have no time for research at all.

A painful lesson I had to learn in the academy was that, as a
woman, you are rarely *given* time for research, particularly if it has the
potential to make you more marketable. I had to learn to *take* time,
and wade through layers of potent internalised narratives telling me
that I was being selfish if I took time to write instead of being in my
office and universally available. In my early years as a writer, I also
had external pressure too – countless phone calls from colleagues on
trivial matters whenever I said I was writing. This micropolitical sabotage was very effective in unsettling me emotionally and breaking my
intellectual concentration. Writing demands temporary withdrawal
from interaction with others. Thus 'selfishness' with all its negative
connotations is an essential prerequisite for writing. Minh-ha (1989:
7) identified guilt as a major obstacle for women writers to overcome.
Brackenbury, writer and teacher of creative writing, described how
she learned to recognise that 'Real writing flourishes with space

around it (Brackenbury, quoted in Sellers, 1989: 44). This is a profoundly gendered issue, and many women do not have the support and encouragement to contradict socially constructed patterns of women's accessibility (Morley, 1995b).

Feminist principles of collectivity are oppositionally located to the individualism of the academic research industry. Academic resources are organised and distributed in ways that discourage cooperation and guarantee competition (Fox-Keller and Moglen, 1987). A senior lecturer indicated how collaboration diluted her academic standing:

> from a research point, I'm sure it [feminism] has made a difference because of a lot of the work I do is collaborative with other women. On one of the projects that I've worked on we have had nine women involved in that. We published a paper recently and it had nine names on it and I suppose sooner or later somebody is going to say, 'Hang on a minute, you're watering down your scores, do you need to put the name of ...?' One of the people who had worked on the project was a black woman who we had employed to interview women in Urdu ... and we included her name in the publication. I mean she didn't write for it at all, but it was her work we had included within the discussion and actually felt morally obliged to put her name on it, but I suppose that had I been anywhere else and possibly not working for this institution they would start saying, 'You have got to knock some of the names off.' It probably has affected me so far in terms of I've applied for a couple of jobs and I'm sure that the fact that I have lots of collaborative work, and not much that has been single-authored, has worked against me. And all of my research projects are working with community groups or working with other women again I don't think they like that really. Collectivity is not one of the aims, is it, in the academy?

The comments about including the interpreter's name is a reminder about power inequalities between women. In this case, a feminist intervention was the refusal to render the black woman invisible by delegitimising her skills. This action meant the work had less academic value. The issue of names, credit and reputation was raised by a lecturer in an old university who explained how all the professors in her department were men. They were the 'big names' which attracted research funding, and therefore had to be included in every research proposal, regardless of who would be actually conducting the research. The 'unknowns', who were often women, were expected to do the majority of work while constantly being told that their names would weaken the application if included. When research applications were successful, they were simply added to the overflowing curriculum vitae of the male professors. This strategic approach to research applications ensured that many women forever remained 'unknown'. This lecturer also commented how there was subtle micropolitical slippage, so that the 'unknowns' became perceived as 'unknowing', while the 'big names' were invested with unlimited intellectual authority.

Research success demands a type of individualistic self-promotion that involves a discomforting visibility for many women, and invisibility for others. Women, who have traditionally been subjected to the objectifying and critical male gaze, can experience discomfort in self-promotion. A Swedish associate lecturer describes how second-class citizenship erodes the confidence required by competitive research processes:

> Promotion in Sweden – you have to compete all the time if you want to be promoted. You have to apply for tenured positions and you have to apply for research money and then you are evaluated by your colleagues and other people at the University. And in this process it can sometimes be very hard for women to come through.

A senior lecturer identified how feminist research was part of a wider community of women:

> I do feel some responsibility to a kind of group that might be calling themselves feminist researchers wherever they are. I feel a responsibility and accountability.

Accountability has to work both ways, with research funding processes being more open to scrutiny. For example, a Swedish associate professor commented on how the gendered allocation of research funding had been empirically researched in Sweden:

> I don't know if you have heard about the medical research council in Sweden. Two women made an investigation of how they had distributed money for ten years and it was shown very very clearly that men got money ten times more often than women, even if they had less competence. So now they have changed the board of this whole research council, but this is the way it works. You have to have people within the system to guard and to watch what is going on and to try to change and to try and prevent discrimination.

Discrimination can be more subtle, with funding priorities directly linked to areas of inquiry in which women are under-represented. The publish or perish cliché oversimplifies the conditions under which feminist academics labour. I worked for eleven years with a male who never published anything and who did not perish. On the contrary, he enjoyed protection and patronage from management, fulfilling the micropolitical function of a sick child. Allowances were always made for his failure to do research, while no credit was given for my successes. In other words, he lost nothing from his inactivity, and I gained nothing from my productivity. A woman member of the Association of University Teachers reports how she was described as publishing 'excessively' by her male interviewer in a formal appraisal interview situation. She was told to wait for promotion and 'allow her male colleagues to catch up', in other words stop doing research and publishing (AUT, 1991: 2). It would appear that in women's hands, research and writing are often constructed as forms of arrogance, exhibitionism and self-aggrandisement.

An Australian study (Cass et al., 1983) found that productivity in higher positions was the same for men and women, but conditions at the lower levels, where the majority of women are situated, militated against publication. Park (1992: 236) discovered that there were more senior men than senior women who had ceased to publish after their promotion. She argued: 'Contrary to much "accepted" opinion, these results suggest that women's representation in senior ranks would actually improve if publication became a standard measure of suitability.'

So, something else is going on in promotions procedures which does not appear to be related to the declared criteria, as controlling for the same features still produces glaring inequalities. Park (1992: 237) also observed that: 'University women are about three times less likely to be professors than men when age and publication rate are taken into account.' I can only speculate that micropolitical factors are involved such as coalitions, networks and alliances which subtly reproduce male power and discriminate against women.

SUMMARY

Fox-Keller and Moglen (1987: 508) asked:

> But what does it mean to be a good feminist in a real world, where real power, real issues of professional survival and real opportuni-

ties are at stake ... where power, excellence and the capacity or ability to influence are not ever distributed equally?

As agents for change, feminist academics frequent a territory in which micro- and macro-processes are analytically related. A gendered deconstruction of the academy reveals the social and psychic labour involved in the daily negotiation of patriarchal power in the academy. Academic feminists speak from a position of deviance which can alienate them from feminists outside the academy and from academic colleagues on the inside. It can also mean, like Bakhtin's notion of carnivalesque (1968), that they occupy a strange border location or period of licence – a site in which conventions of the academy are permitted to be challenged, on a limited basis, with random consequences for career development and personal well-being.

8 Concluding Comments: The Dangers of Certainty

Conclusions to studies are hard to write, as there are often expectations of concrete recommendations demanding immediate action, authoritative findings and monolithic solutions. This strategy can be dangerous. To denote required changes implies a new kind of rationality, with the risk of hegemonic arrogance about what constitutes progress. In one of his last interviews, (quoted in Dreyfus and Rabinow, 1982: 232) Foucault said: 'My point is not that everything is bad, but that everything is dangerous.' Power relations, as this study has indicated, take diverse forms. The women's stories from three European countries demonstrate how power is structural, interpersonal and intrapersonal, often coagulating to create confused and contradictory readings. As a theoretical framework, feminism has described and analysed the dangers of exclusion, suppression and domination in the academy. It also continues to be scrutinised for the dangers embedded in its theories and praxis, particularly in relation to difference and diversity.

Elam (1994: 101) argues that 'the radical epistemological move on the part of women's studies deconstructs the whole notion of the university.' In this analysis, if feminist influence were given free rein, there would be no universities left as we know them. Hierarchies, departments, disciplines, curriculum, pedagogies, processes would all be called into question. However, this is one reading of future developments. I will not attempt to offer ambitious predictions. Furthermore, as a qualitative inquiry, with a relatively small data set, it could be dangerous to over-generalise from my findings. All I can do is describe some of the patterns, paradoxes and preoccupations which appear to have emerged from these transnational, transdisciplinary feminist readings of the academy.

Comparative work can acknowledge commonalities without automatically implying denial of differences. My study included a variety of voices across nations, disciplines, age, 'race', sexualities and social classes, indicating how power relations rarely operate in isolation, and how different structures of inequality are conceptually and materially interrelated. A key finding of my study has been that, in spite of location in differing logics, political frameworks and economies, voices chorused similar concerns about the prolonged subordination of women in the academy. Feminism has had some success, in all three countries, in disrupting continuities of masculinist hegemonic discourses, but it is also a lived force field, with a range of layers of engagement. As a negotiated subject position, feminism is more or less in constant flux. This implies an exciting dynamism, but also possibilities for dilution and diversion from some of feminism's original radical aims. A further finding of my study was how respondents expressed fears that feminism was providing a ladder for opportunists who had no political or emotional connection with the women's movement.

Another finding of my study is that, whereas feminism has destabilised some of the dominance in traditional academic disciplines, it appears to have developed on a separate trajectory from equity discourses. Equity discourses, heavily criticised by some for conceptual flaws, and by others for manipulative micropolitical functions, have failed to bring about wider organisational changes. It appears that even in Sweden, with its widespread political commitment to equity politics, neither employment issues nor the nature of the academic 'product' have been substantially challenged. The rigid hierarchical and selective nature of the academy provides structural opportunities for differentiation. This both reinforces and reproduces social inequalities. While it is dangerous to draw universal conclusions from limited evidence, it would appear that employment disadvantage affects women in the academy in many locations (Stiver Lie et al., 1994). This seems to have had a detrimental effect on the development of feminism in the academy. Employment issues are inextricably linked with epistemology. Ball (1987: 73) observes that 'lack of opportunity for and discrimination against women ensures the continued dominance of the male perspective'. However, several informants in my study were significantly concerned about women's disadvantaged career status in the academy, while paradoxically displaying political discomfort with the entire notion of career development in alienating, discriminatory hierarchies. Seniority was often perceived as betrayal and compliance with management's regulatory functions. This provided an interesting contradiction – if feminists are concentrated on the lower rungs of the hierarchy, their influence is limited; if they ascend to higher ranks, their commitment to feminism can be called into question.

My study indicated that even in Sweden, where feminism was

ostensibly well resourced and politically inserted into the academy, many feminist students and teachers felt angry, disadvantaged and vulnerable. Having lived through liberalising measures of state welfarism, Swedish feminists in my study felt that quota systems, equality politics and state interventions were new regulatory ways of silencing feminism, inside and outside the academy. In Greece, I spoke to women who had lived through the period of military dictatorship and who had fought monolithic power structures and succeeded in getting first women and then feminism into the academy, only to find many younger women denying sexual discrimination in the post-feminist belief that everything is equal now. In Britain, feminists in the academy can often be change agents, while also being victims of massive political reform in education. While the issue of reform or revolution became a cliché of the Left, it has not been so easy to predict the extent and consequences of a revolution from the Right. A current fear in Britain is that the New Labour government will simply continue, rather than challenge these processes. Policy changes have had varying effects on universities in Britain, with elite institutions staying relatively protected, while newer, mass universities have been more directly influenced by marketisation and new managerialism. There has been a New Right revolution, with many feminists precariously located on the wrong side of it. Access of under-represented groups to non-elite institutions has changed, particularly at undergraduate level. However, the class origins of students in elite institutions remain largely unchanged. There is now a more covert form of binary divide in the academy. With proposals to introduce fees for universities, there are severe dangers of a return to pre-1960s elitism.

A further finding was that in all three countries, feminism is ambiguously related to many parts of the academy. A fundamental point demonstrated in my study was that micropolitical competence seems to be as important as intellectual ability in the struggle for survival in the academy.

Nicolson (1996: xiii) said: 'I came to realise that the psychological survival of women in organizations is a key issue for feminist psychology.' My study indicated that many women are surviving in the academy, particularly at undergraduate level. Few are flourishing at postgraduate level or in terms of employment. This represents a major contradiction. Feminist courses appear to be prospering, but many women academics are languishing at the bottom of university hierarchies, often managing programmes on a voluntary basis.

Feminist students, many of whom have had to wait a long time for access to the academy, are often intellectually exhilarated by their experiences. However, many are also disappointed at the industrialisation of higher education.

An additional finding in my study has been that feminists have learned that in order to initiate the smallest changes they have had to mine their political, intellectual and emotional energies to an extent that threatens them personally and professionally. In a stimulating discussion I had with my colleague Jenny Shaw, on the subject of emotional labour in the public services, we concluded that marketisation had impacted on human resources in the same way as industrial capitalism has destroyed the natural resources of the planet. This was demonstrated in my study too. Feminist academics, as a limited resource, have had to mine themselves deeper and deeper without sustainable renewal. In this framework, a new compliance culture is emerging, in which opposition is in danger of being worn down and made docile. It can also mean that energies have to be focused on one small area for change, such as curriculum development, rather than involvement with policy initiatives for wider organisational change. The metaphor of depletion and replenishment has also been applied to women's studies, as a subject. As Campbell (1992: 2) suggests, there is a

> metaphor of the academy harbouring feminism: building it up and replenishing it in some ways, yes, but at the same time given to running it dry, keeping it within walls, seeing to its overall containment.

Feminism verges on the possibility of turning into yet another form of thematic criticism appropriated by the academy (Elam, 1994: 7). However, there is also the possibility that the more access women have to feminism in the academy, the more it could influence demands to change it.

CHANGING THE SCRIPT

In spite of my reservations about the rationality and common-sense feel of recommendations for change, I asked informants to identify the types of changes they would like to see in the academy. Not surprisingly, many of them drew a deep breath and asked, 'Where do I start?' As so much of our knowledge is oppositional, it was hard for women to fantasise about new ways of creating and organising knowledges. Equally, there are dangers inherent in this exercise too. In the power/counterpower discourse, imagining another system can weld us more firmly to the present one. This implies that desired changes are framed by existing regimes, rendering interventions reformist and ameliorative. This can lead to a type of nihilism that immobilises change agency, and feminism is essentially concerned with political and social change. After initial hesitations and reservations, informants produced creative ideas for a new order. However, they were mostly in relation to current discontents and disenchantment.

Several wanted to see the expansion of women's studies, with explicit feminist foundations. It was suggested by one student that women's studies should be mandatory for all undergraduate students. Diversity was also emphasised in relation to both students and staff, with Swedish students commenting strongly on the low participation rate of working-class students in Swedish universities. Space was a subject many highlighted – some wanted a return to women-only colleges, many suggested women-only spaces in universities, perhaps with appointed women's support officers. The issues of women's representation and role-modelling were perceived as crucial, and one student felt that feminists have to evolve strategies for confronting 'women students' overwhelming lack of self-confidence'. Women's disadvantaged employment position was repeatedly mentioned. Some felt that any woman would be preferable to a man in a senior position, whereas others felt strongly that there need to be more feminists as chairs, heads of departments and deans. Opportunities and mentorship for younger women, particularly research students, was desired. Maternity, motherhood and parent-friendliness were also raised.

Many wished for more effective equity measures, with policies more thoughtfully integrated into practices and more attention given to racial as well as sexual discrimination. In Britain, many commented on the miseries of new managerialism, particularly in relation to the constant preoccupation with finance, measurement, marketing and accountability. There was a longing to be free of these bureaucratic burdens which were perceived as regulatory devices to create an atmosphere of fear and uncertainty, rather than merely to save/make money and assure quality. More time and resources for feminist research were desired, and women wanted feminist publications to have the same academic legitimacy and cultural capital rate as 'mainstream' publications. The labelling of the feminist product was an item of concern, with one student stating that she wanted to see women's studies 'stamp down gender studies into the dirt!' Others felt it did not matter how feminism was labelled, so long as it had a substantial presence in the academy.

HOW DOES ONE MOVE ON IF THE VERY NOTION OF LINEARITY IS IN QUESTION?

Connected politically, professionally and emotionally to a worldwide movement for social change, feminists in the academy have uneasy relations with the confines of the reified patriarchy of the academy. Yet intellectual work continues to attract and fascinate. Feminists in the academy seem to occupy a strange border territory. Enigmatic, their utterances and interventions shock, irritate, delight, unsettle and ultimately reposition. They are licensed to provoke, entertain and sustain simultaneously. Ambiguously located in dominant organisa- tions of knowledge production, they are both connected to the wider social and political world of women and to enlightenment principles of reason and rationality. This hybridity produces some painful tensions. As Stanley (1997: 3) asked: 'How is it possible to be so subservient as to "be reasonable" in the face of inequality, exploita- tion, oppression?'

Feminists' 'unreasonable' readings, knowledges, articulations disturb and dislocate. They can push the boundaries, but have to stay within a hierarchy which ultimately disempowers and constrains.

It would be easy to depict feminists in the academy as micropoliti- cal martyrs – Christ-like figures being tested by adversity to rise triumphantly at the end. This reifies power relations by reinforcing the reductive victim/oppressor binary. It also overlooks power rela- tions between women, implying unitary subjectivities. Just as power can be both oppressive and productive, so too can counter-powers. For some, academic feminism can represent a new hegemonic force which marginalises other structures of inequality such as sexualities, 'race', disability. In relation to lesbian studies, Wilton (1995: 1) believes that while

> it is true that women's studies is 'more fully developed' as an acad- emic presence, it has been too saturated with homophobia to develop a radical critique of the erotic, or to offer an intellectually adequate milieu for lesbians.

While this may indeed be the case, it demonstrates the precariousness of academic feminism, and how it is frequently under attack from a range of views on the political spectrum. In New Right discourses of post-feminism, feminism is represented as a coercive orthodoxy. Criticised for being exclusionary, repressive, non-academic, *passé*, feminism continues to occupy a tentative position in the academy.

In the context of marketisation in Britain, it is too simple and reductive to conclude that feminism has flourished from economic necessity. There are deeper issues at stake, with striking cross-cultural commonalities. To speak of margins/mainstream or insiders/outsiders dichotomises complex psycho-social processes of change. Postmodernism has challenged the notion of meta-narratives and rational interventions for change, drawing attention to the inevitability of segmentation and discontinuities. It has also scrutinised feminism itself, questioning whether interventions in message systems, such as feminist pedagogy, are new regimes of power, with regulatory functions. But we live in contradictory times with theoretical tensions. In spite of the influence of postmodernism on intellectual processes, new managerialism, with its modernist rationality, has become a dominant organising principle in the academy in Britain. It could also be concluded that policies of the New Right, with their combination of conservatism and morality, simply entered fragmented institutions and reinforced pre-existing power relations.

The very notion of the academy is in flux. Distance learning, cyberspace and the information superhighway suggest that, in the future, the university may only exist as an electronic network. This could render current debates on feminist pedagogy redundant, and pose new challenges for social relations. Researching micropolitics is challenging, as so much is elusive, personal and relies on senses, innuendo, hunches and suspicions. As a vehicle for both radical dissent and opportunity, academic feminism has developed its own micropolitics, while simultaneously becoming micropolitically competent in reading organisational cultures. It would appear from my study that feminism exposes the micropolitics of the academy in a particularly transparent and disturbing way. Micropolitics enables an understanding of the interweaving of feminism and academic life. Micropolitics can also inhibit and promote feminist change. Feminism, to a certain extent, exemplifies the contradictory and conflictual bases of organisational life. The academy, like most organisations, can be experienced as domination, but it also offers possibilities for creativity and critical challenge. For many feminist students and academics, it is experienced both as oppressive and stim-

ulating. Universities are not consensual institutions, but are fragmented, discontinuous and in flux. Dominance is maintained by
patriarchal structures and practices, but paradoxically, these both
feed and contain the growth of academic feminism. The academy, like
other institutions, is a site of ideological struggle, with epistemologies, life chances and careers at stake in the battle. At the end of my
study, I am left wondering if this is the only way of organising knowledge.

References

Aaron, J. and Walby, S. (eds) (1991) *Out of The Margins: Women's Studies in the Nineties*. London: Taylor and Francis.

Acker, J. (1990) Hierarchies, Jobs, Bodies: a Theory of Gendered Organizations, *Gender and Society* 4, pp. 139–58.

Acker, J. (1992) Gendering Organizational Theory, in A. Mills and P. Tancred (eds) *Gendering Organizational Analysis* (pp. 248–60). London: Sage.

Acker, S. et al. (eds) (1984) *World Year Book of Education: Women and Education*. New York: Kogan Page.

Agger, B. (1993) *Gender, Culture and Power: Towards a Feminist Postmodern Critical Theory*. Westport: Praeger.

Ainley, P. (1994) *Degrees of Difference*. London: Lawrence and Wishart.

Albrow, M. (1992) *Sine Ira et Studio* – or Do Organizations Have Feelings? *Organization Studies* 13(3), pp. 313-29.

Alvesson, M. and Billing, Y. D. (1992) Gender and Organization: Towards a Differentiated Understanding, *Organization Studies* 13/12, pp. 73–102.

Amos, V. and Parmar, P. (1984) Challenging Imperial Feminism, *Feminist Review* 17 (July), pp. 3–19.

Arends, J. and Volman, M. (1995) Equal Opportunities in the Netherlands and the Policy of the ILEA, in L. Dawtrey, J. Holland, M. Hammer and S. Sheldon (eds) *Equality and Inequality in Education Policy* (pp. 113–22). Clevedon: Multilingual Matters.

Arnot, M. (1995) Feminism, Education and the New Right, in L. Dawtrey, J. Holland, M. Hammer and S. Sheldon (eds) *Equality and Inequality in Education Policy* (pp. 159–81). Clevedon: Multilingual Matters.

Aronowitz, S. and Giroux, H. (1991) *Postmodern Education: Politics, Culture and Social Criticism*. Minneapolis: University of Minnesota Press.

Association of University Teachers (AUT) (1991) *AUT Woman* No. 23, Summer.

Association of University Teachers (AUT) (1994) *AUT Woman*, 33.

Bagilhole, B. (1993) How to Keep a Good Woman Down: an Investigation of the Role of Institutional Factors in the Process of Discrimination against Women Academics, *British Journal of Sociology of Education* 14(3), pp. 262–74.

Bakhtin, M. (1968) *Rabelais and His World*. Cambridge, MA: MIT Press.

Balaska, J. (1994) 2,500 Years after Plato: Greek Women in Higher Education, in S. Stiver Lie, L. Malik and D. Harris (eds) *The Gender Gap in Higher Education* (pp. 85–94). London: Kogan Page.

Ball, S. (1987) *The Micropolitics of the School*. London: Routledge.

Ball, S. (1990) Management as Moral Technology: A Luddite Analysis, in S. Ball (ed.) (1990) *Foucault and Education: Disciplines and Knowledge*, (pp. 153–66). London: Routledge.

Ball, S. (1994a) *Education Reform – a Critical and Post-Structuralist Approach*. Milton Keynes: Open University Press.

Ball, S. (1994b) Researching inside the State: Issues in the Interpretation of Elite Interviews, in D. Halpin and B. Troyna (eds) *Researching Education Policy: Ethical and Methodological Issues* (pp. 107–20). London: The Falmer Press.

Bandura, A. (1977) Self-Efficiency: Toward a Unifying Theory of Behavioural Change. *Psychological Review* 82(2), pp. 191–215.

Bartky, S. L. (1988) Foucault, Femininity and the Modernisation of Patriarchal Power, in I. Diamond and L. Quilby (eds) *Feminism and Foucault: Reflections on Resistance* (pp. 61–6). Boston: Northeastern University Press.

Beauvoir, S. de (1972) *The Second Sex* (trans. H. M. Parshley). Harmondsworth: Penguin Books.

Benhabib, S. (1992) *Situating the Self: Gender, Community and Postmodernism in Contemporary Ethics*. Oxford: Polity Press.

Benn, R. (1995) Higher Education, Non-Standard Students and Withdrawals, *Journal of Further and Higher Education* 19 (3) (Autumn), pp. 3-12.

Bernard, J. (1972) *The Sex Game*. New York: Atheneum.

Bettleheim, B. (1979) *The Informed Heart: Autonomy in a Mass Age*. New York: Avon.

Bhavnani, K-K. (1993) Tracing the Contours: Feminist Research and Feminist Objectivity. *Women's Studies International Forum* 16(2), pp. 95–104.

Blase, J. (ed.) (1991) *The Politics of Life in Schools*. Newbury Park: Sage.

Blase, J. and Anderson, G. (1995) *The Micropolitics of Educational Leadership*. London: Cassell.

Bourdieu, P. (1979) *Distinction: a Social Critique of the Judgement of Taste* (trans. R. Nice). London: Routledge and Kegan Paul.

Bourdieu, P. (1988) *Homo Academicus*. Cambridge: Polity Press.

Bourdieu, P. and Passeron, P. (1990) *Reproduction in Education, Society and Culture*. London: Sage.

Bowe, R., Ball, S. and Gold, A. (1992) *Reforming Education and Changing Schools: Case Studies in Policy Sociology*. London: Routledge.

Bowles, G. and Klein, R. (eds) (1987) *Theories of Women's Studies*. London: Routledge and Kegan Paul.

Braidotti, R. (1986) Ethics Re-visited: Women and/in Philosophy, in C. Pateman, and E. Gross (eds) *Feminist Challenges* (pp. 44–60). London: Allen and Unwin.

Braidotti, R. (1992) Origin and Development of Gender Studies in Western Europe, in European Network for Women's Studies Workshop, *Establishing Gender Studies in Central and Eastern European Countries,* Wassenar, The Netherlands, 5–8 November. pp. 23–32.

Bricker-Jenkins, M. and Hooyman, N. (1987) Feminist Pedagogy in Education for Social Change, *Feminist Teacher* 2(2), pp. 36–42.

Brown Packer, B. (1995) Irrigating the Sacred Grove: Stages of Gender Equity Development, in L. Morley and V. Walsh (eds) *Feminist Academics: Creative Agents for Change* (pp. 42–55). London: Taylor and Francis.

Burrell, G. (1993) Eco and the Bunnymen, in J. Hassard and M. Parker (eds) *Postmodernism and Organizations* (pp. 71–82). London: Sage.

Butler, A. and Landells, M. (1995) Taking Offence: Research as Resistance to Sexual Harassment in Academia, in L. Morley and V. Walsh (eds)

Feminist Academics: Creative Agents for Change (pp. 156–68). London: Taylor and Francis.

Butler, J. (1993) *Bodies that Matter: On the Discursive Limits of 'Sex'*. London: Routledge.

Cacoullos, A. (1991) Women, Science and Politics in Greece: Three is a Crowd, in V. Stolte-Heiskanen et al. (eds) *Women in Science: Token Women or Gender Equality?* (pp. 135–46). Oxford: Berg.

Cain, M. (1986) Realism, Feminism, Methodology and the Law. *International Journal of the Sociology of Law*, 14(3/4), pp. 255–67.

Cain, M. (1990) Realist Philosophy and Standpoint Epistemologies OR Feminist Criminology as a Successor Science, in L. Gelsthorpe and A. Morris (eds) *Feminist Perspectives in Criminology* (pp. 124–40). Milton Keynes: Open University Press.

Cain, M. (1993) Foucault, Feminism and Feeling: What Foucault Can and Cannot Contribute to Feminist Epistemology, in C. Ramazanoglu (ed.) *Up against Foucault: Explorations and Some Tensions Between Foucault and Feminism* (pp. 73–96). London: Routledge.

Calas, M. and Smircich, L. (1992) Rewriting Gender into Organizational Theorizing: Directions from Feminist Perspectives, in M. Reed and M. Hughes (eds) *Rethinking Organization: New Directions in Organization Theory and Analysis*, (pp. 227–53). London: Sage.

Campbell, K. (ed.) (1992) *Critical Feminism: Argument in the Disciplines*. Milton Keynes: Open University Press.

The Carnegie Foundation for the Advancement of Teaching (1990) Women Faculty Excel as Campus Citizens, *Change*, 22, pp. 39–43.

Carroll, B. (1990) The Politics of Originality: Women and the Class System of the Intellect. *Journal of Women's History* 2 (2), pp. 136–63.

Carter, P. and Jeffs, T. (1995) The Don Juans, *Times Higher Educational Supplement* 10, pp. 16–17.

Cass, B. et al. (1983) *Why So Few? Women Academics in Australian Universities*. Sydney: Sydney University Press.

Cherryholmes, C. (1988). *Power and Criticism: Poststructural Investigations in Education*. New York: Teachers College Press.

Chodorow, N. (1978) *The Reproduction of Mothering: Psychoanalysis and the Sociology of Gender*, Berkeley: University of California Press.

Chodorow, N. (1995) Gender as a Personal and Cultural Construction, *Signs*, 20(3), pp. 516–44.

Clarke, M. and Stewart, J. (1992) Empowerment: a Theme for the 1990s, *Local Government Studies* 1, pp. 18–26.

Clarke, J., Cochrane, A. and McLaughlin, E. (1994) *Managing Social Policy*. London: Sage.

Clegg, S. (1993) *Modern Organizations: Organization Studies in the Postmodern World*. London: Sage.

Cochrane, A. (1993) *Whatever Happened to Local Government?* Milton Keynes: Open University Press.

Cockburn, C. (1989) Equal Opportunities: the Long and Short Agendas, *Industrial Relations Journal* 20 (3), pp. 213–25.

Cockburn, C. (1991) *In the Way of Women: Men's Resistance to Sex Equality in Organizations*, Basingstoke: Macmillan.

Coffield, F. and Vignobles, A. (1997) *Widening Participation in Higher Education by Ethnic Minorities, Women and Alternative Students* Report No. 5. The National Committee of Inquiry into Higher Education.

Coleman, G. (1991) *Investigating Organizations: a Feminist Perspective.* University of Bristol: School for Advanced Urban Studies.

Commission of University Career Opportunity (CUCO) (1994) *A Report on the Universities' Policies and Practices in Employment.* London: CUCO.

Condor, S. (1986) Sex Role Beliefs and 'Traditional' Women: Feminist and Intergroup Perspectives, in S. Wilkinson (ed.) *Feminist Social Psychology: Developing Theory and Practice* (pp. 97–118). Milton Keynes: Open University Press.

Conger, J. (1989) Leadership: the Art of Empowering Others, *The Academy of Management Executive* (1), pp. 17–24.

Conway, D. (1992) Do Women Benefit From Equal Opportunities Legislation?, in C. Quest (ed.) *Equal Opportunities: A Feminist Fallacy* (pp. 53–67). London: IEA Health and Welfare Unit.

Coppock, V., Haydon, D. and Richter, I. (1995) *The Illusions of 'Post-Feminism': New Women, Old Myths.* London: Taylor and Francis.

Corrin, C. (1994) Lesbians in Higher Education, in S. Davies, C. Lubelska and J. Quinn (eds) *Changing the Subject: Women in Higher Education* (pp. 58–74). London: Taylor and Francis.

Cowan, J. K. (1996) Being a Feminist in Contemporary Greece: Similarity and Difference Reconsidered, in N. Charles and F. Hughes-Freeland (eds) *Practising Feminism: Identity, Difference, Power* (pp. 61–85). London: Routledge.

Cox, D. (1992) Crisis and Opportunity in Health Service Management, in R. Loveridge, and K. Starkey (eds) *Continuity and Crisis in the NHS.* Milton Keynes: Open University Press.

The Croham Report (1987) *Review of the University Grants Committee,* Cmnd. 81. London: HMSO.

Culley, M. and Portuges, C. (eds) (1985) *Gendered Subjects: the Dynamics of Feminist Teaching.* London: Routledge and Kegan Paul.

Currie, D. and Kazi, H. (1987) Academic Feminism and the Process of De-radicalization: Re-examining the Issues, *Feminist Review* 25, pp. 77–98.

Dahlerup, D. (1987) Confusing Concepts – Confusing Reality: a Theoretical Discussion of the Patriarchal State, in A. Showstack Sassoon (ed.) *Women and the State* (pp. 93–127). London: Hutchinson.

Davies, C. (1995) *Gender and the Professional Predicament in Nursing.* Milton Keynes: Open University Press.

Davies, C. and Holloway, P. (1995) Troubling Transformations: Gender Regimes and Organizational Culture in the Academy, in L. Morley and V. Walsh (eds) *Feminist Academics: Creative Agents for Change* (pp. 7–21). London: Taylor and Francis.

Deem, R. (1992a) Feminist Interventions in Schooling 1975–89, in A. Rattansi and D. Reeder (eds) *Rethinking Radical Education: Essays in Honour of Brian Simon* (pp. 118–41). London: Lawrence and Wishart.

Deem, R. (1992b) School Governing Bodies – Public Concerns and Private Interests', Paper presented to the International Conference on

Accountability and Control in Educational Settings, CEDAR, University of Warwick.

Deem, R. (1996) Border Territories: a Journey through Sociology, Education and Women's Studies, *British Journal of Sociology of Education* 17(1) pp. 5–19.

De Groot, J. and Maynard, M. (eds) (1993) *Women's Studies in the 1990s: Doing Things Differently*. Basingstoke: Macmillan.

Delphy, C. (1996) Rethinking Sex and Gender, in D. Leonard and L. Adkins (eds) *Sex in Question: French Materialist Feminism* (pp. 30–41). London: Taylor and Francis.

Department of Education and Science (1987) *Higher Education: Meeting the Challenge*. London: HMSO.

Department of Education and Science (1991) *Mature Students in Higher Education 1975–1988*. London: HMSO.

Dewey, J. (1933) *How We Think*. Chicago: Henry Regnery.

Dewey, J. (1966) *Democracy and Education*. New York: Free Press.

Dreyfus, H. and Rabinow, P. (1982) Afterword to *Michel Foucault: Beyond Structuralism and Hermeneutics*. Chicago: University of Chicago Press.

Dubois, B. (1983) Passionate Scholarship: Notes on Values, Knowing and Method in Feminist Social Science, in G. Bowles, and R. Duelli Klein (eds) *Theories of Women's Studies* (pp. 105–16). London: Routledge and Kegan Paul.

Dyhouse, C. (1995) *No Distinction of Sex? Women in British Universities 1870–1939*. London: UCL Press.

Edelman, M. (1977) *Political Language: Words that Succeed and Policies that Fail*. New York: Academic Press.

Eduards, M. (1991) Toward a Third Way: Women's Politics and Welfare Policies in Sweden. *Social Research* 58(3) (Fall) pp. 677–705.

Edwards, R. (1993) *Mature Women Students*. London: Taylor and Francis.

Eichler, M. (1988) *Non-Sexist Research Methods*. London: Allen and Unwin.

Eisenstein, H. (1984) *Contemporary Feminist Thought*. London: Unwin.

Elam, D. (1994) *Feminism and Deconstruction*. London: Routledge.

Ellsworth, E. (1989) Why Doesn't This Feel Empowering? Working through Repressive Myths of Critical Pedagogy. *Harvard Educational Review* 59(3), pp. 297–324.

Epstein, D. (1995) In Our (New) Right Minds: The Hidden Curriculum and the Academy, in L. Morley, and V. Walsh (eds) *Feminist Academics: Creative Agents for Change* (pp. 56–72). London: Taylor and Francis.

Evans, M. (1991) The Problem of Gender for Women's Studies, in J. Aaron and S. Walby (eds) *Out of the Margins: Women's Studies in the 1990s* (pp. 67–74). London: Taylor and Francis.

Evans, M. (ed.) (1994) *The Woman Question* (2nd edition). London: Sage.

Evans, M. (1995) Ivory Towers: Life in the Mind, in L. Morley and V. Walsh, (eds) *Feminist Academics: Creative Agents for Change* (pp. 73-85). London: Taylor and Francis.

Faludi, S. (1992) *Backlash – the Undeclared War Against Women*. London: Chatto and Windus.

Farish, M. et al. (1995) *Equal Opportunities in Colleges and Universities*. Milton Keynes: SRHE/Open University Press.

Farnham, C. (1987) *The Impact of Feminist Research in the Academy*. Bloomington: University of Indiana Press.

Ferguson, K. (1983) Bureaucracy and Public Life, *Administration and Society* 15(3) 295–322.

Ferguson, K. (1984) *The Feminist Case Against Bureaucracy*. Philadelphia: Temple University Press.

Finch, J. (1984) It's Great Having Someone to Talk To: the Ethics and Politics of Interviewing Women, in C. Bell and H. Roberts (eds) *Social Researching: Politics, Problems and Practice* (pp. 70–87). London: Routledge and Kegan Paul.

Fine, M. (1992) *Disruptive Voices*. Ann Arbor: University of Michigan Press.

Fine, M. (1994) Dis-stance and Other Stances: Negotiations of Power Inside Feminist Research, in A. Gitlin (ed.) *Power and Method: Political Activism and Educational Research* (pp. 13–35). London: Routledge.

Fine, M. and Gordon, S. M. (1991) Effacing the Center and the Margins, *Feminism and Psychology*, 1(1), pp. 19–25.

Fineman, S. (ed.) (1993) *Emotion in Organizations*. London: Sage.

Fisher, S. (1994) *Stress in Academic Life: The Mental Assembly Line*. Milton Keynes: Open University Press.

Fonow, M. and Cook, J. (eds) (1991) *Beyond Methodology: Feminist Scholarship as Lived Research*. Bloomington: Indiana University Press.

Forbes, I. (1989) Unequal Partners: The Implementation of Equal Opportunities Policies in Western Europe. *Public Administration* 67(1) (Spring), pp. 19–38.

Forbes, I. (1991) Equal Opportunity: Radical, Liberal and Conservative Critiques, in E. Meehan and S. Sevenhuijsen (eds) *Equality Politics and Gender*. (pp. 17–35), London: Sage.

Foucault, M. (1980) Body/Power, in C. Gordon (ed.) *Michel Foucault: Power/Knowledge*, Brighton: Harvester Press.

Fox-Keller, E. and Moglen, H. (1987) Competition and Feminism: Conflicts for Academic Women, *Signs* 12(3), pp. 493–511.

Franzway, S., Court, D. and Connell, R. (1989) *Staking a Claim: Feminism, Bureaucracy and the State*. Cambridge: Polity Press.

Freire, P. (1973) *Pedagogy of the Oppressed*. Harmondsworth: Penguin Books.

Freire, P. (1985) *The Politics of Education: Culture, Power and Liberation*. South Hadley, MA: Bergin and Garvey.

Freud, A. (1937) *The Ego and the Mechanisms of Defence*. London: Hogarth Press.

Fuchs Epstein, C. (1988) *Deceptive Distinctions: Sex, Gender and the Social Order*. New Haven: Yale University Press.

Fuss, D. (1989) *Essentially Speaking: Feminism, Nature and Difference*. London: Routledge.

Garber, L. (ed.) (1994) *Tilting the Tower: Lesbians, Teaching, Queer Subjects*, New York: Routledge.

Gherardi, S. (1994) The Gender We Think, The Gender We Do in Our Everyday Organizational Lives. *Human Relations* 47(6), pp. 591–610.

Gherardi, S. (1995) *Gender, Symbolism and Organizational Cultures*. London: Sage.

Gibson, R. (1996) Deaf Women in Higher Education, in L. Morley and V.

Walsh (eds) *Breaking Boundaries: Women in Higher Education* (pp. 67–77). London: Taylor and Francis.

Gilligan, C. (1982) *In a Different Voice: Psychological Theory and Women.* Cambridge, MA.: Harvard University Press.

Gipps, C. (1993) The Profession of Educational Research, *British Educational Research Journal* 19(1), pp. 3–16.

Giroux, H. (1983) *Theory and Resistance in Education: a Pedagogy for the Opposition.* London: Heinemann.

Giroux, H. (1985) Teachers as Transformative Intellectuals, *Social Education* 38(2), pp. 33–9.

Giroux, H. (1988) *Schooling and the Struggle for Public Life: Critical Pedagogy in the Modern Age.* Minneapolis: University of Minnesota Press.

Giroux, H. (1991) *Postmodernism, Feminism and Cultural Politics.* Albany, NY: Albany State University Press.

Gitlin, A. (ed.) (1994) *Power and Method: Political Activism and Educational Research*, London: Routledge.

Glaser, B. and Strauss, A. (1967) *The Discovery of Grounded Theory.* Chicago: Aldine Publishing.

Gore, J. (1992) What Can We Do For You? Struggling over Empowerment in Critical and Feminist Pedagogy, in C. Luke and J. Gore (eds) *Feminisms and Critical Pedagogy* (pp. 54–73). London: Routledge.

Gore, J. (1993) *The Struggle for Pedagogies.* London: Routledge.

Gramsci, A. (1971) *Selections from the Prison Notebooks.* London: Lawrence and Wishart.

Griffiths, M. (1993) Self-Identity and Self-Esteem: Achieving Equality in Education, *Oxford Review of Education* 19(3) pp. 301–17.

Griffiths, M. (1995a) Making a Difference: Feminism, Post-modernism and the Methodology of Educational Research, *British Educational Research Journal* 21(2), pp. 219–35.

Griffiths, M. (1995b) *Feminisms and the Self: The Web of Identity.* London: Routledge.

Guardian (1995) 10 February, p. 7.

Haavio-Mannila, E. et al. (eds) (1985) *Unfinished Democracy: Women in Nordic Politics.* Oxford: Pergamon Press.

Habermas, J. (1981) New Social Movements, *Telos* 49, pp. 33–8.

Habermas, J. (1984) *The Theory of Communicative Action. Vol. 1, Reason and Rationalization of Society* (trans. Thomas McCarthy). Boston, MA: Beacon Press.

Habermas, J. (1987) *The Philosophical Discourse of Modernity* (trans. F. Lawrence). Cambridge: Polity Press.

Halsey, A. (1992) *Decline of Donnish Dominion: The British Academic Profession in the Twentieth Century.* Oxford: Oxford University Press.

Halsey, A. (1993) Trends in Access and Equity in Higher Education: Britain in International Perspective, *Oxford Review of Education* 19(2), pp. 129–40.

Ham, C. and Hill, M. (1993) *The Policy Process in the Modern Capitalist State.* London: Harvester Wheatsheaf.

Hanmer, J. (1991) On Course: Women's Studies – a Transitional Programme, in J. Aaron and S. Walby (eds) *Out of the Margins: Women's Studies in the Nineties* (pp. 105–14). London: Taylor and Francis.

The Hansard Society (1990) *The Report of the Hansard Society Commission on Women at the Top*. London: The Hansard Society.

Haraway, D. (1988) Situated Knowledges: The Science Question in Feminism and the Privilege of the Partial Perspective, *Feminist Studies* 14(3) (Fall), pp. 573–99.

Harding, S. (1991) *Whose Science? Whose Knowledge?* Milton Keynes: Open University Press.

Hardy Aitken, S. et al. (1987) Trying Transformations: Curriculum Integration and the Problem of Resistance, *Signs* 12(2), pp. 255–75.

Hargreaves, A. (1994) *Changing Teachers, Changing Times: Teachers' Work and Culture in the Postmodern Age*. London: Cassell.

Harrison, M. J. (1994) Quality Issues in Higher Education: A Post-modern Phenomenon?, in G. Doherty (ed.), *Developing Quality Systems in Education* (pp. 52–67). London: Routledge.

Haug, F. (1989) Lessons from the Women's Movement in Europe, *Feminist Review* 3(1), pp. 107–16.

Haug, F. (1992) *Beyond Female Masochism: Memory Work and Politics*. London: Verso.

Hayek, F. A. (1944) *Road to Serfdom*. London: Routledge and Kegan Paul.

Hearn, J. (1994) The Organization(s) of Violence: Men, Gender Relations, Organizations and Violences, *Human Relations* 47(6), pp. 731–54.

Hearn, J., Shepphard, D., Tancred-Sheriff, P. and Burrell, G. (eds) (1989) *The Sexuality of Organization*. London: Sage.

Hearn, J. and Parkin, W. (1987) *Sex at Work*. Brighton: Wheatsheaf Books.

Hearn, J. and Parkin, W. (1993) Organizations, Multiple Oppressions and Postmodernism, in J. Hassard and M. Parker (eds) *Postmodernism and Organizations* (pp. 148–62). London: Sage.

Hennessy, R. (1993) *Materialist Feminism and the Politics of Discourse*. London: Routledge.

Henry, M. (1994) Ivory Towers and Ebony Women: The Experiences of Black Women in Higher Education, in S. Davies, C. Lubelska and J. Quinn (eds) *Changing the Subject: Women in Higher Education* (pp. 42–57). London: Taylor and Francis.

Henwood, K. and Pidgeon, N. (1995) Remaking the Link: Qualitative Research and Feminist Standpoint Theory, *Feminism and Psychology*, 5(1), pp. 7–30.

Her Majesty's Inspectorate (HMI) (1991) *Aspects of Education in the USA: Quality and its Assurance in Higher Education*. London: HMSO.

Her Majesty's Inspectorate (HMI) (1993) *Aspects of Women's Studies Courses in Higher Education*, 371/92/NS. London: HMSO.

Heseltine, M. (1980) Ministers and Management in Whitehall, *Management Services in Whitehall*, 35.

Heward, C. and Taylor, P. (1993) Effective and Ineffective Equal Opportunities Policies in Higher Education, *Critical Social Policy* 37, pp. 75–94.

The Higher Education Quality Council (HEQC) Report (1994) *Choosing to Change*. London: HEQC.

Hill Collins, P. (1990) *Black Feminist Thought: Knowledge, Consciousness and the Politics of Empowerment*. London: Routledge.

Holland, J. and Ramazanoglu, C. (1995) Accounting for Sexuality, Living Sexual Politics. Can Feminist Research be Valid? in J. Holland, M. Blair and S. Sheldon (eds) *Debates and Issues in Feminist Research and Pedagogy* (pp. 273–91). Clevedon: Multilingual Matters/Open University Press.

Holloway, W. (1994) Relations among Women: Using the Group to Unite Theory and Experience, in G. Griffin et al. (eds) *Stirring It: Challenges for Feminism* (pp. 211–22). London: Taylor and Francis.

hooks, b. (1987) Feminism: A Movement to End Sexist Oppression, in A. Phillips (ed.), *Feminism and Equality*. New York: New York University Press.

hooks, b. (1989) (ed.) *Talking Back: Thinking Feminist – Thinking Black*. London: Sheba.

hooks, b. (1991) *Yearning: Race, Gender and Cultural Politics*. London: Turnaround Press.

hooks, b. (1993) *Sisters of the Yam*. London: Turnaround Press.

hooks, b. (1994) *Teaching to Transgress*. London: Routledge.

Hoyle, E. (1982) Micro-politics of Educational Organisations, *Educational Management and Administration* 10, pp. 87–98.

Hughes, D. (1995) Significant Differences: the Construction of Knowledge, Objectivity, and Dominance, *Women's Studies International Forum* 18(4), pp. 395–406.

Iannello, K. (1992) *Decisions Without Hierarchy: Feminist Interventions in Organization Theory and Practice*. New York: Routledge.

Iantaffi, A. (1996) Women and Disability in Higher Education: a Literature Search, in L. Morley and V. Walsh (eds) *Breaking Boundaries: Women in Higher Education* (pp. 180–86). London: Taylor and Francis.

Ince, M. (1996) Chipping Away at the Glass Ceiling, *Times Higher Educational Supplement*, 26 July, pp. 16–17.

Jackson, D. (1989) *Changes in Higher Education In Australia*, Report to the Association of Commonwealth Universities.

Jackson, D. (1990) Women Working in Higher Education: a Review of the Position of Women in Higher Education and Policy Developments, *Higher Education Quarterly* 44(4), pp. 297–324.

Jacobs, J. (1992) *Systems of Survival: A Dialogue on the Moral Functions of Commerce and Politics*. London: Hodder and Stoughton.

Jaggar, A. (1983) *Feminist Politics and Human Nature*. Brighton: Harvester-Wheatsheaf.

Janeway, E. (1971) *Man's World, Woman's Place*. New York: Delta.

Jaques, E. (1955) Social Systems as a Defense against Persecutory and Depressive Anxiety, in M. Klein, P. Heinmann and R. Money-Kyrle (eds) *New Directions in Psychoanalysis* (pp. 478–98). London: Tavistock.

Jarratt Report (1985) *Report of the Steering Committee for Efficiency Studies in Universities*. London: CVCP.

Jeffs, T. and Smith, M. (1994) Young People, Youth Work and A New Authoritarianism, *Youth and Policy* 46 (Autumn), pp. 17–32.

Jewson, N. and Mason, D. (1986) The Theory and Practice of Equal Opportunities Policies: Liberal and Radical Approaches, *Sociological Review* 34(2), pp. 307–34.

Jewson, N., Mason, D., Bowen, R., Mulvaney, K. and Parmar, S. (1991)

Universities and Ethnic Minorities: the Public Face, *New Community* 17(2), pp. 183–99.

Kandola, R. S. et al. (1991) *Equal Opportunities Can Damage Your Health: Stress Among Equal Opportunities Personnel*. Oxford: Pearn Kandola Downs.

Kanter, R. (1977) *Men and Women of the Corporation*. New York: Basic Books.

Kassimati, K. (1993) Female Education and Employment: Problems of Equal Opportunities in Greece, in A. Yotopoulos-Maraugopolous (ed.) *Women's Rights, Human Rights* (pp. 164–80). Athens: Hestia Publications.

Kelly, L., Regan, L. and Burton, S. (1992) Defending the Indefensible? Quantitative Methods and Feminist Research, in H. Hinds, A. Phoenix and J. Stacey (eds) *Working Out: New Directions for Women's Studies* (pp. 149–60). London: Taylor and Francis.

Kenway, J. (1995) Feminist Theories of the State: To Be or Not to Be?, in M. Blair, J. Holland, and S. Sheldon (eds) *Identity and Diversity: Gender and the Experience of Education* (pp. 123–42). Clevedon: Multilingual Matters.

Kenway, J. and Modra, H. (1992) Feminist Pedagogy and Emancipatory Possibilities, in C. Luke, and J. Gore (eds) *Feminisms and Critical Pedagogy* (pp. 138–66). London: Routledge.

Kickert, W. (1991) 'Steering at a Distance': a New Paradigm of Public Governance in Dutch Higher Education. Paper for the European Consortium for Political Research, University of Essex.

Kitzinger, C. and Perkins, R. (1993) *Changing Our Minds: Lesbian Feminism and Psychology*. London: Onlywoman Press.

Kogan, M. (1993) The End of the Dual System?, in C. Gellert (Ed.) *Higher Education in Europe* (pp. 47–58). London: Jessica Kingsley Publications.

Kriesberg, S. (1992) *Transforming Power: Domination, Empowerment and Education*. New York: State University of New York.

Kulke, C. (1993) Equality Politics and Difference: Approaches to Feminist Theory and Politics, in J. De Groot and M. Maynard (eds) *Women's Studies in the 1990s: Doing Things Differently*. London: Macmillan.

Lacey, C. (1977) *Socialization of Teachers*. London: Methuen.

Ladwig, J. G. and Gore, J. M. (1994) Extending Power and Specifying Method within the Discourse of Activist Research, in A. Gitlin (ed.) *Power and Method: Political Activism and Educational Research* (pp. 227–38). London: Routledge.

Lather, P. (1986) Research as Praxis. *Harvard Educational Review* 56(3), pp. 257–77.

Lather, P. (1991) *Getting Smart: Feminist Research and Pedagogy With/in the Postmodern*. New York: Routledge.

Laurence, J. (1991). Re-membering that Special Someone: On the Question of Articulating a Genuine Feminine Presence in the Classroom. *History of Education Review* 20(2), pp. 53–65.

Le Grand, J. and Bartlett, W. (eds) (1993) *Quasi-markets and Social Policy*. Basingstoke: Macmillan.

Legge, K. (1987) Women in Personnel Management: Uphill Climb or Downward Slide?, in A. Spencer and D. Podmore (eds) *In a Man's World:*

Essays on Women in Male-Dominated Professions (pp. 33–60). London: Tavistock.

Leicester, M. (1993) *Race for a Change in Continuing and Higher Education.* Buckingham: SRHE/Open University Press.

Leicester, M. and Lovell, T. (1994). Equal Opportunities and University Practice: Race, Gender and Disability: a Comparative Perspective. *Journal of Further and Higher Education* 18(2), pp. 220–24.

Lennon, K. and Whitford, M. (eds) (1994) *Knowing the Difference: Feminist Perspectives in Epistemology.* London: Routledge.

Lewis, M. (1990) Interrupting Patriarchy: Politics, Resistance and Transformation in the Feminist Classroom, *Harvard Educational Review* 60(4), pp. 467–88.

Lewis, M. (1994) *Without a Word: Teaching Beyond Women's Silence.* New York: Routledge.

Lieberman, M. (1981) The Most Important Thing for You to Know, in G. Desole and L. Hoffman (eds) *Rocking the Boat: Academic Women and Academic Processes.* New York: Modern Languages Association of America.

Lieblich, A. and Josselson, R. (eds) (1994) *Exploring Identity and Gender: the Narrative Study of Lives.* London: Sage.

Lipsky, M. (1980) *Street-Level Bureaucracy.* London: Russell Sage.

Lloyd, M. (1995) Does She Boil Eggs? Towards a Feminist Model of Disability, in M. Blair, J. Holland and S. Sheldon (eds) *Identity and Diversity: Gender and the Experience of Education*, (pp. 211–24). Clevedon: Multilingual Matters.

Loden, M. (1986) *Feminine Leadership or How to Succeed in Business Without Being One of the Boys.* New York: Time Books.

Lorde, A. (1984) *Sister Outsider.* Trumansberg, NY: The Crossing Press.

Lown, J. (1995) Feminist Perspectives, in M. Blair, J. Holland, and S. Sheldon (eds) *Identity and Diversity: Gender and the Experience of Education* (pp. 107–22). Clevedon: Multilingual Matters.

Luke, C. (1994) Women in the Academy: The Politics of Speech and Silence, *British Journal of Sociology of Education* 15(2), pp. 211–30.

Luke, C. and Gore, J. (eds) (1992) *Feminisms and Critical Pedagogy.* London: Routledge.

Lukes, S. (1974) *Power: A Radical View.* London: Macmillan.

Lusted, D. (1986) Why Pedagogy? *Screen* 27(5), pp. 2–14.

Lynch, K. and O'Neill, C. (1994) The Colonisation of Social Class in Education, *British Journal of Sociology of Education*, 15(3), pp. 307–24.

MacGwire, S. (1992) *Best Companies for Women.* London: Pandora Press.

Maguire, M. (1996) In the Prime of Their Lives: Older Women in Higher Education, in L. Morley and V. Walsh (eds) *Breaking Boundaries: Women in Higher Education* (pp. 24–36). London: Taylor and Francis.

Mahony, P. (1988) Oppressive Pedagogy: The Importance of Process in Women's Studies. *Women's Studies International Forum* 11(2), pp. 103–8.

Maidment, R. and Thompson, G. (eds) (1993) *Managing the United Kingdom: an Introduction to its Political Economy and Public Policy.* London: Sage.

Marshall, C. and Anderson, G. (1994) Rethinking the Public and Private Spheres: Feminist and Cultural Studies Perspectives on the Politics of

Education, *Journal of Education Policy Politics of Education Yearbook*, pp. 169–82.

Marshall, J. (1986) Exploring the Experiences of Women Managers: Towards Rigour in Qualitative Methods, in S. Wilkinson (ed.) *Feminist Social Psychology*, (pp. 193–209). Milton Keynes: Open University Press.

Marshall, J. (1995) *Women Managers Moving On*. London: Routledge.

Martin, J. (1990) Deconstructing Organizational Taboos: the Suppression of Gender Conflict in Organizations. *Organization Science* 1(4), pp. 339–59.

Martin, L., Gutman, H. and Hutton, P. (eds) (1988) *Technologies of the Self: a Seminar with Michel Foucault*. London: Tavistock.

Maynard, M. (1993) Feminism and the Possibilities of a Postmodern Research Practice, *British Journal of Sociology of Education* 14(3), pp. 327–31.

Maynard, M. (1994) Methods, Practice and Epistemology: the Debate about Feminism and Research, in M. Maynard and J. Purvis (eds) *Researching Women's Lives from a Feminist Perspective* (pp. 10–26). London: Taylor and Francis.

Maynard, M. (1996) Challenging the Boundaries: Towards an Anti-racist Women's Studies, in M. Maynard and J. Purvis (eds) *New Frontiers in Women's Studies: Knowledge, Identity and Nationalism* (pp. 11–29). London: Taylor and Francis.

Maynard, M. and Purvis, J. (eds) (1994) *Researching Women's Lives from a Feminist Perspective*. London: Taylor and Francis.

McAuley, J. (1987) Women Academics: A Case Study in Inequality, in A. Spencer and D. Podmore (eds) *In a Man's World: Essays on Women in Male-Dominated Professions* (pp. 158–81). London: Tavistock.

McDermott, P. (1994) *Politics and Scholarship: Feminist Academic Journals and the Production of Knowledge*. Chicago: University of Illinois Press.

McIntosh, P. (1985) *Feeling Like a Fraud*, Work in Progress Paper No. 18. Wellesley, MA: The Stone Center.

McNay, L. (1992) *Foucault and Feminism*. Cambridge: Polity Press.

McNeil, M. (1993) Dancing with Foucault, in C. Ramazanoglu (ed.) *Up Against Foucault: Explorations and Some Tensions Between Foucault and Feminism* (pp. 147–75). London: Routledge.

McRobbie, A. (1982) The Politics of Feminist Research, *Feminist Review* (12), pp. 46–57.

McWilliam, E. (1996) Touchy Subjects: a Risky Inquiry into Pedagogical Pleasure, *British Educational Research Journal* 22(3), pp. 305–17.

Measor, L. (1985) Interviewing: a Strategy in Qualitative Research, in R. Burgess (ed.), *Strategies of Educational Research: Qualitative Methods* (pp. 55–77). Lewes: The Falmer Press.

Menzies, I. (1990) The Functioning of Social Systems as a Defense against Anxiety: an Empirical Study of the Nursing Service of a General Hospital, in E. Trist and H. Murphy (eds) *The Social Engagement of Social Science, Vol. 1* (pp. 439–75). London: Tavistock.

Mercer, G. (1997). Feminist Pedagogy to the Letter: a Musing on Contradictions, in L. Stanley (ed.), *Knowing Feminisms*. London: Sage.

Messer-Davidow, E. (1991) Know-How, in J. Hartman and E. Messer-

Davidow (eds) *(En)gendering Knowledge* (pp. 281–309). Knoxville, TX: University of Tennessee.

Milan Women's Bookstore Collective (1990) *Sexual Difference: a Theory of Social-Symbolic Practice*, Bloomington: Indiana University Press.

Miller, A. (1987) *The Drama of Being a Child*. London: Virago.

Mills, A. J. (1988) Organization, Gender and Culture, *Organization Studies* 9 (3), pp. 351–69.

Mills, A. and Tancred, P. (eds) (1992) *Gendering Organizational Analysis* London: Sage.

Minh-ha, T. T. (1989) *Woman, Native, Other: Writing Postcoloniality and Feminism*. Bloomington: Indiana University Press.

Mirza, H. S. (1995) Black Women in Education: Defining a Space/Finding a Place, in L. Morley and V. Walsh (eds) *Feminist Academics: Creative Agents for Change* (pp. 145–55). London: Taylor and Francis.

Modood, T. (1993) The Number of Ethnic Minority Students in British Higher Education: Some Grounds for Optimism, *Oxford Review of Education* 19(2), pp. 167–82.

Moglen, H. (1983) Power and Empowerment, *Women's Studies International Forum* 6(2), pp. 131–3.

Morley, L. (1991) Towards a Pedagogy for Empowerment in Community and Youth Work Training, *Youth and Policy* 35 (December), pp. 14–19.

Morley, L. (1992) Women's Studies, Difference and Internalised Oppression, *Women's Studies International Forum*, 15(4), pp. 517–25.

Morley, L. (1993) Women's Studies as Empowerment of 'Non-Traditional' Learners in Community and Youth Work Training, in M. Kennedy, C. Lubelska and V. Walsh (eds) *Making Connections: Women's Studies, Women's Movements and Women's Lives*, (pp. 118–29). London: Taylor and Francis.

Morley, L. (1994) Glass Ceiling or Iron Cage: Women in UK Academia, *Journal of Gender, Work and Organization* 1(4), pp. 194–204.

Morley, L. (1995a) Empowerment and The New Right, *Youth and Policy*, 51, pp. 1–10.

Morley, L. (1995b) Measuring the Muse: Creativity, Writing and Career Development, in L. Morley, and V. Walsh (eds) *Feminist Academics: Creative Agents for Change* (pp. 116–30). London: Taylor and Francis.

Morley, L. (1995c) An Agenda for Gender: Women in the University, *European Journal Of Women's Studies* 22(2), pp. 271–5.

Morley, L. (1995d) The Micropolitics of Women's Studies, in M. Maynard, and J. Purvis (eds) *(Hetero)sexual Politics* (pp. 171–85). London: Taylor and Francis.

Morley, L. (1997) A Class of One's Own: Women, Social Class and the Academy, in P. Mahony and C. Zmroczek (eds) *Class Matters* (pp. 109–22). London: Taylor and Francis.

Morley, L. and Walsh, V. (eds) (1995) *Feminist Academics; Creative Agents for Change*. London: Taylor and Francis.

Morley, L. and Walsh, V. (eds) (1996) *Breaking Boundaries: Women in Higher Education*. London: Taylor and Francis.

Morris, J. (1993) Feminism and Disability, *Feminist Review* 43 (Spring), pp. 57–70.

Morris, J. (1995) Personal and Political: a Feminist Perspective on Researching Physical Disability, in J. Holland, M. Blair and S. Sheldon (eds) *Debates and Issues in Feminist Research and Pedagogy* (pp. 262–72). Clevedon: Multilingual Matters.

Morris, M. (1988) The Pirate's Fiancée: Feminists and Philosophers, or Maybe Tonight it Will Happen, in I. Diamond and L. Quilby (eds) *Feminism and Foucault* (pp. 21–42). Boston: Northeastern University Press.

Moussourou, L. and Spiliotopoulis, S. (1984) Women at Work in Greece: the Sociological and Legal Perspectives, in M. J. Davidson and C. L. Cooper (eds) *Women at Work* (pp. 123–50). Chichester: John Wiley.

Neal, S. (1995) Researching Powerful People from a Feminist and Anti-Racist Perspective: a Note on Gender, Collusion and Marginality, *British Educational Research Journal* 21 (4), pp. 517–31.

Nemiroff, G.H. (1989) Beyond 'Talking Heads': Towards an Empowering Pedagogy of Women's Studies, *Atlantis* 15 (1), pp. 1–15.

Newman, J. (1994) The Limits of Management: Gender and the Politics of Change, in J. Clarke, A. Cochrane and E. McLaughlin (eds) *Managing Social Policy* (pp. 182–209). London: Sage.

Newman, J. (1995) Gender and Cultural Change, in C. Itzin and J. Newman (eds) *Gender, Culture and Organizational Change* (pp. 11–29). London: Routledge.

Newman, J. and Williams, F. (1995) Diversity and Change: Gender, Welfare and Organizational Relations, in C. Itzin and J. Newman (eds), *Gender, Culture and Organizational Change* (pp. 108–23). London: Routledge.

Nicolson, P. (1996) *Gender, Power and Organisation*, London: Routledge.

O'Brien, M. and Whitmore, E. (1989) Empowering Women Students in Higher Education, *McGill Journal of Education*, 24(3), pp. 305–20.

Orner, M. (1992) Interrupting the Calls for Student Voice in 'Liberatory Education': a Feminist Poststructuralist Perspective, in C. Luke and J. Gore (eds) *Feminisms and Critical Pedagogy* (pp. 74–89). New York: Routledge.

Orwell, G. (1945) *Animal Farm*. London: Penguin Books.

Park, A. (1992) Women, Men, and the Academic Hierarchy: Exploring the Relationship Between Rank and Sex, *Oxford Review of Education* 18(3) pp. 227–39.

Patai, D. and Koertge, N. (1994). *Professing Feminism: Cautionary Tales from the Strange World of Women's Studies*. New York: Basic Books.

Pearce, L. (1992) Demanding More Attention, *AUT Woman* 25 (Spring), p. 2.

Personnel Management (1994) 5(6) June.

Phoenix, A. (1994) Practising Feminist Research: the Intersection of Gender and 'Race' in the Research Process, in M. Maynard and J. Purvis (eds) *Researching Women's Lives from a Feminist Perspective* (pp. 49–71). London: Taylor and Francis.

Pollitt, C. (1993). *Managerialism and the Public Services: Cuts or Cultural Change in the 1990s*, (2nd edition). Oxford: Basil Blackwell.

Polsky, A. J. (1991) *The Rise of the Therapeutic State*, Princeton, NJ: Princeton University Press.

Popkewitz, T. and Brennan, M. (1997) Restructuring of Social and Political Theory in Education: Foucault and a Social Epistemology of School Practices. *Education Theory* 47(3), pp. 287–313.

Potts, T. and Price, J. (1995) 'Out of the Blood and Spirit of Our Lives': the Place of the Body in Academic Feminism, in L. Morley and V. Walsh (eds) *Feminist Academics: Creative Agents for Change* (pp. 102–15). London: Taylor and Francis.

Pring, R. (1992) Access to Higher Education, *Oxford Review of Education*, 18(2), pp. 125–36.

Purvis, J. (1994) Feminist Theory in Education, *British Journal of Sociology of Education* 15(1), pp. 137–40.

Quest, C. (ed.) (1992) *Equal Opportunities: A Feminist Fallacy*. London: IEA Health and Welfare Unit.

Ramazanoglu, C. (ed.) (1993) *Up against Foucault: Explorations and Some Tensions between Foucault and Feminism*. London: Routledge.

Ramazanoglu, C. (1995) Back to Basics: Heterosexuality, Biology and Why Men Stay on Top, in M. Maynard and J. Purvis (eds) *(Hetero)sexual Politics* (pp. 27–41). London: Taylor and Francis.

Ransom, J. (1993) Feminism, Difference and Discourse: the Limits of Discursive Analysis for Feminism, in C. Ramazanoglu (ed.) *Up against Foucault: Explorations and Some Tensions between Foucault and Feminism* (pp. 123–46). London: Routledge.

Ranson, S., and Stewart, J. (1994) *Management for the Public Domain: Enabling the Learning Society*. London: Macmillan.

Rassool, N. (1995) Black Women as 'Other' in the Academy, in L. Morley and V. Walsh (eds) *Feminist Academics: Creative Agents for Change* (pp. 22–41). London: Taylor and Francis.

Raymond, J. (1985) Women's Studies: a Knowledge of One's Own, in M. Culley and C. Portuges (eds) *Gendered Subjects: the Dynamics of Feminist Teaching*, (pp. 49–63). London: Routledge and Kegan Paul.

Reinharz, S. (1983) Experiential Analysis: a Contribution to Feminist Research, in G. Bowles and R. D. Klein (eds) *Theories of Women's Studies* (pp. 162–91). London: Routledge.

Richards, H. and Tysome, T. (1996) £5.8 billion, *Times Higher Education Supplement*, 20 September, p. 1.

Robbins (Lord) (1963) *Committee on Higher Education Report*, CMND. 2154. London: HMSO.

Roberts, H. (ed.) (1981) *Doing Feminist Research*. London: Routledge and Kegan Paul.

Robinson, H. A. (1994) *The Ethnography of Empowerment: The Transformative Power of Classroom Interaction*. Washington: Taylor and Francis.

Rose, H. (1994) *Love, Power and Knowledge: Towards a Feminist Transformation of the Sciences*. Oxford: Polity Press.

Rosser, S. (1988) Good Science: Can it Ever Be Gender Free? *Women's Studies International Forum* 11 (1), pp. 13–19.

Rothschild, J. and Davies, C. (1994) Organizations Through the Lens of Gender: Introduction to the Special Issue, *Human Relations* 47(6) pp. 583–90.

Rowan, J. and Reason, P. (eds) (1981) *Human Inquiry*. Chichester: Wiley.

Rowbothom, S. (1973) *Woman's Consciousness, Man's World*. Harmondsworth: Penguin Books.

Rowntree Foundation Inquiry into Income and Wealth (1995) chaired by Sir Peter Bailey.

Said, E. (1994). *Representations of the Intellectual: The 1993 Reith Lectures*. London: Vintage.

Savage, M. and Witz, A. (eds) (1992) *Gender and Bureaucracy*. Oxford: Basil Blackwell.

Sawicki, J. (1988) Feminism and the Power of Foucauldian Disclosure, in J. Arac (ed.) *After Foucault: Humanistic Knowledge, Postmodern Challenges* (pp. 161–78). London: Rutgers Press.

Scheurich, J. (1994) Policy Archaeology: a New Policy Studies Methodology, *Journal of Education Policy* 9(4), pp. 297–316.

Schniedewind, N. (1987) Teaching Feminist Process, *Women's Studies Quarterly XV* (3 & 4) (Fall/Winter), pp. 15–31.

Seller, A. (1994) Should the Feminist Philosopher Stay at Home? in K. Lennon and M. Whitford (Eds) *Knowing the Difference: Feminist Perspectives in Epistemology* (pp. 230–48). London: Routledge.

Sellers, S. (ed.) (1989) *Delighting the Heart: a Notebook by Women Writers*. London: The Women's Press.

Shaw, J. (1995) *Education, Gender and Anxiety*. London: Taylor and Francis.

Shaw, J. and Perrons, D. (eds) (1995) *Making Gender Work: Managing Equal Opportunities*. Milton Keynes: Open University Press.

Shilling, C. (1991) Social Space, Gender Inequalities and Educational Differentiation, *British Journal of Sociology of Education* 12(1), pp. 23–44.

Shilling, C. (1993) *The Body and Social Theory*. London: Sage.

Shor, I. (1980) *Critical Teaching and Everyday Life*. Boston: South End Press.

Shor, I. and Freire, P. (1987) *A Pedagogy for Liberation: Dialogues on Transforming Education*, South Hadley, MA: Bergin and Garvey.

Shore, I. and Roberts, S. (1995) Higher Education and the Panopticon Paradigm: Quality Assessment as 'Disciplinary Technology', *Higher Education* 27(3), pp. 8–17.

Shotter, J. and Gergen, K. (1989) *Texts of Identity*. London: Sage.

Shrewsbury, C. (1987) What is Feminist Pedagogy? *Women's Studies Quarterly*, XV(3 & 4), pp. 6–14.

Sidgewick, S., Mahony, P. and Hextall, I. (1994) A Gap in the Market? A Consideration of Market Relations in Teacher Education, *British Journal of Sociology of Education* 15(4), pp. 467–79.

Siim, B. (1987) The Scandinavian Welfare States: Towards Sexual Equality or a New Kind of Male-Domination? *Acta Sociologica* 30(3/4), pp. 255–70.

Sinfield, A. (1993) *Cultural Politics* Professorial Lecture given at the University of Sussex, 9 March 1993.

Sinfield, A. (1994) *Cultural Politics*, London: Routledge.

Siraj Blatchford, I. (1995) Critical Social Research and the Academy: the Role of Organic Intellectuals in Educational Research, *British Journal of Social Research* 16(2), pp. 205–20.

Skeggs, B. (1991) Postmodernism: What is all the Fuss about? *British Journal of Sociology of Education* 12(2), pp. 255–67.

Skeggs, B. (1994a) The Constraints of Neutrality: The 1988 Education Reform Act and Feminist Research, in D. Halpin and B. Troyna (eds) *Researching Education Policy: Ethical and Methodological Issues* (pp. 75–93). London: The Falmer Press.

Skeggs, B. (1994b) Situating the Production of Feminist Ethnography, in M. Maynard and J. Purvis (eds) *Researching Women's Lives from a Feminist Perspective* (pp. 72–92). London: Taylor and Francis.

Skeggs, B. (1995) Women's Studies in Britain in the 1990s: Entitlement Cultures and Institutional Constraints, *Women's Studies International Forum* 18(4), pp. 475–85.

Smith, D. (1989) Sociological Theory: Methods of Writing Patriarchy, in R. Wallace (ed.) *Feminism and Sociological Theory: Key Issues in Sociological Theory* (pp. 34–64). London: Sage.

Smith, D. (1992) Sociology from Women's Experience: a Reaffirmation. *Sociological Theory* 10 (1), pp. 88–98.

Smyth, A. (1992) A (Political) Postcard from a Peripheral Pre-Modern State (of Mind) or How Alliteration and Parentheses Can Knock You Down Dead in Women's Studies, *Women's Studies International Forum* 15(3) pp. 331–7.

Sparkes, A. (1987) Strategic Rhetoric: A Constraint in Changing the Practice of Teaching, *British Journal of Sociology of Education* 8(1), pp. 35–54.

Spence, J. (1992) The Artist and Illness-interview in *Artpaper – (Art/Community/ Cultural Activism)* 11(5) (January), pp. 11–13.

Spender, D. (1980) Talking in Class, in D. Spender and E. Sarah (eds) *Learning to Lose* (pp. 148–54). London: The Women's Press.

Spender, D. (1982) *Invisible Women: the Schooling Scandal.* London: Writers and Readers Co-operative.

Spivak, G. C. (1987) *In Other Worlds: Essays in Cultural Politics*, London: Methuen.

Stacey, J. (1988) Can There Be a Feminist Ethnography? *Women's Studies International Forum* 11(1), pp. 21–7.

Stanley, L. (1991) Feminist Auto/Biography and Feminist Epistemology. In J. Aaron and S. Walby (eds), *Out of the Margins: Women's Studies in the 1990s* (pp. 204–19). London: Taylor and Francis.

Stanley, L. (ed.). (1997) *Knowing Feminisms.* London: Sage.

Stanley, L. and Wise, S. (1983) *Breaking Out.* London: Routledge.

Stanley, L. and Wise, S. (1991) Feminist Research, Feminist Consciousness and Experiences of Sexism, in M. Fonow and J. Cook (Eds) (1991) *Beyond Methodology: Feminist Scholarship as Lived Research* (pp. 265–83). Bloomington: Indiana University Press.

Stanley, L. and. Wise, S. (1993) *Breaking out Again: Feminist Ontology and Epistemology.* London: Routledge.

Stiver Lie, S., Malik, L. and Harris, D. (eds) (1994) *The Gender Gap in Higher Education.* London: Kogan Page.

Stiver Lie, S. and Malik, L. (1994) Trends in the Gender Gap in Higher Education, in S. Stiver Lie, L. Malik and D. Harris (eds) *The Gender Gap in Higher Education* (pp. 205–13). London and Philadelphia: Kogan Page.

Strauss, A. and Corbin, J. (1990) *Basics of Qualitative Research: Grounded Theory Procedures and Techniques.* London: Sage.

Stuart Mill, J. (1869) *The Subjection of Women* (reprinted in *Three Essays*, 1975 edn). London: Oxford University Press.

Scott-Clark, C., Driscoll, M. and Steiner, R. (1996) Privilege and Prejudice, *Sunday Times*, 7 July, p. 12.

Sutherland, M. (1994) Two Steps Forward and One Step Back: Women in Higher Education in the United Kingdom, in S. Stiver Lie, L. Malik and D. Harris (Eds) *The Gender Gap in Higher Education* (pp. 171–81). London and Philadelphia: Kogan Page.

Tannen, D. (1992) *You Just Don't Understand: Women and Men in Conversation*. New York: Random House.

Taylor, P. (1992) *Ethnic Group for University Entry*, Project Report for CVCP Working Group on Ethnic Data, The Centre for Research in Ethnic Relations, University of Warwick.

Tierney, W. G. (1994) On Method and Hope, in A. Gitlin (ed.) *Power and Method: Political Activism and Educational Research* (pp. 97–115). London: Routledge.

Thomson, R. (1995) Unholy Alliances: The Recent Politics of Sex Education, in L. Dawtrey, J. Holland, M. Hammer and S. Sheldon (eds) *Equality and Inequality in Educational Policy* (pp. 281–99). Clevedon: Multilingual Matters.

Toren, N. (1993) The Temporal Dimension of Gender Inequality in Education, *Higher Education 25*, pp. 439–55.

Tritter, J. (1995) The Context of Educational Policy Research: Changed Constraints, New Methodologies and Ethical Complexities, *British Journal of Sociology of Education*, 16(3), pp. 419–30.

Troyna, B. (1994a) Reforms, Research and Being Reflexive about Being Reflective, in D. Halpin and B. Troyna (eds) *Researching Education Policy: Ethical and Methodological Issues* (pp. 1–14). London: The Falmer Press.

Troyna, B. (1994b) Critical Social Research and Education Policy, *British Journal of Education Studies*, 42(1), pp. 70–84.

Troyna, B. (1994c) Blind Faith? Empowerment and Educational Research, *International Studies in Sociology of Education* 4(1), pp. 3–24.

Van Maanen, J. and Kunda, G. (1989) 'Real Feelings': Emotional Expression and Organizational Culture, in L. L. Cummings and B. M. Shaw (eds) *Research in Organizational Behaviour* 11 (pp. 43–104). Greenwich, CT: JAI Press.

Vince, R. and Broussine, M. (1996) Paradox, Defense and Attachment: Accessing and Working with Emotions and Relations Underlying Organizational Change, *Organization Studies*, 17(1), pp. 1-21.

Von Franz, M. L. (1972) *Creation Myths*. Dallas, TX: Spring Publications.

Wagner, L. (1989) Access and Standards: an Unresolved (and Unresolvable?) Debate, in C. Ball and H. Eggins (eds) *Higher Education Into the 1990s* (pp. 29–37). Milton Keynes: Open University Press.

Walby, S. (1990) *Theorising Patriarchy*. Oxford: Basil Blackwell.

Walby, S. (1994) Towards a Theory of Patriarchy, in *The Polity Reader in Gender Studies* (pp. 22–8). Oxford: Polity Press.

Walford, G. (1992) The Reform of Higher Education, in M. Arnot and L. Barton (eds) *Voicing Concerns: Sociological Perspectives on Contemporary Education Reforms* (pp. 186–200). Wallingford: Triangle Books.

Walford, G. (ed.) (1994) *Researching the Powerful in Education*. London: UCL Press.

Walkerdine, V. (1986) Progressive Pedagogy and Political Struggle, *Screen* 27 (5) pp. 54–60.

Walkerdine, V. (1990) *Schoolgirl Fictions*: London: Verso.

Warwick, A. and Auchmuty, R. (1995) Women's Studies as Feminist Activism, in G. Griffin (ed.) *Feminist Activism in the 1990s* (pp. 182–91). London: Taylor and Francis.

Weber, M. (1948) Bureaucracy, in H. H. Gerth and C. Wright Mills, (eds) *From Max Weber: Essays in Sociology* (pp. 196–244). London: Routledge and Kegan Paul.

Weiler, K. (1991) Freire and a Feminist Pedagogy of Difference, *Harvard Educational Review* 61(4), pp. 449–74.

Weiner, G. (1994) *Feminisms in Education*. Milton Keynes: Open University Press.

White, S. K. (1986) Foucault's Challenge to Critical Theory, *American Political Science Review*, 80(2) 419–31.

Wildavsky, A. (1979) *Speaking Truth to Power: the Art and Craft of Policy Analysis*. Boston: Little, Brown.

Wilton, T. (1995) *A Lesbian Studies Primer*. London: Routledge.

Women's Studies Network UK Association (WSN) (1995*) Courses Handbook and Members' Handbook*. London: Institute of Education.

Yates, L. (1994) Feminist Pedagogy Meets Critical Pedagogy Meets Poststructuralism, *British Journal of Sociology Of Education* 15(3), pp. 429–37.

Young-Eisendrath, P. and Wiedemann, F. (1987) *Female Authority*. London: The Guilford Press.

Zmroczek, C. and Duchen, C. (1991) What are Those Women Up To? Women's Studies and Feminist Research in the European Community, in J. Aaron and S. Walby, (eds) *Out of the Margins: Women's Studies in the 1990s* (pp. 11–29). London: Taylor and Francis.

Index